page 43

BJ
1012
.C57
1987

Clark, Henry, 1930-

Altering behavior

$28.00

| DATE | | | |
|---|---|---|---|
| | | | |
| | | | |
| | | | |
| | | | |
| | | | |
| | | | |
| | | | |
| | | | |
| | | | |
| | | | |
| | | | |
| | | | |

# Altering Behavior

Faces along the bar
Cling to their average day;
The lights must never go out;
The music must always play.
Lest we should see where we are,
Lost in a haunted wood,
Children afraid of the night
Who have never been happy or good.

W. H. Auden, "September 1, 1939"
(Reprinted by permission of Random House)

Henry B. Clark

# *Altering Behavior*

## The Ethics of
## Controlled
## Experience

*with a foreword by*
Perry London

**SAGE** PUBLICATIONS
The Publishers of Professional Social Science
Newbury Park   Beverly Hills   London   New Delhi

*For information address:*

SAGE Publications, Inc.
2111 West Hillcrest Drive
Newbury Park, California 91320

SAGE Publications Inc.          SAGE Publications Ltd.
275 South Beverly Drive         28 Banner Street
Beverly Hills                   London EC1Y 8QE
California 90212                 England

SAGE PUBLICATIONS India Pvt. Ltd.
M-32 Market
Greater Kailash I
New Delhi 110 048 India

Printed in the United States of America

Library of Congress Cataloging-in-Publication Data

60229127

Clark, Henry, 1930-
    Designing the self.
    Bibliography: p.
    1. Ethics.   2. Social ethics.   I. Title.
BJ1012.C57   1987        174'.915        86-3710
ISBN 0-8039-2765-7

FIRST PRINTING

# Contents

To my friends and colleagues

in

The Society for Values in Higher Education

# Foreword

Perry London

*Harvard Graduate School of Education*

Most serious essays on behavior control are concerned with its dangers. There is good reason for such concern. Most people involved in the technology of behavior control are interested in controlling others. Their purpose is usually for the good of those controlled, as is clearly the case in most (nonpsychiatric) medical applications. Even so, ethicists, scientists, politicians, and the general public are properly sensitive to the harmful possibilities inherent in behavior control. The warnings of *Brave New World* and *Nineteen Eighty Four* remain fresh, however dated the books themselves become.

Henry Clark approaches behavior control with full knowledge of its harmful applications and, in the business jargon of our day, its "downside risk." But the aim of his work is to make us see the positive side of the subject, not just in terms of its technical possibilities but also in terms of its ethical choices and imperatives. Writing with freshness, clarity, and gusto, Clark gives us a liberal ethicist's perspective on behavior control technology as a means for promoting self-control and, in so doing, offers easier possibilities for happiness and fulfillment (as opposed to mere pleasure) than have hitherto been available to human beings.

It is not the possibilities for happiness and fulfillment, of course, that unsettle the antagonists of "EBC" (Clark's shorthand term for "experience and behavior control," i.e., the voluntary control techniques, substances, and devices that he advocates). What disturbs, rather, is the notion that happiness and fulfillment can be come by *easily*, without the ardor or the anguish of body or soul for which, in most popular philosophies, happiness and fulfillment are held out as rewards. Clark challenges this contingent view of

pleasure (which I use here in the broadest philosophic sense of
*hedone*, not merely as sensory gratification) as something that must
be earned. Thus he takes pains to assert that

> it might very well be that the happiness and fulfillment associated with
> EBC-stimulated pleasure are uniquely valuable in themselves. . . . The
> satisfaction that comes from being able to manage one's own expe-
> rience satisfactorily, from having the power to do so, and being free
> from the anxiety of not being able to do so . . . might be very substantial
> indeed.

Clark's philosophical and ethical position in championing EBC
elaborates ideas that are vital to policy decisions regarding these
phenomena. His empirical premise is that the development of
behavior control technology is inevitable because the pressing
needs of medicine and the explosion of biological discovery at all
levels of body and brain function compel it. The main prospects
for discoveries in the relatively near future (some already quite
advanced) are for relief of pain, easing depression, and producing
pleasurable sensations and moods. Clark reviews the current technology of behavior control, giving due attention to behavior modification methods, relaxation, meditation, and biofeedback, and to
relatively esoteric, at least less popular, methods, such as brain
implantation. But much of his attention, understandably, goes to
drugs. It is there that one finds the magical combination of ease of
administration and potent effects almost unlimited in its possibilities for influencing thought, feeling, mood, and action. Clark
believes that memory enhancement, sexual enhancement, and skill
enhancement are all either here or on the threshold of practicality.
A sizable segment of scientists and observers agree with him.

From "Ecstasy" (MMDA) to enkephalins, the rate of mind-
altering drugs being discovered is increasing apace. Clark's novel
contribution to our awareness of what this means day to day comes
in his vignettes on individuals and families and advertisng agencies
promoting and using "Intensity," "Congruity," "Commitment,"
and "Rev Up"—not so far removed, as one ponders it, from tranquilizers, energizers, antidepressants, and over-the-counter sleep
and diet pills in use today.

Journalistic treatment of these developments is sometimes as glib
as social forecasting about them is gloomy. Serious discussion of the

ethical issues involved, with plainspoken and sophisticated commitment to their positive use, is rare indeed. In taking this posture, Clark offers more than voluntary affirmation or apologia for the obligatory. Rather, he is formulating the kind of ethical argument that can be most useful to policymakers and practitioners both on the positive and the cautionary side of implementing behavior control technology—for implement it they surely will.

Clark does not deny the possibilities for misuse to which EBC is subject. Indeed, almost a quarter of the book is devoted to the political safeguards and the philosophical values needed to promote its optimal and ethical use; but the cautionary side of behavior control technology is not central to his purpose. This is more an essay on the ethics of its benefits. "The scope and focus of the book are determined by my interest in spelling out how EBC can be used by ordinary people to make their lives better." It aims at once to explore the "prospects for augmenting pleasure, upgrading ethical responsibility and enlarging capacity in normal persons who voluntarily choose to make use of EBC for these purposes."

That people will choose to use EBC is as plain to Clark as the fact that they have already used virtually everything developed along these lines to which they have access. He neither advocates nor bemoans this fact, though he is plainly sympathetic with it. The use of EBC for pleasure enhancement, he says, is "only one example of a pronounced cultural trends toward greater *individual awareness and choice* in the determination of one's identity and one's life."

While the general contribution of this work to dialogue on the ethics of behavior control is significant, it also makes several contributions that will sharpen and perhaps gladden the thinking of specialists as well. One of these that deserves particular mention is the neat conceptual distinction that Clark draws among "pleasure," "happiness," and "fulfillment," and the argument he makes for their hierarchical development. This offers, I believe, a valuable and novel contribution to existential philosophy.

An even more fascinating contributon comes in his discussions of "artificial happiness," "artificial goodness," and "artificially increased capacity," about each of which there is a separate chapter. Artificial happiness is pleasure that is deliberately induced by drugs such as "Intensity" rather than experienced spontaneously and haphazardly. It is "artificial" only in its opposition to the idea that the more chancey occurrence of such pleasures to which we are accustomed is considered "natural." We are already, of course, more than ready to accept such devices ideologically when they serve the commonly accepted goal of relieving pain and practically when we take vitamin pills instead of conventional food. Clark prepares us to do the same when the devices provide positive pleasure, not just relief. He makes the same case for endorphins and for hot tubs, and it is a difficult case to fault.

For the general reader and specialist alike, *Altering Behavior: The Ethics of Controlled Experience* is an important and engaging work that should take an honored place in the continuing discourse of this field.

# Acknowledgments

My interest in controlling experience and behavior began almost twenty years ago when a professional book club sent me its dual selection of the month, Perry London's *Behavior Control* and Jose Delgado's *Physical Control of the Mind.* Thus it is no easy task for me to remember all of the individuals, and all the institutions, who have contributed to my research and thinking on this topic. With sincere apologies, then, to anyone who is inadvertently omitted, here's a list of those to whom I am especially grateful.

Ed Cornish, founding father of The World Future Society and editor of *The Futurist,* gave me initial encouragement by publishing my review article on the books by London and Delgado. The Duke University Research Council provided funds for summer travel and research. David Malone and Ron Gottesman, the guiding spirits of the Center for the Humanities at the University of Southern California, supported a major conference on "The Ethics of Experience and Behavior Control" in the winter of 1976 and the publication of a monograph based on the highlights of that conference. Colleagues in the School of Religion at USC have given me a forum for expounding my ideas on the subject and an abundance of helpful criticism. The same may be said of colleagues in the American Society of Christian Ethics and the American Academy of Religion, before whom I have delivered papers on EBC. The National Conference of Christians and Jews, Furman University, and the University of the Pacific also provided occasions when I could present my thoughts to a discerning audience.

The project came to fruition in a sabbatical leave in London in 1982. Those who were most instrumental in helping to arrange for this period of study and to carry it out were Perry London, Henry Slucki, Victor Meyer, Stanley Rachman, Gerald Davison, John Taylor, Gerald Stover, Jose Delgado, Mrs. Jose Delgado, Ian Kennedy, and Paul Abrecht.

I am especially grateful to the following publishers for granting permission to quote from works for which they hold the copyright:

The American Enterprise Institute [no author named], *Proposals to Reform Drug Regulation Laws* (Washington, D.C., 1981).

The American Psychiatric Association, Szasz, Thomas J., "The Ethics of Addiction," *American Journal of Psychiatry,* Vol. 128 (1971), pp. 542-543. Copyright 1971, the American Psychiatric Association. Reprinted by permission.

Cambridge University Press, Erwin, Edward, *Behavior Therapy: Scientific, Philosophical and Moral Foundations* (New York, 1978).

Center for Ethics, Society and the Life Sciences, Bakalar, James and Lester Grinspoon, "Drug Abuse Policy and Social Attitudes Toward Risk-Taking," in *Hastings Center Report* (August, 1983).

Dow Jones, Inc., Shaffer, Richard A., "Mastering the Mind," *The Wall Street Journal,* Vol. 97, No. 30 (1977).

Harcourt Brace Jovanovich, Hughes, Richard and Robert Brewin, *The Tranquilizing of America* (New York, 1979); Orwell, George, *1984* (New York, 1949); Pines, Maya, *The Brain Changers* (New York, 1973).

Harper and Row, Publishers, Inc., Brown, Barbara, *New Mind, New Body* (New York, 1974).

Little, Brown and Co., Packard, Vance, *The People Shapers* (New York, 1977).

*Los Angeles Times,* Timnick, Lois, "'Brain Pacemaker' Success Reported." (May 3, 1977).

Pergamon Press, Rachman, Stanley and G. T. Wilson, *The Effects of Psychological Therapy* (New York, 1980).

Random House, Inc., Auden, W. H., "September 1, 1939" in *W. H. Auden: Collected Poems,* edited by Edward Mendelson (New York, 1945).

Rowman and Allanheld, Publishers, Richard, David A. J., *Sex, Drugs, Death and the Law: An Essay on Human Rights and Overcriminalization* (Totowa, New Jersey: Rowman and Littlefield, 1982).

The Saturday Review, Inc., Houston, Jean, "Putting the First Man on the Earth," *Saturday Review* (February 22, 1975).

Taylor, John G., *The Shape of Minds to Come* (London, 1971).

# Chapter 1

# INTRODUCTION

Human beings have always tried to control what they experience and how they behave. As sociologists of knowledge have shown, what we call "reality" is itself a social construct that is intended to make us feel good about what happens, and to tell us what it is right for us to do. Art, philosophy, religion, etiquette, and role definitions of all kinds can be seen in this light, as can the mental, verbal, and societal rituals that express or reinforce the conventions of cultural interpretation and social interaction.

The substances and techniques we have used to shape experience and behavior have been rather imprecise, unreliable, unsafe, and, in short, ineffective. Education often fails to reach uncomprehending minds and exhortation often falls on deaf (or resistant) ears. The drugs used to produce desired states of mind or moods often have undesirable side effects or cause damage through prolonged use. Scientific knowledge has, of course, brought progress, but our attitude toward most unconventional interventions in the operation of the human organism is defined by the medical model: We tend to believe that pharmaceutical substances and clinical procedures are to be used only for *therapeutic* purposes; that is, they are to be sought and resorted to only when you are sick and need medicine and/or a medicine man to make you well.

The fact is, however, that we now have at our disposal an array of new substances and techniques that could make us far more effective than ever before in controlling experience and behavior. We could use our new technologies of experience and behavior control (EBC) to create increased happiness, goodness, and human capacity:

(1) Pleasure is an important aspect of happiness—and new kinds of chemical stimulation of the brain (CSB) and electrical stimulation of the brain (ESB) may be used to produce pleasurable sensations or euphoric moods that would not be contaminated by the deleterious consequences of many drugs commonly used today (such as heroin, cocaine, "speed," or alcohol).

(2) The most important aspect of goodness is good *actions* (i.e., *deeds* that result in benefit to one's neighbors)—and behavior modification may be used to extinguish undesirable behaviors and to create long-term behavior patterns that express the moral values of the person concerned.

(3) Increased capacities of body, mind, and spirit enrich the possibilities of life—and various processes ranging from biofeedback through orthomolecular nutritional programs to hypnotism may be used to enhance learning, memory, longevity, sleeping, dreaming, para-normal psychic states, and physical vigor (including sexual energy).

It must be emphasized, of course, that the technologies of EBC do not constitute a "technical fix" that completely solves all of the per-plexities and difficulties of the human condition. The very notion of a technical "fix" may be misleading if applied to complex goals, for it is only very specific problems originating in unambiguous causes that can be "fixed" by particular technological innovations. Yet indi-vidual technological *breakthroughs* (such as the serums that protect us against polio or typhoid fever) are possible, and each such break-through is a constructive contribution to life that we are right to utilize and for which we ought to be properly grateful. To speak of the possibility of greatly augmented happiness, goodness, and capacity is therefore to claim that the cumulative thrust of a host of new breakthroughs in EBC is a manifestation of progress in human af-fairs that deserve to be noted, refined, and exploited to the fullest.

Many observers are filled with Promethean ardor when they con-template the "fourth Copernican Revolution" that may be wrought through EBC breakthroughs. Just as Copernicus shattered the as-sumptions of medieval theology by showing that the earth was not the center of the universe, just as Darwin put the uniqueness of humanity in perspective with his theory of the evolution of the species, and just as Freud challenged the all-sufficiency of the rational mind, even so does the advent of EBC herald a dramatically new vision of the human potential. One may be justifiably skeptical of Kenneth Clark's hope that world peace can be ensured by means of antihostility pills in the medicine chest of every world political leader with access to a nuclear button,[1] and one may entertain some reservations about Joseph Fletcher's contention that nothing is more quintessentially human (or more praiseworthy in human beings) than our ability to manipulate, extend, and otherwise use artifice to improve the human organism and its felicity.[2] But despite skepticism and disagreement regarding details, most twentieth-century Americans probably agree with Jose Delgado's trenchant dictum on the historical significance of EBC: Heretofore the cardinal maxim of moral wisdom has been "Know thyself"—but now it is "Use your intelligence to construct a better self."[3]

This book is intended to be an explanation of new breakthroughs in the area of EBC and a discussion of exactly how they might be implemented (and limited) in such a way as to promote true human fulfillment. Thus, it is inevitably an analysis of the prevailing norms, attitudes, and values that keep us from making the most of the opportunities presented by EBC. Indeed, because the author is a social ethicist rather than a scientist or a psychologist, the bulk of the analysis is devoted to the philosophical and ethical convictions that ought to govern individual choice and social policy concerning wise use of EBC. Many of the most familiar and time-honored givens of the philosophical and religious heritage of our culture will be challenged and/or reinterpreted. As Gerald Jonas observes, "Western science can question some cherished assumptions of Western civilization without cutting itself adrift from the traditional strengths of Western thought."[4]

No one can be certain that the technical breakthroughs envisioned in this book will be perfected in the next decade. But I believe that most of them will be; moreover, I believe that Perry London and Gerald Klerman are correct in predicting that nontherapeutic applications of EBC will be increasingly common:

> The biggest social changes engendered by drugs and behavior modification technologies do not arise from what people can do to each other, though those political dangers are potentially real enough, but

from what people will want to do to themselves. The social consequences of greatest potential concern in a benevolent, free society are not the impositions of malicious intentions and hostile restraints, but of benign intentions and amicable enhancements. *It is amicable enhancements, so common in daily life that we take them for granted*, that constitute the most important kinds of consequences of these technologies [italics added]. They are matters of how people want to treat themselves because they are things which individuals want to do, or want done to them. The social and ethical problems which result are those of the incursions these treatments make on society's values, for they challenge the tradition of Puritan ethics and move further and further, faster and faster, towards a hedonic or pleasure-oriented ethic. This trend is resulting, as we believe, from the interactions of an improving technology for the self control of mood and behavior with an abundant economy and a political tradition of relatively great individual liberty. The continuation of this trend will occur as long as those forces are operating.[5]

The italicized phrase emphasizes a central assumption of this book: The "amicable enhancements" of EBC can become "so common in daily life that we take them for granted," and their inclusion in the texture of ordinary life may occur without rending the social fabric or creating upheavel in the personality or the character of individuals who avail themselves of these enhancements. I agree with London and Klerman in their focus on nontherapeutic utilization of EBC; however, I would like to emphasize a point that they do not stress: Promoting a higher order of ethical responsibility is at least as important as augmenting pleasure in making use of the "amicable enhancements" now becoming available.

## WHAT THE FUTURE WILL HAVE TO OFFER

The practical possibilities for "artificial" pleasure, virtue, and enhanced performance of mind and body through nontherapeutic applications of EBC come to life when one imagines the kinds of advertisements that will be common in a decade or so. Imagine, for example, that you are watching your favorite prime-time TV sitcom on a weekday evening, when the following ad reaches out to you and thirty million other viewers:

A TV Spot for a Drug Called "Intensity"[6]

(Camera shows a middle-aged couple seated on the left side of a tour bus, just across the aisle from a very attractive younger couple. Former looks disgruntled; latter, *radiant*.)

MIDDLE-AGED HUSBAND: Sure, Edna, those mountains are kind of pretty. But I don't know whether this tour is worth all it's costing us.

MIDDLE-AGED WIFE: You're right, Frank. We could have stayed at home and bought some color slides. I *certainly* don't see why those young people are carrying on so.

(Camera zooms in on the younger couple, both of whom are oohing and ahing over the view out their window.)

YOUNG WIFE: Oh, Tommy—it's so wonderful I just can't *stand* it! Thank you for bringing me to this wonderful spot, darling!

YOUNG HUSBAND: And thank you, sweetheart, for remembering to bring along the Intensity. It sure does heighten the experience!

ANNOUNCER (as camera shows split screen view of both couples, with a picture of a bottle of Intensity superimposed on the lower middle part of the picture): Yes, folks, the sky *is* bluer and the trees are greener with Intensity, the modern sensory perception enhancer used by people who really want to *feel* the beauty and power of Nature. Don't go on your vacation this year without an ample supply of Intensity. And keep the economy-sized family bottle in your medicine chest all year around, so that you don't miss out on any of the delights of the changing seasons.

Remember (camera now shows announcer lifting up different colored bottles), it's Intensity in the blue and green bottle for heightening visual experience, the red bottle for sound, and the pink and purple bottle for touch. You aren't really living unless you're living with Intensity!

Or imagine instead that you are thumbing through the latest issue of *Presbyterian Life* when your eye falls upon this full-page ad:

A Full-Page Ad for "Congruity"
NO MORE EXCUSES!

You *can* do the good you would—and you can avoid the evil you would not! (Romans 5:12)

Yes, Christian friends, at last there is a successful solution to St. Paul's dilemma. Through the Providence of God and modern technology, a *sure cure* for many specific forms of wickedness is now available. For example:

Entangled in a nasty affair? Don't want to
hurt the wife and kids, but you just can't
get enough of *her*?
DON'T GIVE UP HOPE!
THERE IS A WAY OUT!
Sign up for our modestly priced six-week course in Antiadultery Operant Conditioning, and we will *guarantee* disentanglement. (This guarantee is based on studies by an independent research firm which found
that the success rate of this specific Congruity program is 94.3%. A free
copy of the report will be furnished on request.)

Should you happen to pick up a copy of *Commonweal* in the
parish library, you might see a not altogether dissimilar ad designed
to offer you the same kind of help in leading a more earnestly committed moral life:

An Ad for "Commitment"
Are you having trouble sharing as generously as you should? Do you
find yourself depressed by a sense of guilt, yet unable to shake off the
yoke of "keep up with the Joneses" consumerism?
YOU CAN CHANGE ALL THAT!
Your unfortunate cultural conditioning can be reversed by countercon-
ditioning. Assume that your present rating on the Christian Self-Denial
Index is less than the 1998 average of 6.1, we can guarantee that your
rate of charitable giving will increase by 300 to 500 percent!

Call 800-212-683-4719 (toll-free) for the name of the authorized
Catholic Behavior Control Clinic in your area.
"WE TAKE UP WHERE THE HOLY SPIRIT LEAVES OFF."

Later in the week, while watching "Wall Street Week in Review,"
you might be intrigued by the following sales pitch:

A TV Spot for "Rev Up"
(The screen shows a fleet of 707s warming up, with the sound of jet
engines rising to a thunderous crescendo, which is softened as the announcer speaks.)

ANNOUNCER: There's no such thing as a free lunch—and those who
want to get a big slice of the pie have got to be operating at top efficiency and full speed.

That's what Rev Up is all about. We provide you with an individually
tailored program of maximum personal development for maximum

production. Better nutrition to increase intelligence, learning speed, and memory. Speed-sleeping to overcome the waste of countless hours in unneeded sleep. Stress control through biofeedback. You tell us what capacities you want to rev up, and we'll get the job done for you.

Remember: leading corporations *expect* their fast-track executives to rev themselves up. As the CEO of EXXON said recently, "In a competitive market situation, the only firms and the only individuals who will prosper are those who develop their full productive potential. The man who cannot remember the details of complicated memos will not be able to perform adequately, and the woman who cannot work twenty-two hours a day, seven days a week, from time to time, when the heat is on, will fall by the wayside. The best people will not only accept these realities, they will welcome the challenge—because the best people are those who always drag the best and the most out of themselves."

DON'T WAIT ANY LONGER—REV YOURSELF UP **TODAY!**

The possibilities envisioned in the foregoing advertisements are not at all farfetched. As argued in Chapter 2, products such as "Intensity" and processes such as "Congruity," "Commitment," and "Rev Up" are either already available in principle or "in the pipeline." Moreover, whatever the timetable on technological innovation, it is high time—now—for us to think through the values that will determine our response to the technological possibilities. What has already happened as a result of the advent of the computer is instructive in this regard: Those who work extensively and intimately with computers are driven to ask philosophical questions about who *they* are as human beings as well as questions about what the computer is. The same impact will be felt by those who become aware of the possibilities created by innovations in EBC, and we will be forced to clarify our convictions about what happiness, goodness, and human capacities really are.

It is inevitable, of course, that the sometimes startling new possibilities will arouse uncertainty and hesitation. Our ability even to understand the possibilities clearly may be hampered by lack of imagination, political apprehensions, and philosophical/ethical objections. Yet, such qualms are healthy and must be dealt with patiently and honestly. After more than ten years of research on the ethics of EBC I am well acquainted with the qualms and with those who are bothered by them. In presenting a number of papers on this topic at professional gatherings, I have often been struck by the astonishment and dismay of my colleagues in the field of religious studies, and my speculations have frequently been greeted with mirth or derision. (One former student congratulated me on reducing the very idea of EBC to a horrible absurdity by my admittedly flamboyant portrayal of the possibilities in the foregoing hypothetical advertisements—and then, when she found out I wasn't kidding, and was in fact in favor of an open attitude toward them, she chastised me severely and told me I ought to be ashamed of myself!)

I believe, in all earnest sobriety, that a satisfactory answer can be given to the qualms that ethically sensitive people understandably have. I believe, in fact, that intelligent, constructive use of EBC is both feasible and desirable, and that the advent of new and more effective ways of ordering experience and behavior, plus new ways of generating higher performance capabilities, will prove to be a significant blessing for humankind.

I can make this point in a negative mode by declaring that I am sick and tired of hearing people con themselves into believing that conventional ways of seeking happiness and goodness are just fine and that all we need to do is try a little harder. That's a pernicious falsehood: To pursue happiness through consumption and accumulation of all the expensive commodities and activities the mass media tell us we ought to want is a blind alley, and to keep hoping that traditional methods of character formation will produce adequate ethical responsibility is a pathetic exercise in vanity. We are far less happy than we might be because (in biblical language) "we see and see, but do not understand," and we "spend our substance for that which does not satisfy." Neither are we as good as we ought to be, and could be, for our definition of goodness is too self-centered and, ultimately, self-congratulatory. Furthermore, we are quite wrong in our insistence that goodness can be attained only by a lengthy process of mind and character development that is increasingly unrealistic in our day and time—and that is now, because of EBC, unnecessary in certain specific ways in regard to many specific issues. To put it bluntly, I do not believe that most people can be happy for very long by devoting themselves to the accumulation of the trinkets and symbols of success, power, status, or fun as currently conceived in our culture —and those who imagine themselves happy with such a life must cope with an immense burden of guilt in their best moments of self-awareness. Nor do I believe that conventional methods of bringing up children or bringing about economic, political, and cultural reform can suffice without the assistance of the technologies of EBC.

I can put it positively by affirming that a substantial measure of the kind of pleasurable experiences and altruistic behavior that are a part of the good life can be attained through EBC and that we would be foolish not to take advantages of what it has to offer. If technical innovations do indeed make possible the degree of precision, safety, and reliability envisioned in this book and if the necessary political safeguards can be implemented, it is up to moralists, social philosophers, and thoughtful citizens of all kinds to formulate the revised view of human nature and destiny that will enable us to make optimal use of EBC.

## SOME IMPORTANT STIPULATIONS

This introductory chapter is not complete without listing a number of stipulations that require special emphasis:

(1) The scope and focus of the book are determined by my interest in spelling out how EBC can be used by ordinary people to make their lives better. Much has been written about laboratory experiments and the use of EBC in clinics and prisons, but these are not my primary concerns. I am interested, rather, in the prospects for augmenting pleasure, upgrading ethical responsibility, and enlarging capacity in normal persons who voluntarily choose to make use of EBC for these purposes. The book is not addressed to wild-eyed "psychotropic hedonists" or to "pharmacological Calvinists." Rather, it is addressed to thoughtful Americans who have jobs and families (or the equivalents thereof), who pay their taxes and aspire to a well-balanced life leading to long-term fulfillment in joy and accomplishment, and who see in particular forms of EBC a means to be better and happier persons. (Readers who think that only slightly reckless persons—those who are willing to undergo drastic changes in their lives—will dare fool around with EBC should pay special attention to the vignettes at the beginning of Chapters 3, 4 and 5.)

(2) It must be stressed that this entire study is based on the assumption that EBC should not be forced upon anyone and that "informed choice" is something that must be a part of the picture. Even if "free will" is an illusion, it is a unversal illusion, and philosophical doctrines about its illusory nature have no practical influence on the fact

that people do *decide* what course of action to take (or not to take) when presented with (apparent!) options. Thus, even behaviorists will find themselves in situations where "the history of previous contingencies of reinforcement" will dispose them to use a certain type of EBC or not to do so; and ordinary people in the same situation, imagining that they have free choice, will go right ahead and choose.

(3) The book presupposes certain technical preconditions that actually cannot be taken for granted: I stipulate that acceptable applications of EBC must be safe, reliable, nonaddictive, and—in principle, or insofar as possible—reversible in their effects. In referring to the happiness, goodness, and increased capacity attainable through EBC as "artificial," I intend merely to emphasize that its interventions in the normal functioning of the organism are extraordinary; that is, out of the ordinary in the sense that they go beyond what people in our society usually do at present in order to obtain certain consequences in structuring experience or behavior. As Jose Delgado puts it, they are interventions that do not make use of "the normal portals of entry" to the brain, or that do not depend upon conventional methods of education or socialization: They require the ingestation of pills, the eating of unusual quantities or types of foods, electrical stimulation, or submission to laboratory or clinical manipulations that are substantially different from what individuals in our society typically do.

The chapter titles present the progression of the argument in a fairly straightforward manner. Chapter 2 describes recent technological developments that reveal how close we are to products like "Intensity" and procedures such as "Congruity," "Commitment," and "Rev Up." Each of the next three chapters is divided into two sections. The first section consists of a matter-of-fact description of the applications of EBC that I regard as feasible (and, in many cases, as a *probable* component in the mix of possibilities available by the year 2000). The second section is devoted to a normative analysis of some of the most significant philosophical and ethical issues at stake.

Chapter 3 takes the position that the good life is a complex whole composed of pleasure, happiness, and fulfillment and that artificially enhanced pleasure can be a valuable ally of the best kind of happiness and fulfillment. Chapter 4 makes the case for artificial goodness, and in doing so it argues that the new means to good actions differ from older means only in being more effective in producing good consequences for our fellow human beings. Chapter 5 describes some of the benefits we may expect from increased human capacity and answers the charge that developing hitherto unrealized capacities is "playing God" in some inappropriate way. All three of these chapters begin with a vignette describing benign and constructive use of EBC in the lives of ordinary Americans. These vignettes are intended to show that average people, given access to technologically enhanced happiness, goodness, and capacity, will have no difficulty at all in using EBC to enrich their lives in accordance with their own values and that they will be able to do so without undergoing drastic changes in personality or character. The vignettes demonstrate that EBC can be incorporated smoothly into the lives of thoroughly responsible citizens and will be welcomed by thoughtful persons who believe in taking control of their own lives and realizing their best potential as human beings.

Chapter 6 deals with the political ramifications of EBC, and Chapter 7 sketches the normative understanding of human nature and destiny on which are based all of the particular judgments about the ethics of EBC made in the rest of the book.

## NOTES

1. Kenneth Clark, "The Pathos of Power," *American Psychologist*, Vol. 26, No. 12 (December 1971), p. 1055.

2. Joseph Fletcher, *The Ethics of Genetic Control*, pp. 35-36.

3. Jose Delgado, "Triunism: A Transmaterial Brain-Mind Theory," *Brain and Mind* (1979), p. 392.

4. Gerald Jonas, *Visceral Learning*, p. 27.

5. Perry London and Gerald Klerman, "Mental Health and Behavior Control," unpublished paper prepared for a consultation at the Institute for Society, Ethics and the Life Sciences in 1976, pp. 142-143.

6. So far as I know, it is pure coincidence that the comic strip "Doonesbury" made mention of a drug called "Intensity" in the summer of 1985. As early as 1972 I began to use that name for the benign euphoric in my scenarios for the future.

# Chapter 2

# THE TECHNICAL POSSIBILITIES

No one who is exposed to the mass media can fail to be aware of the novel forms of experience and behavior control being practiced or experimented with during the past couple of decades. The publicity given to increased drug use and to drug abuse has aroused curiosity, hope, and fear concerning mind and mood manipulation. News of war, terrorism, and rising crime rates has called attention to the dangers of excessive or improperly exercised controls. Books with names like *The Brain Changers, The People Shapers, Mind and Supermind*, and *The Brain Revolution* and *The Aquarian Conspiracy* dazzle readers with reports of what has already happened in the laboratory and beguiling speculations about what may happen outside it in the very near future.

Because the primary aim of this book is to explore the philosophical and ethical dimensions of the technical possibilities alluded to in the many popular articles, documentaries, and journalistic books on EBC that have appeared in recent years, no comprehensive survey of these possibilities will be attempted here. But it will be helpful to review the highlights of the scientific research that has opened up the path to artificial happiness, goodness, and increased human capacity.

## WILL THESE THINGS REALLY HAPPEN?

Perhaps we should begin with a comment on the probabilities. Will the research discussed in this chapter actually lead to the development and marketing of products and processes such as those hypothesized in Chapter 1? Will the predictions ventured in the next twenty-five pages or so come true? What are the odds that the seemingly "far-out" possibilities envisioned for the not-too-distant future will ever be realized?

The answer is (of course), nobody knows for sure. The possibilities are by no means inconceivable, and there are many knowledgeable experts who predict that *something like* the pharmaceuticals and the techniques described above will be available before long, and that ordinary citizens will be able to make use of them to generate the experiences and behaviors they desire and approve.

Nobody knows for sure. But it is a fact that technological forecasting has typically been astonishingly conservative in its predictions regarding the pace and direction of change. When, for example, the first commercial computers were built in the late 1940s, early projections of technical capability and probable demand foresaw very limited applicability and stipulated that total saturation of the market would occur in only a few years. Learned opinion concerning foreseeable improvements postponed until the end of the century certain applications that in fact became commonplace within two decades.

Actually, the uses of EBC portrayed in the preceding chapter are not drastically different from practices that are already in evidence. If the advertisements sound familiar, that is because they make claims and inspire hopes that are very similar to claims and hopes we hear articulated almost every day; moreover, they appeal to the same anxieties and dreams toward which present-day advertisements are directed. The main difference is simply that a degree of safety, precision, reliability, and effectiveness not often present in current technologies is presupposed.

In some cases, the change envisioned is not so much a technical breakthrough as it is a more widespread application of existing technologies. Behavior modification, for instance, is a technique that most people in our society tend to think of as extreme or even scary, and it is administered mainly by health care professionals or researchers in situations defined by both the professionals and the clients (or patients) as therapeutic. But as more and more people become familiar with behavior modification techniques through smoking cessation clinics, weight control programs, assertiveness training, and the highly practical advice of popular radio psychologists and columnists, their apprehensions will diminish and self-administered schedules of reinforcement will become increasingly common.

The pattern of usage of MDMA—3, 4-methylenedioxymethamphetamines, or the drug that has come to be called "Ecstasy" by non-therapeutic users—offers another illustration of the same trend. MDMA has been used by therapists for more than a decade, and its reputation as a producer of mellow euphoria has encouraged a growing number of people (notably students and urban professionals) to use it for recreational purposes. Users claims that it "open[s] up great emotional sharing, relaxes inhibitions and enhances communication," and therapists report "almost no negative side effects when MDMA is taken under supervision."[1] Yet street use has led to abuses, and the Drug Enforcement Agency has temporarily classified it as taboo. Supporters of MDMA are lobbying for a change in classification that would at least allow its continued use in psychotherapy and many favor a Schedule III classification, which would put the drug in company with other prescription pharmaceuticals such as codeine.[2] David Nichols of Purdue University declares that the present classification is a very unfortunate mistake that "will make it virtually impossible to continue research into MDMA." Nichols sees this as a real tragedy "because I think we've come across something new and important here, something we've never seen before....Even if MDMA isn't the answer," says Nichols, "second- or third-generation versions of it might be." Dr. Rick Ingrasci contends,

> The real question—the one that won't be addressed by the DEA—is how we use drugs in this society. A tacit decision has been made that it's okay to use drugs to ease pain. It's okay to take aspirin or Valium, both of which may well be more dangerous than MDMA. But it's not okay to use drugs to gain insight.
>
> My hope is that MDMA will force us to reevaluate our attitude about that. Say they throw MDMA in the wastebasket, as they probably will. What happens then? Well, there are maybe 50 other molecules sitting

on the shelf, waiting to be used. Before you blink an eye, MDMA will be replaced by another drug that will do essentially the same thing.[3]

So the demand for "better things for better living through chemistry" and other forms of EBC on the part of consumers is matched by the promise of a vastly increased supply resulting from the rapid pace of scientific discovery. A professor of pharmacology at Yale University asserts that "brain chemistry is catching fire," and a neurophysiologist at Purdue says, "Discoveries are coming so fast it's like going from the candle to the lightbulb overnight."[4] A science journalist from the *Boston Globe* sums it up this way:

> The secrets of the chemicals of consciousness are being unearthed daily by endocrinologists, physiologists, biophysicists, psychiatrists, biochemists and many others in laboratories [all over the world]. . . .
>
> The more scientists probe the chemical secrets of the brain, the more some of them become full of wonder, and more mystically appreciative of the human brain and whatever it is we all know as consciousness. [As] Nobel Prize-winning psychobiologist Roger Sperry wrote in the 1981 *Annual Review of the Neural Sciences:* "Current concepts of the mind-brain relation involve a direct break [with the old notion of mind-body separation] that has dominated neuroscience for many decades."[5]

A British observer declares that the next decade will see "a hundredfold increase in the number and types of drugs capable of affecting the mind," adding that future drugs will be able to "pick out very localized drive centers in the brain—and therefore control specific moods."[6] Scientists in both Europe and America are working on the production of synthetic enkephalins that may be the most potent painkillers ever developed, and certain Swedish scientists feel that "within a few years" they will produce a nonaddictive version of an enkephalin analog that is "30,000 times more powerful than the brain's own version."[7]

For the purposes of this book, then, it is not necessary to assemble overwhelming scientific evidence that proves beyond doubt that specific technological miracles will occur by such and such a date. It is enough to point out that scientific research is moving rapidly in the direction of the applications described here and that a host of technical possibilities for greatly enhanced pleasure, goodness, and capacity are on the horizon.

## ELECTRICAL STIMULATION
## OF THE BRAIN (ESB)

Apart from the kinds of psychosurgery that effect a permanent alteration in brain tissues, the most radical interventions in the ordinary functioning of the mind or body of members of our species are those that require, and are made possible by, the implantation of electrodes in the skull and subsequent electrical stimulation of particular areas of the brain. This procedure—nicely described in terms that a layperson can understand in ESB pioneer Jose Delgado's *Physical Control of the Mind*—is by now thoroughly well established; nevertheless, it is delicate, expensive, and (especially from the perspective of those who are contemplating the prospect of having the procedure executed upon themselves) drastic. Thus, most of the experiments carried out so far have been done with animals or with victims of some disorder (such as epilepsy) sufficiently serious to justify a therapy as ambitious as ESB. However, the results achieved are sometimes spectacular.

Dr. Jose Delgado, Director of the Centro Ramon Y Cajal in Madrid, is the world's foremost authority on ESB. His most famous demonstration of what it can accomplish—and of his own absolutely serene confidence in its reliability—took place in a bull ring. Delgado, after having implanted electrodes in the brain of a bull, got into the arena with the dangerous beast, armed with nothing but the knowledge that he would be able to stop the bull in his tracks by pressing the button on a hand-held transmitter that would activate a charge in the crucially placed electrodes.[8] Even more significant in their implications for social psychology are his experiments with a monkey colony:

—When the dominance/aggression area of the chief monkey's brain was electrically dulled, his normally swaggering, threatening behavior was eliminated. Other monkeys, who would normally cower in the chief's presence or flee, sensed the change in his "personality" and behaved impudently or aggressively toward him.

—When the current was turned off, all of the monkeys abandoned their new postures and resumed the old deferential ways of relating to the chief. Their subsequent behavior gave no indication that they had been affected by their temporary experience with a changed hierarchy of authority.[9]

In experiments with human subjects, Delgado has produced motor movements that the patient usually considered spontaneous (i.e., self-generated) and for which the patient "always offered a reasonable explanation."[10] He has been able to generate specific memories, including recall of passages of music and a powerful sense of deja vu.[11]

Photographs of early experiments with ESB show bulky devices attached to the heads of subjects, with a tangle of wires connecting these devices to the experiment's control panel. But thanks to the microminiaturization of radio receivers, these hampering complications are no longer necessary: Delgado has now created a transdermal stimoceiver capable of two-way communication (it can be hooked up to a computer to provide constant monitoring of activity in precise brain locations and make possible messages sent by the computer in response to what is happening inside the skull). The coin-sized stimoceiver can be inserted just beneath the head's skin covering, where it can function without wires or any other visible signs of its presence (other than a slight lump, which can easily be concealed by hair).[12] A similar mechanism called a dialytrode can be used to add chemical intervention and communication to the range of possibilities.[13]

It can be done; of that there is no doubt. But most authorities doubt that we will ever see the day when large numbers of people are lining up to have electrodes put into their heads. A scientific procedure regarded as routine by a physician may still seem frightening to a prospective client, and cosmetic implications that seem negligible to the scientist may seem terribly distasteful to a client. Furthermore, according to some authorities, the matter of safety is not to be dismissed as inconsequential. Both Dr. James Olds, who is famous for his experiments on the putative "pleasure center" of the brain in the 1950s, and Eliot Valenstein, author of a highly regarded book, *Brain Control*, are worried about the hazards of ESB. They contend that the presence of even the tiniest wires extending deep into the cranial cavity might lead to the formation of scar tissue that could cause epilepsy or other damaging lesions. They also fear that a sudden movement of the head forward, backward, or circular (such as might occur in certain common recreational activities or in a minor auto-mobile collision) could do irreparable mischief to the unfeeling yet delicate tissues of the brain.[14]

Delgado, who has performed more experiments involving elec-trode implantation than anyone else in the medical profession, and John Taylor, whose *The Shape of Minds to Come* is still one of the best single works on the subject in the English language, see these fears about the safety of EBC as groundless. But Delgado doubts that the procedure he has perfected will be feasible for anything except therapeutic applications and research[15] and Olds has said that he foresees few applications of this research to human beings. "This methodology," he declares, "is extremely gross, in the sense that we have no idea what we are really doing when we put a probe in the brain." He goes on to say,

> Actually, there are no brain centers. There is a bundle of fibers running through this region carrying all the possible emotional messages of the animal. It's as if we tapped into a trunk line from Chicago to New York. Almost every stimulated brain effect ever discovered happens in the [lateral part of the hypothalamus]. This is the whole bundle of the brain's motivational and autonomic fibers brought through one small tube. Well, the so-called centers are just chance conglomerations of fibers, or stems, which carry the main emotional outflow of the brain past a certain point. It's not a very good way to do anything specific.[16]

Before his death, Olds admitted that he was not sure his earlier use of the term "pleasure center" was accurate: "Maybe the brain probe causes the subject to itch and brain stimulation is the only way he can scratch it."[17]

Thus, ESB may not be a major part of the most probable future in nontherapeutic EBC. Perhaps Gerald Leach is correct in predicting that "ESB will remain a research and therapeutic tool," the main value of which will be its utility in helping scientists gain a better understanding of brain activity.[18] Even so, informed observers of the current state of the art conjure up arresting visions of what may very soon be commonplace. Albert Rosenfeld, the outstanding journalist whose several books on various science-related topics are models of the important role played by writers who can translate scientific findings into reports that are accessible to nontechnical readers, ventures the following predictions:

> One can easily imagine people in the future wearing self-stimulating electrodes (it might even become the "in" thing to do) which might render the wearer sexually potent at any time; that might put him to sleep or keep him awake, according to his need; that might curb his appetite if he wanted to lose weight; that might relieve him of pain; that might give him courage when he is fearful, or render him tranquil when he is enraged.[19]

## CHEMICAL STIMULATION
## OF THE BRAIN (CSB)

As long ago as 1969, Rosenfeld asserted that chemical stimulation of the brain would someday be capable of much greater precision (and, therefore, utility) than ESB.[20] This assertion is evidently an echo of the "magic bullet" paradigm of drug effects described by Paul Ehrlich in these words:

> If we picture an organism as infected by a certain species of bacterium, it will obviously be easy to effect a cure if substances have been discovered which have an exclusive affinity for these bacteria and act deleteriously or lethally on these and these alone, while at the same time they possess no affinity whatever for normal constituents of the body and cannot therefore have the least harmful or other effect on that body. Such substances would then be able to exert their final action exclusively on the parasite harbored within the organism, and would represent, so to speak *magic bullets* which seek their target of their own accord.[21]

Unfortunately, the realities of chemical intervention are usually more complex, and critics of the "magic bullet" image often argue that Ehrlich's "myth of specificity" is in large measure "a fiction created by . . . labelling processes." In reality, say the critics, drugs almost always have a variety of effects on various parts of an organism, and it is misleading to *label* desired effects as the main effects when "all other changes are labeled as 'side effects,' regardless of whether they may be positive, negative, uncomfortable, dangerous, or massive."[22]

But one does not have to subscribe to the myth of specificity or believe in magic bullets in order to acknowledge that ever greater effectiveness in achieving specific desired consequences is being attained by current research on CSB. Both experience and behavior can be controlled by a host of chemical agents that alleviate pain, relieve anxiety, mitigate depression, stimulate (or dull) sexual interest and/or potency, heighten the concentration or energy that can be brought to bear on particular tasks, strengthen (or becloud) memory and learning abilities, enhance pleasurable sensations or create euphoric moods, and generate hallucinations. Impressive evidence for this claim can be found in the spectacular advances made during the past decade in research on peptides.

## Peptides

Those who are exercised about the matter of artificiality may be encouraged to learn that one of the most promising lines of research now being developed centers on the discovery and therapeutic value of various body chemicals that seem to be correlated with reduction of pain, relief of depression, lowering of stess, and, in short, easing (or even in effect *curing*) certain maladies that are a source of distress for millions of people. These bodily substances, for which the most general term is *peptides*, have been identified by research that used as its point of departure the knowledge that the brain is filled with "receptor sites" that are crucial in the alleviation of pain through drugs such as morphine. Knowing that these receptor sites are in fact situated in the part of the brain that controls moods as well as pain, scientists began (especially during the 1970s) to search for the natural bodily substances that make contact with these sites and act as neurotransmitters to affect moods or lessen pain. Among the brain peptides (sometimes called "enkephalins," meaning "in the head") they found an amino acid chain called beta analgesic which animal experiments demonstrate to be "48 times more potent than morphine when injected directly into the brain and three times more potent when injected intravenously."[23]

Practical applications of this new knowledge were soon devised. In 1977, a major effort to experiment with the possible uses of beta endorphin with treatment-resistent patients suffering from mental illnesses such as schizophrenia, autism, and depression were launched. Although the results have not been unfailingly positive, dramatic improvements have been brought about in some patients, and researchers are hopeful that more and more applications will be certified effective as scientific knowledge goes forward. By 1980, chronic pain patients were already inducing their brains to secrete additional beta endorphin by "holding a small transmitter over their chests, where an electric receiver had been implanted." The receiver, located in the brain, activates electrodes that stimulate the pituitary to produce beta endorphin.[24]

Other peptides have been shown to be useful in combatting several other common human problems:

—Depression seems to be correlated with an insufficiency of another natural bodily substance, norepinephrine. Amphetamines "slow down the pumps that ordinarily suck [norepinephrine] back from the synapse into the brain cell." Future drugs that can regulate a person's supply of norepinephrine may be able to eliminate the subjective feeling we call depression even though objective realities that might cause rational anxiety or discouragement continue to exist in the patient's life.

—Hypertension and insomnia can be significantly mitigated by another transmitter named serotonin, which dampens the action of the portion of the brain that is responsible for alertness.

> Psychiatrists at Boston State Hospital have demonstrated that insomniacs fall asleep twice as fast when given small doses of L-tryptophan, the chemical from which the body makes serotonin, and they awaken the next morning without the drugged, groggy feeling that sleeping pills often cause.[25]

One theory about the tranquil mood states of some mystics or practitioners of meditation is that they have learned how to increase the amount of serotonin in their system. The correlation between high quantities of serotonin and feelings of calm restfulness have earned it the nickname "sleep juice" in some laboratories. The recently established link between long-standing practice of meditation and atypical youthfulness may be related to serotonin and suggests that the rate of aging may be chemically manipulable. A physiologist from the University of California at Los Angeles claims, for example, that "people who have been meditating twice daily for more than five years are physiologically 12 to 15 years younger than a non-meditating control group."[26]

—Serious joggers and other devotees of strenuous exercise generate high levels of endorphin in their system, and it is possible that the often-noted phenomenon of the "runner's high" is related to this fact. Because endorphin receptors are found in the deep brain area where emotions are seated as well as in the "pain pathways" of the brain, interventions in the brain that increase endorphins in the right place at the right time may be a formidable euphoric capable of extensive applications.

—Even something as specific (and as notorious) as alcoholism may be subject to an effective cure through chemical stimulation of the brain. When THP (tetrahydropapaveroline) is injected into the brains of experimental animals, they develop an insatiable appetite for alcohol (which they normally do not consume). To R. D. Myers, a neurophysiologist at Purdue University, who has directed this research, "the outcome suggests that alcoholism isn't the product of psychological or social influences" but is, instead, "a physical disease stemming from a defect in the brain cells that results in too much THP." Myers hopes to find, then, "a drug that cures alcoholism, or even prevents it."[27]

In saying that those who are bothered by artificiality may take heart from the research findings just alluded to, what I have in mind is this. Even though the peptides that control experience or behavior may have to be stimulated by chemical or electrical interventions originating from outside the person concerned, the fact that the substances that produce the desired effect are body chemicals may make the overall process appear to be more "natural" and therefore more acceptable. Yet, the fact that external interventions based on scientific knowledge would be necessary, for example, to trigger release of the natural substances, establishes the process as a technology of experience and behavior control. If some users of EBC are partial to peptide-related approaches because they are in some sense less artificial, that's fine, so long as others are free to choose a different approach (operant conditioning, for example) that strikes them as faster, more reliable, or (for whatever reason) more advantageous.

## Orthomolecular Research

A second possible breakthrough in the area of CSB comes from the field of orthomolecular research. Some of the miracle treatments proclaimed by exponents of this approach have been challenged by skeptics, but there is no question that certain forms of schizophrenia and depression that are extremely resistant to conventional psychiatric techniques (especially psychoanalysis) have responded marvelously to megavitamin therapies or treatments by certain cheap, readily obtainable chemicals such as lithium. Dr. Ronald Fieve's prediction that "traditional psychotherapy and analysis will become, for the most part, obsolete" is not accepted by many practitioners, and there is still a good deal of skepticism about the claim that "for the first time in history there are specific medicines that are effective against emotional illnesses in as many as 80 percent of cases."[28] But few specializations within the medical arts look as promising in the next couple of decades as this branch of psychopharmacology.

## Consciousness Expansion

A third type of CSB breakthrough is possible with what the popular literature calls "consciousness expansion" drugs. Gerald Leach predicts that "new synthetic hallucinogens will surely be produced and people will surely go on using them," for the desire "and the need for temporary escape into Aldous Huxley's 'artificial paradise' is ingrained too deeply into human culture for it to be otherwise." This development may be all the more promising if Leach is correct in assuming that important progress can be expected in "reducing their toxicity and in understanding why people react to them differently." Thus, "Huxley's wish for highly potent, non-toxic, non-addictive 'escape' drugs without any of the physically incapacitating or damaging effects of today's could well be realized."[29] It should be emphasized, of course, that exponents of consciousness-expanding drugs do not view them as a means of "escape." On the contrary, they believe that one's perceptions of the most important realities of the psyche and, sometimes, of the cosmos are intensified—and by the time Aldous Huxley wrote *Island*, he postulated the availability of a drug that opened the gates of perception to a serene and utterly sublime vision of the universe (see Chapter 3).

## BEHAVIOR THERAPY

Another major technology of EBC, one that is frequently (often pejoratively) called "behavior modification" in common parlance, is behavior therapy. The risks of oversimplification and prejudicial half-truths are staggering when one attempts to give an ordinary language explanation of this specialty. So perhaps it would be wise to begin by correcting a number of misconceptions:

(1) The label preferred by professionals in the field is "behavior therapy," and it includes a wide range of clinical techniques that deal with specific problems (e.g., desensitization, operant conditioning, modeling, and cognitive restructuring). A "client"[30] suffering from a phobia, for example, may be desensitized by being given an opportunity to learn to tolerate the thought or the presence of what he or she fears little by little, step by step. For a person afraid of being touched by her own urine, for example, this learning process might proceed in the following way:

(1) She learns deep relaxation techniques (which can be used as a first step in coping with almost any kind of phobia).
(2) She learns to tolerate being in the same room, and then at the same table, with a tightly sealed bottle of urine.
(3) She learns to handle the sealed bottle.
(4) She learns to handle the unsealed bottle.
(5) She learns to allow one drop to be put on her arm . . . and once she can tolerate this, it is usually not difficult to tolerate several drops, or contact with a piece of cloth soaked in urine, etc.

The client may still find the presence, smell, or touch of urine offensive (most people in our culture do), and she may always have to live with occasional feelings of anxiety as well as continuing distaste for the experience of being touched by urine. But if she overcomes the feeling of *panic* that typically goes along with a phobia, and is able to cope with ordinary life situations where the chance of being touched by urine exists, the problem is for all practical purposes solved.[31]

A patient suffering from addiction learns "stimulus control" and "substitution of alternative behaviors." He identifies the situations that stimulate a desire for the addictive substance and learns to avoid or restructure them; not only that, he also learns to do something else when conscious of a desire for the addictive substance. Thus, a smoker who wants to quit stays away from the social situations in which he is most fond of smoking and chews gum or drinks a glass of water when he is conscious of a desire to light up.

(2) Contrary to popular misconceptions, most behavior therapy is both voluntary and nonaversive. Many experts contend that no lasting modification of behavior *can* be accomplished without the assent and the consistent cooperation of the client, and one of the most pronounced trends within this relatively novel discipline is toward increased understanding, control, and self-administration by the client. "Cognitive restructuring," for instance, requires the client to learn to alter his or her own behavior by replacing "maladaptive characteristics" and the assumptions on which they are based with other inclinations and ideas that are in harmony with the behaviors they seek to develop.

Aversive techniques are not in favor simply because they are considered less effective than positive reinforcement in producing desired behaviors. But when used in situations in which they do serve as useful supplements to other parts of the meticulously categorized step-by-step process of behavior shaping, they are likely to be logically related to the unwanted behavior being extinguished. Thus, one aspect of smoking cessation programs may be "rapid smoking," in which you inhale quickly and deeply—say, one complete cigarette every five minutes—until you can take no more without vomiting or passing out. Doing this helps make you aware of the physiological consequences that always accompany smoking but to which you are usually oblivious because they are gradual or not concentrated. And if aversive techniques are used, they are usually so mild as to be experienced as merely "irritating" or "annoying" rather than actually painful or hurtful.

(3) There is, finally, a trend toward increasingly complex multi-component programs of behavior therapy that supplement laboratory or clinical exercises with a host of other expriences or learned skills:

> As with other clinical disorders, the application of limited techniques (such as aversive therapy) to isolated aspects of the alcoholic's behavior has given way to more sophisticated analyses of the nature of [the problem] and an emphasis on multi-component social learning

treatment programmes. Among the several behavior-therapy techniques that are now commonly used ... are social skills training; self-
control procedures including self-monitoring, goal-setting and self-
evaluation, self-reinforcement and self-instruction; stress-reduction
techniques; modeling . . . ; contingency management focused on
reinforcing alternative behavior; and social reinforcement . . .
through group support.[32]

This trend is a logical concomitant of the genius of behavior modification—to "shape" what one does, to do what one is capable to do,
and to become accustomed to break complicated behavior se-
quences and attendant attitudes into separate components that can
be encouraged or discouraged, according to the wishes of the client.

## BIOFEEDBACK

Biofeedback is both natural and artificial. It leads to learned behaviors that can be produced again and again at will. One might not
be able to produce learned behaviors without the use of the technical equipment that provides reinforcement in the form of information about one's success in producing the desired states and without
the systematic ordering of the exercises by means of which one
learns. What happens in biofeedback training is this: Electronic
monitoring devices are attached to those parts of the body where
they can pick up heartbeat, blood pressure, brain waves, tension
levels, or whatever you want to have measured—and then you learn,
by trial and error, to influence various bodily operations in such a
way as to create the effects you want to create. Barbara Brown,
whose *New Mind, New Body* is an excellent one-volume treatment
of the subject, describes biofeedback in these words:

Actually, there are two aspects of bio-feedback [*sic*—Brown consistently uses this spelling, which is hardly ever used today]. First is the
technology, the use of biomedical devices that are capable of taking a
reading of your physiologic activity, such as temperature, heart rate,
etc., and second is the aspect of training, i.e., what you do with the
device....

In some forms of bio-feedback you simply watch or listen as the
monitor sign or a selected body function fluctuates.... If you continue
to work with the device, ... then over time some association appears

between certain changes in the body sign and different subjective feelings. . . . In essence the monitor gives you information about your successes. In time you develop control over fluctuations of the sign, and
often may learn to exercise precise control, at will, over how the body
signs change. . . .

There is a popular misconception about bio-feedback by some tradi-
tionalist psychologists that in order for bio-feedback to be effective one
must be strapped to a bio-feedback instrument for a lifetime. This is un-
true. Many research studies have demonstrated surprisingly long-lasting
effects of bio-feedback *once the concept has been realized.*[33]

It is not at all difficult to understand why biofeedback ought to
help us in many important ways:

One has only to look to disorders of the cardiovascular system to see
that the control over blood pressure, heart rate and peripheral vasodi-
lation and vasoconstriction will add immeasurably to a patient's
comfort and life expectancy. . . . Control over both respiration and
the secretions of the respiratory mucosa will ameliorate the discom-
forts and serious sequelae of asthma, bronchitis, emphysema,
sinusitis, and so on. Learned control over muscle systems, individual
muscles, and even muscle cells will provide extraordinary help in all
types of muscle problems, ranging from the simple muscle tension of
anxiety to the rehabilitation of inactive or disordered muscles. So it is
with each body system.[34]

The extended list of possible benefits, both therapeutic and nontherapeutic, is quite impressive: "an early warning system for the
detection of developing illnesses," the sort of learned muscle relaxation that could be used to mitigate both the length and the intensity
of some illnesses, sleep control (including control over "even the exact depth of sleep desired"), greater benefits from "such sleep
substitutes as rest, cat-napping and momentary relaxation," greater
rapport with physicians (because of heightened bodily awareness),
marked reduction of psychosomatic illness, "control over dream
life," faster and more complete rehabilitation and openness to new
states of consciousness, or actual experience of them (including
"sensations of floating, a feeling of dissolving into the feedback
signal, the loss of time perception, detachment and other non-
ordinary states and feelings").[35]

Of course, biofeedback per se is no panacea, and many of the
claims made for it may be advanced without adequate scientific

proof of its efficacy. According to Dr. Ronald Melzack, a psychologist at McGill University who is famous for his formulation of the "gate-control theory" of pain, few research reports on the impact of biofeedback satisfy basic criteria deemed essential to a sober evaluation of its benefits. In Melzack's opinion, the value of biofeedback cannot be assessed unless the following conditions are satisfied:

(1) Controlled studies must make allowances for the placebo effect that is almost always operative in situations involving a medical professional and a patient in distress or a research subject eager to please the researcher.
(2) Changes induced "must be of sufficient magnitude and duration to have clinical significance."
(3) The procedures learned in a therapeutic or experimental setting must be "as effective in a person's normal, variable environment as they are in a clinic or a laboratory."
(4) "Biofeedback training, once acquired, [must] last long enough to be meaningful."[36]

Melzack found that learning to produce alpha brain waves does not necessarily reduce chronic pain and that biofeedback may have to be supplemented by another therapy (e.g., hypnosis) in order to have the desired analgesic effect. Other researchers have discovered that biofeedback can sometimes create a boomerang effect: A person who is trying to learn to govern some bodily function may worry so much about the difficulty of the learning process that his symptoms are aggravated instead of alleviated.[37]

## MISCELLANEOUS POSSIBILITIES

In addition to these four main technologies of EBC that have direct applications to the quest for artificial happiness and goodness, there are a host of other areas of research that are relevant to the concerns of this study (and have a special bearing on the possibilities for increased human capacity discussed in Chapter 5):

—Research on nutrition is pertinent particularly in its effects on mental illness. Relief of emotional illness may be the most noteworthy development in orthopsychiatry at the moment, but in the long run the impact on memory and increased learning ability may be even more significant, for it may result in heightened intellectual capacity in general (resulting in larger, heavier brains) or enhanced ability to learn or remember particular skills or knowledge learned at a particular time. Certainly David Krech's experiments with laboratory animals (see Chapter 5) seem to prove that "good brains can be cultivated" through a combination of nutritional and environmental enrichment. In fact,

many scientists are now predicting that within a few years there will be drugs, or stimulated environmental regimes, or both combined, capable of raising human "intelligence" by up to 20 I. Q. points.[38]

—Memory research may turn out to be of enormous significance. Experiments with vasopressin (a hormone located in the pituitary gland) show dramatic increases in short-term memory, and a completely safe version of synthesized vasopressin may be available by 1987. If tests now being conducted show similar effects on long-term recall,

vasopressin may help you sharpen your memory and enhance your learning ability. The regular use of vasopressin may even sustain your brain's memory mechanism so that you could be spared the forgetfulness that usually accompanies old age.[39]

This area of investigation is regarded by some experts as "the most difficult and challenging field in the brain sciences," for:

it has defeated, so far, the best efforts of some of the world's most imaginative scientists, including men who dropped all their previous research for its sake. It has attracted such Nobel Prize winners as Marshall Nirenberg, Jacques Monod, Francis Crick and—perhaps most revealingly—the brilliant and ambitious James Watson, author of The Double Helix, whose competitive instincts have been aroused by the race. The leading contenders for the key to memory are now laboring at white heat, in considerable secrecy, fully aware of the immense possibilities involved.[40]

There is even some speculation about the prospects for "imprinting" certain kinds of knowledge or quasi-instinctual response patterns or abilities in the minds of very young children (thus awaking the specter of Huxley's *Brave New World*, in which human embryos stored in incubators were conditioned to be content with their future as workers, clerks, or leaders in a highly stratified society).

—Sleep research may teach us how to refresh our bodies adequately with fewer hours of the "right" kind of sleep, or chemicals may provide the body with the same kind of refreshment normally provided by sleep, so that, in effect, our waking lives are extended for an additional ten or twenty years. It may teach us how to dream more or less, to direct the direction and content of our dream life, and to find ways of relating dreams to aesthetic creativity.[41]

—Split-brain research holds out the promise of fascinating new insights into the relation between the "rational" left brain and the "feeling" right brain. As knowledge of this kind moves forward, we should be able to improve both the balance between the activity of each hemisphere and the versatility of our minds in perceiving, thinking, and imagining.[42]

—Experiments with hypnosis, extrasensory perception, mental telepathy, kirlian auras, and other paranormal powers of mind may reveal a capacity for mental operation barely conceived of by most people in our culture today. Commenting on recent signs that artificial intelligence enthusiasts are now less confident about their ability to construct computers that equal the human brain, George Leonard observes,

> What we are learning is not that computers are any less wonderful than we had imagined but that human abilities are far more wonderful than we had dreamed.... The Age of Computers may indeed turn out to be golden after all, if only because it reveals to us the miracle inherent in what we consider most ordinary in our lives.[43]

## SAFETY

This analysis of the ethics of EBC by a nonscientist presupposes a number of technical conditions and feasibilities that the reader is simply asked to accept as plausible. One of these technical factors—safety—is so important that a general statement concerning its limits and the sense in which it is assumed is necessary.

There are two kinds of unintended negative consequences that may be particularly troublesome in situations in which EBC (especially CSB) is being used to promote artificial happiness and good-ness. In the first category are the undesirable side effects that may be caused, especially if these side effects cannot be easily identified as having been caused by the intervention being used to create some desired outcome. This may be a difficult problem in clinical situa-tions, because even if a drug is successful in overcoming the malady for which it is being prescribed, it may actually cause secondary symptoms that are attributed to the illness rather than the medica-tion:

> A whole range of drug-induced effects, from sexual indifference to a robot-like depersonalization, may either go unnoticed by the patient or be attributed to his or her "sickness" and taken as further evidence of the need for medication.[44]

The second type of unintended negative consequence is a long-range effect that cannot be foreseen in advance. Extensive use of a drug that is very effective in eradicating symptom X (and is therefore a tremendous boon to those who suffer from it) may in time produce unanticipated effects that constitute a new problem for the long-term user. Ritalin, for example, may help a "hyperactive" child improve her ability to concentrate and learn in the short run—but prolonged use may actually *impair* learning ability, and it may increase a child's heart and blood pressure rate to a harmful degree. Likewise,

> prolonged phenothiazine therapy, in addition to controlling disruptive behavior, may impair cognitive functioning and exacerbate symptoms in some non-paranoid forms of acute schizophrenia, and so actually prolong recovery.[45]

What posture can be sensibly adopted in regard to the limits of safety? Because the possibility of harmful side effects and deleterious long-range consequences cannot be eliminated, what principle should govern our attitude toward them?

The principle most commonly applied in our society is that of ac-ceptable risk. Decisions about safety are in reality judgments about acceptable risk and involve two very different mental operations: "measuring risk, an objective but probabilistic pursuit, and judging the acceptability of that risk (judging safety), a matter of personal and social value judgment" [italics added].

Ascertaining degree of risk involves an empirical analysis of two variables—that is, probability of harm and severity:

> Thus in a familiar example, it is said that in the present year Americans on the average run a risk of about one in 4000 of dying in an automobile accident. The probability is that one out of 4000 injuries will be lethally severe.... This expresses the overall risk to society; the risk to any particular individual obviously depends on his exposure, how much he is on the road, where he drives and in what weather, whether he is psychologically accident prone, what mechanical condition his vehicle is in and so on.[46]

Assessment of the acceptability of risk requires a decision about the probable costs and benefits of the activity in question. For example, legislative deliberations about the problem of automobile safety might focus on the following questions (in which the issue of *risk* is expressed in Roman type and that of acceptability in italics):

> A legislature asks questions about seat belts: How effective will they be? Will people wear them? What reduction in injuries can be expected from seat belts? How much do they cost? Can manufacturers make them available in all new cars? *How much does society value the injury reduction? Are the belts an acceptable solution? Should they be required by law?*[47]

A conclusion is reached by evaluating empirical factors such as risk, efficacy ("the probability and intensity of beneficial effects"), and costs in the light of the value-laden variables rooted in convictions about the importance of hoped-for benefits and the seriousness of possible dangers.

Thus, different individuals will differ in their appraisal of the safety of various kinds of EBC. If they are careful, they may want to obtain a profile of their own psychological and physiological makeup before they decide which types of EBC to expose themselves to. If the benefits promised by a given drug or procedure strike them as sufficiently enticing, they may be willing to undergo considerable risk. If, on the other hand, they have reason to believe that they are especially vulnerable to a particularly severe negative side effect, no conceivable benefit may suffice to persuade them to risk exposure. Thus, both information and cultivated judgment are of great importance in wise use of EBC for artificial happiness, goodness, and increased capacity.

# NOTES

1. Jerry Adler, Pamela Abramson, Susan Katz, and Mary Hager, "Getting High on 'Ecstasy,'" *Newsweek* (April 15, 1985), p.96.

2. Anastasia Toufexis, "A Crackdown on Ecstasy," *Time* (June 10, 1985), p. 64.

3. Joe Klein, "The Drug They Call 'Ecstasy,'" *New York* (May 20, 1985), p. 43.

4. Richard A. Shaffer, "Mastering the Mind," *The Wall Street Journal*, Vol. 97, No. 30 (August 12, 1977), p. 1.

5. Judy Foreman, "Mind-Body Separation Has Become Obsolete," *Los Angeles Times* (Dec. 27, 1981), Part VII, p. 24.

6. Gerald Leach, *The Biocrats*, p. 236.

7. Charles Panati, *The Book of Breakthroughs*, p. 124.

8. Maya Pines, *The Brain Changers*, p. 43.

9. Jose Delgado, *Physical Control of the Mind*, pp. 128-129.

10. Pines, *Changers*, p. 45.

11. Delgado, *Physical Control*, pp. 150-154.

12. Pines, *Changers*, p. 46.

13. *Ibid.*, p. 47.

14. Eliot Valenstein, *Brain Control*, pp. 162ff.

15. Personal conversation with Jose Delgado, Madrid, June 1982. If Delgado is right on this point, the "experience machine" hypothesized by Robert Nozick in *Anarchy, State and Utopia* (pp. 42-45) is an absurd impossibility, useful only as a theoretical entity that can be used to pose philosophical questions. Its use for this purpose by Jonathan Glover in *What Sort of People Should There Be?* (pp. 92ff.) is intriguing.

16. Pines, *Changers*, p. 51.

17. *Ibid.*, p. 52.

18. Leach, *Biocrats*, p. 232.

19. Vance Packard, *The People Shapers*, p. 59.

20. Albert Rosenfeld, *The Second Genesis*, p. 227.

21. Paul Ehrlich, Address delivered at the Georg-Speyer-Haus, Sept. 6, 1966, in P. Himmelweit [ed.], *The Collected Papers of Paul Ehrlich*, Vol. 3. Quoted in Henry L. Lennard et al., "Hazards Implicit in Prescribing Psychoactive Drugs," *Science*, Vol. 169 (July 31, 1970), p. 43.

22. *Ibid.*

23. Foreman, "Mind-Body," p. 25.

24. *Ibid.*

25. Shaffer, "Mastering," p. 1.

26. Foreman, "Mind-Body," p. 24.

27. Shaffer, "Mastering," p. 1.

28. Roland Fieve, "Medicine for Melancholy," in Albert Rosenfield [ed.], *Mind and Supermind*, p. 229.

29. Leach, *Biocrats*, p. 235.

30. Not "patient," a designation that tends to stigmatize the subject as a deviant, and thus, compromises the matter-of-fact stance preferred by theorists of behavior therapy.

31. Morton Hunt, "A Neurosis Is Just a Bad Habit," *New York Times Magazine* (June 4, 1967), pp. 38-48.

32. Stanley Rachman and G. T. Wilson, *The Effects of Psychological Therapy*, p. 174.

33. Barbara Brown, *New Mind, New Body,* pp. 6-7, 10.

34. *Ibid.,* pp. 8-9.

35. *Ibid.,* pp. 370-408.

36. Ronald Melzack, "The Promise of Biofeedback: Don't Hold the Party Yet," *Psychology Today* (July 1975), p. 21.

37. Personal conversation with Victor Meyer, London, March 1982.

38. Panati, *Breakthroughs,* p. 115.

39. *Ibid.*

40. Pines, *Changers,* pp. 153-154.

41. Packard, *Shapers,* pp. 57-58.

42. Pines, *Changers,* pp. 135ff.

43. Leonard, George, "In God's Image," *Saturday Review* (February 22, 1975), p. 13.

44. Elizabeth Dalton and Kim Hopper, "Ethical Issues in Behavior Control," *Man and Medicine*, Vol. 2, No. 1 (1976), p. 24.

45. *Ibid.,* p. 23.

46. William Lowrance, *Of Acceptable Risk,* pp. 8, 70.

47. *Ibid.,* p. 76.

# Chapter 3

# ARTIFICIAL HAPPINESS

Strictly speaking, it is not accurate to say that the only kind of positive increase in happiness one can expect from EBC is in the form of sensory delights or euphoric moods. The happiness that comes from amicable interpersonal relationships, for example, can be augmented by several of the technologies and techniques described in Chapter 2. Moreover, EBC can be instrumental in the production of peak experiences that are so joyful or profound that they must be classified as fulfilling, not just happy: Thus, some psychiatrists use psychotropic drugs or biofeedback-engendered altered states as a way of unlocking tranformative insights, and some devotees of mystical experiences believe that EBC can lead to the ultimate depths of philosophical or religious awareness. But the average person is likely to be less interested in these possibilities than in some form of "Intensity."

## PETER AND SALLY: A VIGNETTE

Peter has always been the kind of "good all-around guy" who gets voted "most popular" or "most likely to succeed" in high school senior class voting. At 35 he has established himself as a steady performer in a large Los Angeles bank where people who want security and not too much hassle can enjoy a comfortable career. He enjoys sailing with his daughter, golf with his son, and a fairly active social life with his wife, Sally. Similar to many of the upper-middle-class people in whose circles they move, they have given up smoking (except for an occasional joint to remind them of college days) and taken up jogging.They drink a reasonable amount (more wine than whiskey in recent years) and are addicted at a typical American level to coffee and television.

Because they are constantly exposed to the kinds of television programs and magazines in which products such as "Intensity" are advertised, they have begun to experiment with a variety of pleasure-enhancing substances. Accepting *Consumer Reports'* verdict on prospects for marketable ESB (that it would be at least 15 years before a stimucap capable of stimulating the hypothalamus with an implanted electrode would be available, and that in the meantime ESB was both too risky and too expensive), they have turned their attention to CSB. When they hear about a new item (through the media or through word of mouth) they talk it over, and if they feel like giving it a try, they do so on the next convenient weekend, by themselves or with one or more other couples who share their interests. In order to minimize the danger of drug dependency, they follow recognized behavior control techniques of record-keeping, so they are always aware of their own pattern of drug use and can always spot any unusual increase in or concentration of their typical consumption habits. If the slightest indication of excessive use arises, they manipulate the number of stimulus situations and substitute gratifications in such a way as to break up any emerging pattern that looks unhealthy.

They see themselves, in fact, as the very model of the intelligent modern family that knows how to practice refined hedonism to a degree commensurate with acceptable performance of appropriate economic and civic duties and with a more than superficial realization of the kind of human fulfillment that is rooted in a rational life plan and a philosophically meaningful "sense of the whole." They do not see themselves as intellectuals or as religious virtuosi and they have no compelling desire to be either. Now and then they come into contact with proselytizing gurus who try to get them to use drugs "seriously;" that is, for the purpose of attaining cosmic insights or being transported to unaccustomed spiritual heights. Two years ago, in fact, Peter went to the hills for a weekend trial of some far-out meditation techniques and special drugs used by a particular cult. He found the experience quite remarkable and, on the whole, positive. But he really feels no need for radical transformation in his life, and Sally agrees. So they have decided to stick to their comfortable pattern of seeking artificial pleasure only on recreational weekends and special occasions.

## NEW POSSIBILITIES FOR ARTIFICIAL HAPPINESS

Nothing is more obvious than the self-certification of pleasurable sensations. The delight they furnish does not require elaborate explanation because it is intrinsic to those experiences that give us pleasure. You don't need to *understand* the pleasure of the smell and taste of delicious food to enjoy it; you can revel in the pleasure of being caressed without thinking about it; you can be transported by the sound of beautiful music without finding any cognitive interpretation of it; you can be thrilled by an autumn landscape without reflecting on the meaning of your joy.

In fact, nothing is more puzzling than the question, "But *why* do you receive pleasure from these experiences?" You can put together a string of words that constitute an explanation of sorts and may even find that your pleasure is deepened by the thought you give to formulating an answer to the question. Yet, the answer that springs to mind most quickly is simply, "I just do, that's all!" or "Doesn't everybody?"

No wonder, then, we are pleased to find that our enjoyment of various smells, tastes, sights, sounds, and tactile sensations can be augmented by various expedients. If your enjoyment of music is made greater by being able to look at the sky while you listen, you may go to a lot of outdoor concerts or buy a 35-foot extension cord for your stereo earphones. If your beloved's skin feels even more enchanting in proximity to silk, you may buy nightwear and bedclothes made of that material and enrich your enchantment further by perfume, incense, candlelight, and mood music. And if a glass of bourbon increases your enjoyment of certain occasions, you will not hesitate to intensify it "artificially" by the use of that particular drug.

So what is outlandish or outrageous about the idea of a product such as "Intensity"? Each variant of it is merely a chemical expedient to heighten the pleasure of one kind of sensory stimulus: "Red for sound,…" and so on. No doubt a more general euphoric could yield similar satisfactions without the drawbacks of alcohol or marijuana and the slightly different delights of that option might sometimes be preferred. But the possibility can hardly be called farfetched.

EBC research may have already perfected a number of new euphoria-inducing drugs that we have not yet heard of because of the prevailing conservatism of our present cultural climate. If the patent applications for such products exist, they are being kept safe until a time when they can be greeted by a more sympathetic reception at the Federal Drug Administration, and marketing plans are being kept on the shelf until such time as the general public can be expected to give them a more enthusiastic welcome. Be that as it may, some observers are predicting that pleasure-enhancement agents will soon be easy to purchase in great variety and abundance. A recent article on peptide research notes that "endorphin receptors are found not only in the pain pathways of the brain but also in the deep brain area that rules emotions." It continues,

> That location also raises the most far-out of the possible roles for endorphins, that they may be the body's own pleasure drugs. At Ohio State University, doses of synthetic endorphins seem to cause orgasm in rats. Wyeth Laboratories, the drug company, has found that rats, trained to operate a pump by pressing a lever, will voluntarily shoot endorphins into their brains. And these results recall experiments at Tulane University in which a woman had repeated orgasams after neuro-transmitters were injected into her head.
>
> "It may be that these peptides are the actual source of all reward," suggests Larry Stein, a Wyeth researcher. "By working with them we might come up with the greatest pleasure drug ever."[1]

Another famous social analyst forsees a time when "normal" persons "may carry enlarged pillboxes" that contain the wherewithal to make them "more aggressive, optimistic, creative, euphoric, dynamic, placid or sexed up."[2] And a British observer, after describing the action of a key psychotropic that "does not cause the distortions of perception and interference in intellectual functions that other hallucinogens possess," goes on to write,

> Many more drugs, without the extreme effects of LSD and other hallucinogens, but with some of their more useful properties such as

enhancing self-awareness, will be developed in the near future. Thus drugs will have rapid action and have rapid antidotes when necessary. It is possible to envisage the creation of drug cafes which will exist to cater to the public. It will be possible to order a specific menu, say an hors d'oeuvre of enhanced vision or color or sounds, a main course of sensory hallucinations, ... with a dessert of self-awareness.[3]

The practical utility of ESB for artificial pleasure may depend on the perfecting of some means less intimidating (and costly) than the deep implantation of electrodes, or even, for all but the most daring or determined, of transdermal stimoceivers placed just below the surface of the skin. The scenario evoked by John Taylor arouses fascination as well as skepticism:

There is no doubt that these developments [in ESB] have great relevance for the normal person. It is even now possible for a man to experience primitive noises, sights, and senses on his skin by suitably implanted electrodes. These electrodes cause no damage and can be left permanently implanted in his skull. An operation would be costly, but would be repaid by the extended range of sensations he could create at will, and these sensations would become more and more interesting and powerful to him as the placing and switching of the electrodes becomes better understood. The crucial thing is that an unlimited range of visual, auditory, and sensory experiences will become available to such a person.

It is possible to envisage a time in the future when electrode implantation is an everyday operation, just as operations for straightening noses or increasing the size of a woman's breasts are becoming now. Instead of sitting at home and watching the television such a person could fit on his stimulating cap, connect it up to his stimulator set, and experience a program or play of sensations by a good writer of such plays. He might even have a do-it-yourself stimulator kit, which would allow him to choose his own sensations. And there is the possibility of doing it to each other. Such developments will surely come within the next century.[4]

A lot depends on whether or not the electrical charge that does the trick can be shot to its target receptors without necessitating anything so dangerous as wires (no matter how slender) reaching down from the surface of the skull to the target areas, or anything so cosmetically disadvantageous as coin-sized objects under the skin of the head. If a completely detachable stimucap can accomplish the desired effects, there would be lots of takers—and if a stimoceiver can do the job from just inside the skin, perhaps the contact points of a stimucap could do it just as well from just outside the skin. Moreover, if Delgado is right and Valenstein wrong about the safety of wires extending down into the brain, and if the cost of the procedure goes low enough, the perfection of a totally detachable stimucap may prove to be superfluous.[5]

But if we make the vital distinction between pure *technical possibility* and *overall feasibility*, we may conclude that ESB has very little promise as a means to artificial pleasure. Jose Delgado gives several reasons why this is the case:

(1) The procedure would be extremely expensive.
(2) Many of the relatively few neurosurgeons qualified to carry out the procedure would decline to do so on the grounds that it would be a waste of their talent: They would look upon such requests as relatively frivolous in comparison with the plight of a patient who needed ESB as a remedy for some frightful pathological condition or for chronic pain not amenable to treatment by drugs.
(3) The "pay-offs" of the procedure would probably be very limited. The sensations produced might be experienced as pleasurable at first, but after the novelty had worn off they might come to seem monotonous, boring, or even annoying—and the person who had gone to such great expense and trouble to experience these sensations would probably regret his decision to do so.[6]

Delgado does affirm, however, that ESB has an extremely important role to play in increasing happiness by diminishing pain.

In addition to those forms of EBC that produce pleasurable sensations or euphoric moods directly, these technologies are capable of heightening interest in and appreciation of activities that are normally classified as pleasure-giving anyhow. L-dopa and PCPA are two drugs with demonstrated power as aphrodisiacs and bestowers of potency; indeed, Dr. W. O'Malley of Georgetown University reports that the former can give men in their 60s and 70s more sexual vigor than the average 20-year-old.[7] The value of such drugs for older adults is obvious; what is less obvious, but equally hopeful, is their possible use in promoting greater compatibility between married partners when one person's sexual appetite is much lower than the other's. Direct stimulation of the sex center in the hypothalamus is also conceivable through ESB, and in Taylor's words, "those prepared to afford deep electrode implantation there would very likely have a wonderful return for their investment." There's no telling how far people might go in their exuberance for such possibilities:

> In a permissive society, where there is a great deal of changing of sexual companions, the most favored would be those with enhanced powers. They would be the flames around which the moths would dance. But more people would want to be the favored flames with their sexual powers burning brightly; such treatment would most likely spread very rapidly. It is even possible to envisage such a movement getting out of hand; a far greater amount of time would be spent on sexual intercourse, possibly bringing other activities to a halt. But since there is expected to be more leisure in the automated society of the future, what better way of spending it than in sexual ecstasy.[8]

Those who are appalled rather than amused or titillated by such a prospect will be relieved to know that there is a physiological fact concerning the experience of pleasure that might be used to suggest an ethical principal for determining which types of artificial pleasure are morally licit and which are not. If the stimulation of pleasure receptors in the brain takes place *peripherally* instead of directly—that is, if the impulses are mediated through nerve endings located on the skin or in other parts of the body instead of being administered intracranially—there seems to be a sort of "insulation effect" that protects the organism against excessive (or endless) stimulation:

> Peripheral self-stimulation ceases after a time, unlike the continuation of the intra-cranial self-stimulation to exhaustion. It would seem that there is a built-in mechanism, sitting between the sense organs and the pleasure centers which prevents self-stimulation to exhaustion; the mechanism becomes completely ineffective when intra-cranial stimulation can be achieved. So while the latter is a highly effective reward it is also a highly unnatural one.[9]

The implication of this finding is that ordinary sensory stimuli—all of which come to the brain from the peripheral areas of the body through the nerves connecting brain and periphery—do *not* have the same intensity or duration as do stimuli injected directly into the cranium.

## PHILOSOPHICAL AND ETHICAL ISSUES

The second half of this chapter will address the philosophical and ethical issues arising in connection with the new possibilities for artificial happiness. The first of its three main sections deals with a number of conceptual categories that are crucial to the overall argument; the second, with pleasure enhancement; the third, with a summary statement about the implications of the analysis.

### Conceptual Clarification

Following a reiteration of one of the cardinal assumptions implicit in the whole approach to EBC being undertaken here, there are two major areas of conceptual clarification that must be introduced before the analysis proceeds. What is required, first of all, is a fuller explanation of the idea that happiness (or, better, "the good life") is to be thought of as a compound of pleasure, happiness, and fulfillment. Second, we need a statement of normative presuppositions to serve as a context for understanding and evaluating particular judgments concerning the rights and wrongs of EBC. In both cases, presentation of the conceptual material is intended to remind the reader that many different decisions about technical possibilities make sense according to different value preferences. If certain people's concepts of personal fulfillment leave little room for "mere pleasure" of any kind, obviously the coming availability of all kinds of new ways to secure artificial pleasure will strike them as a threat, not a blessing. And from the vantage point of each of the possible "drug ethics" suggested below, a different priority of goods and attendant choices would follow.

Among the assumptions underlying everything that follows is a crucial one that deserves reiteration: All of the uses of EBC discussed here are part of a very large and varied overall mix of experiences and activities that comprise the life of the persons concerned; their use of EBC for "artificial" happiness is balanced by countless other "natural" events brought about for similar reasons. On grounds that will be stipulated and explained below, the supposition is that persons can choose and enjoy these particular uses of EBC without becoming addicted to them and without destroying other precious human characteristics or capacities. We are talking about actions undertaken by ordinary men and women as new means to realize certain ends sought by ordinary men and women since the origin of the species.

*Pleasure, Happiness, and Fulfillment.* The theory of the good life as a compound of pleasure, happiness, and fulfillment is depicted graphically in Figure 1. The meaning of the key terms can be illustrated as follows:

—"Pleasure" is a word that will be used to refer to good feelings that are primarily *sensory* and *personal:* Pleasure comes from physical sensations that can be enjoyed alone as well as in the presence of other persons. It comes from being vitally in touch with your own body and its senses.

*Examples:* a drink of cold water when you are thirsty or a steak that you cook for yourself in the middle of the night when you suddenly feel a yen for just that kind of taste; listening to music on stereo earphones when you are so caught up in the delightfulness of a Bach fugue or a Mozart *divertimento* that you are conscious of nothing but the glory of that sound and the joy of feeling its rhythms in your body; masturbating in the middle of the night as you lie half asleep in your warm bed, deliciously aware of the silk of your pajamas, the mounting excitement of your entire body, and the satisfaction of its shuddering release.

—"Happiness" is a word that will be used to refer to satisfactions that are more *emotional* and *social* in character. Physical sensations may be involved, but happiness comes primarily from the interpretations put upon what one is perceiving, feeling, and doing. It comes from being in touch with other persons and life events one cares about.

*Examples:* having a special meal with family or friends where specially prepared dishes are a celebration of the importance the people gathered at the table have for each other; going to a concert when a part of the joy of the occasion is being appropriately dressed for and taking the trouble to participate in the ritual of attending the event; making love.

—"Fulfillment" is a word that will be used to refer to the satisfactions one feels in connection with major, long-term commitments of one's energy and time. Fulfillment is happiness with a special dimension of significance; it comes from successful completion of some element of your "rational life plan" (or from having given something important your best shot, whether you succeeded or not); it comes from seeing something fall into place in your "sense of the whole" of

| Category | Examples | Typical Errors |
|---|---|---|
| **Pleasure** Primary satisfactions (elemental experience) | Sensory delight, mirth uncontaminated by ego-preoccupation (being in touch with one's body and one's feelings) | (a) The Puritan Fallacy: pleasure is forbidden (b) The Materialistic Fallacy: pleasure is trivialized in unrefined hedonism or dehumanized in addiction |
| **Happiness** Secondary satisfactions (mental interpretations of experience) | Social approval, friendship, sense of community (being in touch with other persons) | (a) Other-directed role performance (e.g., externalization of life in the struggle for success and status) (b) Unthinking indulgence of one's will-to-power |
| **Fulfillment** Ultimate satisfactions (realization of one's deepest desires for meaning in terms of a "Rational Life Plan," a "Sense of the Whole," or devotion to crucial projects such as parenting and/or experiences characterized by "speechless wonder") | Long-term commitment to intimate others and to a vocation and/or "peak experiences" (being in touch with God, Nature, or something perceived as ultimate) | (a) Preoccupation with honor, fame, or immortality (b) Anomie |

Figure 1    Pleasure, Happiness, and Fulfillment

your life. It may come to you in "peak experiences" when you feel struck by what Greek philosophers called "speechless wonder" at the beauty or terror of life, or it may be associated with a feeling that despite all your failures and mistakes, you have, by God, made some kind of contribution to the world. Fulfillment is "heavy" satisfaction that touches your deepest philosophical and ethical convictions about what is worth living and fighting for in your brief span of years on earth.

*Examples:* Your retirement banquet, when your memory of the food (no matter how deliciously prepared it may be) will be eclipsed by other joys and ruminations; a performance of the *St. Matthew Passion* attended to reverently by someone who is, or even used to be, a devout Christian; making love to your wife of 30 years on the evening after your last child's wedding ceremony.

The distinctions, quite obviously, are somewhat artificial, because the experiences isolated for analytical purposes will inevitably overlap to some extent. Nevertheless, the categories do make sense for thoughtful persons who reflect on the different meaning of different experiences and occasions for them. And the distinctions suggested are important for the defense of "artificial happiness" that I now want to offer.

Because artificial pleasure is the main effect that can be attained directly through the technologies of EBC, that is no doubt one of the reasons why so many people are so resistant to it. If "mere pleasure" is so insignificant in comparison with happiness and fulfillment, why waste time on the pursuit of a lesser good—a good that, in fact, may be instrumentally evil if it distracts your attention and drains your resources in the wrong direction?

What I want to do is to suggest that the relative merits of pleasure and happiness (as defined in contemporary American culture) need to be reassessed. It is my conviction that far too many Americans are engaged in a misguided pursuit of *spurious* notions of "happiness" that are really far less wholesome and far less satisfying than simple pleasures, many of which can be obtained through EBC with much less cost and effort and with far fewer negative dysfunctions than the typical scramble for "happiness" gets us into. People would be a lot more fulfilled as well as a lot happier if they would pluck the fruits of pleasure that are relatively easy to gather and would turn away from some of the crazy ideas about happiness and fulfillment constantly being shoved at them by the mass media in particular and the traditional socialization process in general.

## The Metaphysical Fallacy and the Materialistic Fallacy

Concretely, I urge the thoughtful reader to consider the hollowness and stupidity of both the metaphysical and the materialistic fallacies underlying what most Americans are told about what they ought to want and do in order to be happy and good. In our culture, the most pervasive metaphysical fallacy is that of Puritanism, which warns us to eschew pleasure and tender our lives and our souls on the altar of work (often without asking the important questions of religion and morality that were a part of the doctrine of vocation in classical versions of the Protestant Ethic). The most pervasive materialist fallacy is that of consumerism, which instructs us that happiness and even fulfillment can best be attained by the purchase of innumerable commodities and packaged experiences. Puritanism robs us of the joy of easily found pleasures and gives us dubious notions of fulfillment that many of us cling to only because our spirits have been warped by deprivation of healthy pleasures. High-consumption materialism tricks us into selling our souls and wasting our substance on various messes of pottage that offer little genuine satisfaction and thus leave us vulnerable to the next sales pitch for the next beguiling trinket we see advertised. In addition, counterproductive notions of love and honor needlessly rob us of both pleasure and fulfillment. When we have trouble in interpersonal relationships, for example, it is often because we have a naive conception of how someone else ought to be able to read our minds "if they really love us." There is an element of truth, of course, in the expectation that someone who has been close to another person over a certain length of time may to some extent be able to sense what that person wants without having to have it spelled out. And when social scientists talk about role-sets and "interaction ritual," they are analyzing some of the "rules" of "appropriate" behavior that normal people are supposed to learn as a part of the cultural awareness that they need to function in society. Moreover, Fred Hirsch (in the *Social Limits to Growth*) is quite right to point out that there is a trade-off involved in moving from widely accepted traditional norms on which various parties could count (without having to insist on or bargain for) to a contractual mode of relating in which many things formerly taken for granted have to be negotiated *de novo* again and again as one interacts with individuals who no longer operate in accordance with the old norms.

Even so, one suspects that some of the resistance to EBC as a means of promoting more harmonious interpersonal interaction (as in the very simple "positive reinforcement" schema for resolving family tensions described near the end of Chapter 4 is a manifestation of a romantic sense of honor (or just plain stubborn pride) that cannot be seriously defended on moral grounds. One is perfectly free to cling to what Hirsch calls the "positional good" of tacit communication based on traditional roles and rituals—but one should not claim moral superiority for doing so and should not be self-righteous in one's denunciations of the "dehumanizing" character of operant conditioning techniques that remove the cause of friction by teaching matter-of-fact assertiveness, self-management, and interpersonal negotiating.

But these generalizations may be misleading. Let me try to make my crucial points by discussing something as controversial as it is specific: Consider, if you will, that quintessential symbol of shallow hedonism, the hot tub. It is possible, of course, for one's use of a hot tub to be characterized by enslavement to many of the most perverted ideas concerning happiness now current in our culture. It can be put on display primarily as a status symbol and used more to impress one's associates than to enjoy for its intrinsic pleasures. It can be used in ways that are plainly unethical: It can be used as a device for manipulating or exploiting others; it can be used to excess (and therefore become an instrument of "besotted hedonism" as pernicious as drugs or electrodes); it can be heated in an ecologically irresponsible fashion; it can be used for one's own exclusive pleasure instead of as a not altogether common good that ought to be shared with lots of friends and acquaintances.

But the possibility of abuse does not bar use, as we argue throughout this book: The fact that something is capable of being misused does not mean that proper use should be declared immoral or illegal. And it is certainly possible for a hot tub to be a marvelous source of pleasure and the best kind of happiness as well as a utilitarian aid to better bodily and mental health. If, as is so often the case, the tub is located in a spot where the warmth and relaxation given to the body are supplemented by a pretty view of a garden or a lovely panorama of lake or ocean and if one can listen to good music, sip good wine, and have good conversation with friends while soaking, enjoying a hot tub can be one of the loveliest gratifications life has to offer. And if the expense or the class connotations of owning or having access to a private hot tub are offensive, it is possible now in many parts of the country to rent time in a commercial tub or find a natural hot spring where the natural setting adds something very special to the experience (and puts you into contact with a very different set of fellow hot pool enthusiasts).

This illustration serves to highlight the difficulty of making a rigid line of separation between pleasure and happiness (or even fulfillment). I may be prejudiced in favor of hot tubs, in fact, because my first experience of them was at the Esalen Institute, in a setting so glorious that my mind as well as my senses were overwhelmed with the fullness of joy. This tub was on a cliff overlooking the Pacific Ocean, so the panorama that greeted my eyes was breathtaking (as was the novelty—and, as I got used to it, the deep sense of naturalness and freedom—of being naked in the presence of a lot of other naked people). The sounds of the gulls and sea otters combined with the sound of the wind and the surf to create a feeling of hypnotic enchantment. The alternation of hot and cold water was both invigorating and calming and the giving and receiving of massages added both to the pleasure and the happiness of the occasion. All in all, it was a peak experience that engendered "speechless wonder."

Unfortunately, not all hot tub occasions can measure up to that, and EBC per se cannot give an experience of comparable depth, complexity, and joy. Yet, the occasion I have just described gives some idea of why I think people in technologically advanced high consumption societies would be wise to be more discriminating in their thinking about pleasure and happiness and why I think they ought to put more emphasis on the former and less on prevailing notions about the latter.

A Typology of "Drug Ethics." The second principal area of conceptual clarification needed has to do with a typology of "competing drug ethics" that will serve nicely as a point of departure. In a seminal paper on "Humanizing Drug Choices," Robert Veatch distinguishes five fundamental ethical positions regarding the use of mood-control drugs.[10]

(1) The first drug ethic he identifies is a "back to nature" ethic that condemns modern technology in general and drugs in particular on the grounds that anything artificial is inferior to nature's ways. Veatch rejects this point of view without much argumentation (but on grounds, I think, similar to those given in Chapter 5 of his book). He also rejects a second position that he calls, following Philip Rieff,

(2) the "therapeutic ethic," which views the goal of drug use as "simply to produce happiness, contentment, accommodation, or adjustment," and which destroys a sense of destiny, substituting instead an "accommodation designed to squash tensions and incongruities" that ignores "the realities which are the human condition." The three tenable positions between these two extremes are as follows:

(3) A "Protestant drug ethic," which forbids some chemical agents as "irrelevant to or contrary to the goals of one's life" but treats others as "appropriate or even required." Among these would be "agents used to make man more productive, efficient, and hardworking." (Note that this view is not synonymous with Klerman's "pharmaceutical Calvinism," which is so antipleasure that it in effect means "if it makes you feel good it must be wrong"—see Chapter 5.)

(4) A "Neo-Protestant drug ethic" that is so single-minded in its commitment to a certain kind of enlightenment or mystical union with the Divine that it "justifies the use of psychotropics, including the hallucinogenics," and thus "takes great risks—medical, legal, genetic risks—in order to pursue a particular kind of salvation."

(5) A "Protean drug ethic" in which "variety of chemical experience is valued in itself." "This is the ethic of pluralism," says Veatch, "a peculiarly American ethic" in which "the drive to unify, to integrate, to make sense of one's life, is abandoned in favor of a quest for diversity."

The value of Veatch's typology (as is usually the case with typologies of this kind) is not so much that it describes the empirical realities of what is thought and believed by real-life persons but rather that it helps us put our fingers on some of the most important values that determine attitudes toward drug use—and on the contrary values that are in conflict with them. My interpretation of the import of Veatch's typology is summarized in Figure 2, which may be explained as follows:

(1) The "back-to-nature" ethic values piety or humility vis-à-vis God or Nature above all else. Rather than be guilty of the hubris of challenging the created order, it exhibits exaggerated reverence for a pretechnological concept of the human condition and unwarranted prejudice against human efforts to improve that condition. It reflects commendable awareness of the hazards of pretentiousness and heedlessnesses, but it also shows a lack of both imagination and courage.

(2) The therapeutic ethic has similar defects in its willingness to submit so meekly to the reality principle and all of the surplus-repressions imposed thereby. It may be foolish to try to be a lion, but human beings do not have to settle for being no more than "live dogs," and the person who is too timid to respond to any of the heroic challenges life has to offer is a pitiful and contemptible being.

(3) The Protestant drug ethic puts productivity above all other values, and any admirer of Promethean technology cannot disagree entirely with this emphasis. But all work and no play does make for a pretty dull life, and any conception of God or Right Reason that demands this of human beings does not deserve credence or allegiance.

(4) The Neo-Protestant drug ethic aims at some kind of mystical transport that suggests undue other-worldliness, and if it directs its

| Appellation | Key Principle | Main Flaw |
|---|---|---|
| The "Back to Nature" Ethic | Piety vis-à-vis God and/or Nature | Failure of imagination and loss of nerve |
| The Therapeutic Ethic | Adjustment | Canine view of human potential* |
| The Protestant Drug Ethic | Productivity | Excessive inner-worldly asceticism (obsessive work-compulsiveness) |
| The Neo-Protestant Drug Ethic | Transcendence | Neglect of social responsibility (spiritual self-indulgence) |
| The Protean Ethic | Variety | Aimlessness (fleshly self-indulgence) |

**Figure 2   A Typology of Drug Ethics**
*So called in accordance with a rather curious (and quite uncharacteristic) passage of scripture which declares, "It is better to be a live dog than a dead lion." (Ecclesiastes, 9:4).

followers to abandon this world as hopelessly tainted or unimportant, it may legitimately be accused of undervaluing work, civic responsibility, and a host of other virtues on which civilization depends. In the absence of the organismic theory of society on which medieval monasticism was based (which very few people today would be able to take seriously), any other-worldly ethic is morally irresponsible and may be self-indulgent.

(5) The Protean ethic seems to be the closest thing to what Klerman calls "psychotropic hedonism" in the typology, although it may be possible to adopt this position with greater open-mindedness and scientific detachment than the noun suggests. To explore all possibilities within the limits of acceptable risk in order to see what benefits are to be had (and what perils must be guarded against) is hardly shameful, so long as one is willing to share the knowledge gained with others who may benefit equally. To pursue variety aimlessly and self-indulgently would be morally dubious, particularly if doing so involves a flight from responsibilities in the world.

I should like to think that one can figure out a coherent moral position that partakes of the good points of each of the five schools of thought in Veatch's typology without partaking to a serious degree of their weaknesses. One ought to be able, for instance, to have a measure of the Protean ethic without falling victim to a compulsive emphasis on exploring *every* conceivable route to novel experience (as if "variety for its own sake" were a cherished rule of action). One ought to be able to *optimize* productivity—and certainly to honor the desirability of doing so—without sacrificing humane balance in one's life and personality. And one can certainly be constructively mindful of the "reality principle" and of the folly of hubris without the lack of imagination or courage characteristic of the therapeutic ethic or the "back to Nature" ethic. To put it negatively, I have at least endeavored not to allow my distaste for an extreme version of any of these positions to make me oblivious to the important value(s) each one endeavors to express.

## Philosophical Qualms

EBC promises to increase the pleasure and diminish the pain experienced by millions of human beings. On the face of it, this would appear to be one of the greatest blessings ever vouchsafed to humankind. Why, then, is there so little apparent joy over the prospects?

Part of the answer to that question, of course, has to do with fears about the safety of EBC or about the potential for political abuses. But the skepticism and lack of enthusiasm of many people are in part a function of philosophical qualms that are rooted in the history of the species and in the historical teachings of the dominant value system of Western civilization. To put it bluntly, our culture is characterized by a curious bias against pleasure and an even more curious romanticism about pain which we must now examine.

Disapproval of pleasure is one of the best-known aspects of Puritanism, and the "Puritan work ethic" is frequently blamed for a host of inhibitions and strictures that limit many Americans' joie de vivre. Yet a bias against "mere" pleasure can be detected in both Classical and early Christian thought. In both cases, it is a logical correlate of a metaphysical dualism that tends to associate the world and the flesh with the devil. The realm of matter is inferior to that of the spirit and the lusts of the flesh—which means, especially in monastic thought, attachment to material possessions or worldly concerns of all kinds—are seen as a detriment (even a danger) to a healthy life of the spirit. In the Augustinian tradition (a remarkable blend of Neoplatonic and Biblical elements), the will is dominated by attachment to the things of this world (*cupiditas*) and is quite literally a *drag* on the soul of a person, a weight that drags it lower and lower on the chain of being and thus prevents it from rising toward heaven. Salvation in Christ replaces *cupiditas* with *caritas*, a love of God that

draws the soul upward toward the spiritual fulfillment God intends
for those who are created in His image.[11]

The Renaissance brought a "rediscovery of the world and the individual" that legitimated the healthy lust for life that no culture has
ever been able to suppress more than partially, but its glorification of
the higher goods of the spirit in reason and art soon joined with the
demands of science, technology, and industry to emphasize work
over play, so pleasure (especially in the Protestantism of the Calvinistic tradition that flourished in Northern Europe) continued to be
a somewhat shameful good, a reward that one should enjoy sparingly
and only after paying for it in advance by diligent performance of
one's duties. Hard work is what builds character; sloth, luxury, and
pleasure weaken it.[12]

Romanticism about pain is intimately related to this prejudice
against pleasure. Just as courage in battle or devotion to achievement
in science or industry build and display heroic excellence of
character in an active mode, patient endurance of pain builds and
displays a passive heroism that is regarded as an admirable constit-
uent of strong character. "Strength through adversity" and "salvation through suffering" are two of the most revered themes in
Western letters.[13] Insofar as pain can be utilized to develop strength
and virtue, it is looked upon as a necessary evil that is an instrumental
good.

## Pleasure Enhancement

Everybody pursues pleasure, but almost everyone in our culture
feels ambivalent about it. So it is hardly surprising that a certain
amount of opposition to the prospects for artificial pleasure through
EBC should exist. The qualms of the opponents might be summarized
as follows:

(1) "Mere pleasure" is an unworthy goal for creatures formed in
the image of God. As even the Epicureans and the utilitarians realized, this is particularly true of "base physical appetites" that are
greatly inferior to pleasures of the mind and soul. Happiness ought to
be seen as the by-product of other significant activities, and the pursuit of pleasure is a blind alley that will not engage the energies of a
wise person. A certain amount of pleasure may be necessary, and
thus may be legitimately sought, as a means of *recreating* one's

productive resources; only in this sense and to this extent is pleasure a part of the good life.

(2) The *kind* of pleasure made possible through EBC is unworthy, and the implications of addiction to it are highly disturbing—for it encourages habituation to *isolated self-stimulation,* an individual tickling of the pleasure center of the brain that goes against and tends to deform humankind's nature as a gregarious creature, a social animal whose best enjoyments of life require the presence of other persons and interaction with them.

(3) In a certain sense, then, artifical happiness isn't *real*: It is so inferior to the genuine article that it deserves to be classified as *illusory.*

(4) Certainly an *excess* of pleasure is a detriment to the spirit—and the thing that is particularly alarming about artificial pleasure through EBC is that it will be so intense as to be *irresistible.* Those who are exposed to its insidious delights will fall into a life of drug dependency that is, to speak plainly, subhuman.

(5) The availability of an irresistible escape route would mean that practically nobody would be interested any longer in solving personal or social problems that can so easily be evaded. EBC is *an ignoble cop-out.*

These qualms might be answered by the following counter-arguments.

*"Mere" Pleasure is Unworthy.* There's something odd about being called upon to put in a good word on behalf of something as ubiquitous, basic, natural, and intrinsically self-certifying as pleasure. There is no known culture where pleasure has not been prized and praised by ordinary people (regardless of the misgivings of priests and philosophers), and only the most austere theologians have dared to say nasty things about the delight that all infants and small children feel in the tactile stimulation, warmth, and nourishment they receive at their mothers' bosoms and laps. It helps to know that what is really at stake here is the distinction between "higher" and "lower" pleasures and the fear of ruling elites (including parents) that the latter will prove to be so gratifying that they will interfere with the economic, political, and metaphysical business at hand (the *serious* things that people ought to devote themselves to). Even so, I am obligated to give some kind of justification (no matter how superfluous it may seem) for "mere" pleasure—"pure" pleasure, unadorned by any redeeming intellectual, aesthetic, or spiritual importance.

The first thing to be said is that pleasure really is *necessary* as a recreation of one's physical and psychic resources, and this may be peculiarly true in an age as filled with stress and as alienated from Nature as ours is. Anatole France's observation that "existence would be intolerable if we were never to dream" may be read as an insightful comment regarding the importance of play in everyday life. Psychologist Donald B. Louria puts it this way:

> In a world beset by frustrations, heavy responsibilities, and troubles, all individuals need periodically to find some means of temporarily escaping from the demands of "real life." Escapism of this kind is not irresponsibility, but actually a necessary component of responsible behavior because it provides for the mind what sleep provides for the body—a mechanism for renewing the strength needed to cope with the daily vicissitudes of life.[14]

The forms of escape being recommended as wholesome by Louria are of course broader in scope than sensory pleasure per se, but it would certainly be one class of the activities he declares necessary for mental health. If one prefers a more dispassionate affirmation of the same point, it can be found in a report on "The Social Control of Drug Use" made by South Australia's Royal Commission into the Non-Medical Uses of Drugs in 1978:

> Conflicting with reliance upon drugs is a long established belief that they diminish the capacity of any person to manage personal conduct and above all to undertake 'work' in the way society expects. By this standard, personal drug taking is regarded as irresponsible. We can take this discussion a stage further by asking whether it is improper to use *any drug* not to alter a specially painful mood but *to obtain gratuitous pleasure*. The puritan tradition suspects any pleasure which is not the reward of endurance, hard work or self-sacrifice. One can see that such a puritanical policy has material benefits for a society dependent on manual labour, and so it is as pragmatic as it is idealistic. Nevertheless, those who have no objection to pleasure as such will seek it, perhaps after work, through relaxation or recreation. If 'relaxation' strictly means 'tension relief,' it begins to be seen as having therapeutic value. People talk of 'healthy relaxation.' Is there a corresponding term for 'recreation'? It can be called 'disinhibition euphoria.' Thus neutralised and given connotations of a healthy pursuit, the word 'pleasure' loses its guilty overtones, and becomes a medical benefit.[15]

As a consultant at a recent Hastings Center conference put it,

> Until we solve the problem of ... meaninglessness, we will have to accept the need that a substantial part of the population has for drugs as a support to their sense of well-being.... [Furthermore,] it is hard to see why an adult should be denied this self-indulgence so long as he understands whatever hazards there are in the use of these drugs.[16]

The same fundamental point was made somewhat more flamboyantly by a recent visitor from a foreign country. Amused by Establishment tut-tutting of "permissiveness" and "loss of moral fiber," he opined that "people in this country would be a lot better off if they had a good, healthy orgy once in a while!"[17]

*Honi soit qui mal y pense.* The only other justification for pleasure that needs to be advanced is that people not only need it, they like it, and they want a lot of it. If the culture bearers in our society think that some special justification for pleasure is needed, that says more about them (and about the depravity of our wretched Puritan heritage) than it does about the pleasures of which we are so suspicious. As Lady Chatterly said when her husband sneered that even caterpillars could engage in sex, "How nice for the caterpillars!" If anyone resents having the burden of proof shifted to the other side, let him consider two illustrations of the unfortunate bias against simple pleasure that have damaged the lives of countless persons in mainstream American society: (1) child-rearing practices that display so much nervousness about the natural polymorphous perversity of infants that they begin almost immediately to inculcate discomfort, guilt, and shame concerning the "good body feelings" that all members of the species enjoy until they are inhibited from doing so; (2) textbooks and college courses on "Marriage and the Family" that try to sell unsuspecting young men and women on the pernicious notion that considerations such as similar background, shared interests, and values, and other "rational" criteria of mate selection are what really matter, romantic love and sexual compatibility being of little consequence. Needless to say, sexual happiness is a matter that goes far beyond sensory pleasure—but if the pleasures of the flesh are clouded and blocked by obtrusive preoccupation with "higher" goods, the results can be disastrous.

*EBC Encourages Social Isolation.* There are two ways to respond to this indictment: It won't happen very much, and if it does it won't matter. Put the two apparently contradictory statements together, and you get what is actually a very coherent commonsense reply: Much of the use of EBC will occur in a social context, and where its use is purely private, that is only one of the various ways in which people may appropriately entertain themselves.

The first point is fairly self-evident. Enjoying yourself in the company of other people is one of the most important features of enjoying yourself; the fun you have with your friends is the best kind of fun there is. The pleasure of drugs, in particular, is typically associated with the sociability of a party or the companionship of a drinking buddy and there is no reason to suppose that the pleasure drugs of the future will be utilized in a radically different manner. A person who consumes alcohol *may* become a solitary drinker who retreats from the society of others and from the responsibilities that used to engage his attention, but this doesn't *have* to happen and it doesn't *usually* happen; in fact, when it does, it is considered an aberration. The same set of tacit rules and expectations that apply to alcohol consumption will probably apply to the use of EBC for pleasure, too.

On the other hand, private use is certainly one perfectly legitimate part of the overall pattern of EBC use. The notion of *balance* is crucial: Technologically sophisticated experience control should be thought of as a "flexibility mechanism" that enables a person to enjoy life or cope with the vicissitudes of life in *many different ways*. Friendship, for example, is one of the great joys of life; almost no one, we normally presume, can be sane or happy without friends. Yet the complexities and difficulties of maintaining friendships (e.g., giving criticism to a comrade who needs it but is highly displeased by receiving it, sharing the grief of a loved one, or being mistreated by someone you had counted on) are so great that one is not always able to summon the energy to *deal with* friends, either to enjoy them or serve them. One's own fluctuating emotions and resources are also a factor, obviously: sometimes the reason for one's wanting to be alone, or to do a particular thing alone, lies not in the demands of the relationship but in oneself and one's own limitations. In any event, the fact is that one needs a large repertoire of "coping" mechanisms in life and the ability to control one's experience "artificially" adds greatly to one's enjoyment of everyday life, whether as freedom from stress and distress or as a special avenue to delight (which is sometimes taken in the company of others, sometimes not). To put it more positively, EBC may also facilitate certain very special experiences that one cherishes as private and that one regards as a path not only to pleasure or happiness, but to fulfillment as well.

The analogy to sexual experience may be apropos at this point. Solitary sex in the form of masturbation is not the form of sexual enjoyment most people rate at the top of the scale, and those who have no other "outlet," as Kinsey called all types of "sexual tension relief," are not very happy about it. Why? Because sexual pleasure is far more than an "outlet," and as difficult as interpersonal relationships are (indeed, as painful as love can be!), no one without special reasons for self-denial (e.g., a monk or a nun) would deliberately choose to forego the richness of experience found only in intimate human intercourse, and no one would imagine that the psychic needs best fulfilled by sex-with-love could possibly be satisfied by sensory experience alone (no matter how exquisitely pleasurable, prolonged, and frequent such experience might be).

So why should we fear that human beings who might *occasionally* enjoy "Intensity" privately would want to experience *nothing but* the pleasures afforded in this way? Isn't it much more realistic to envision a life-pattern in which the use of such products is only one part of a healthy mix that includes all kinds of social intercourse, aesthetic enjoyments, communing with Nature, playing cards, shooting pool, and, yes, even watching TV? Isn't it, in fact, rather ridiculous to succumb to hysterical anxieties about "besotted hedonism" as the inevitable outcome of EBC?

On the other hand, just as cultural disapproval of masturbation has been greatly exaggerated, the same is probably true of fears about solitary EBC. As an internationally respected psychologist commented in a conference on EBC several years ago,

> When I was a young man, I was told that masturbation was unwholesome because it led to substitution behavior and retarded social development by giving young persons a way to evade the often difficult task of cultivating interpersonal relationships. Now that I am older, I see that these predictions concerning the effects of masturbation are pretty accurate: it *does* lead to great emphasis on solitary activities and less gregariousness. The only difference is, now I don't see anything wrong with that provided it's not the only behavioral response in the person's repertoire forever and ever.[18]

Once again, a lot hinges on the prediction that artificial pleasure will be only one of the many ways in which a person pursues both pleasure and happiness. Given a world in which energy shortages may make traveling more difficult and improved telematic communication and information processing may make it less necessary, the ability to be self-sufficient in entertaining oneself may be a capability most people will want very much to cultivate, and self-stimulation may be one extremely valuable way of meeting one's needs and maintaining one's ability to function well in one's vital social roles.

As for the charge that *artificial pleasure isn't "real,"* it usually translates into the judgment that other kinds of pleasure are in some sense superior and therefore more worthy of being sought. The same line of thought that leads many people to despise food additives and to prefer organically grown foods would suggest that "natural" pleasures are more wholesome in the same double sense of being better and better for you.

If this is a judgment about the putatively harmful side effects of "adulterated" foods or pleasures, then it is a prudential argument that hinges on the question of acceptable risk. One makes empirical assessments of the damage caused by various substances (the known effects of given quantities of alcohol on the liver or the blood vessels, for example), and then one makes a value judgment about the trade-offs: Are the satisfactions of consuming alcohol in such and such quantities at such and such a rate sufficient to justify a given level of risk? By this mode of intellectual analysis one reaches a decision about where to draw the line: The risks of a certain level of consumption are judged to be acceptable in consideration of the satisfactions they offer, beyond this level, the risks are unacceptably high. The same procedure can be applied to EBC-generated pleasure, and the complaint about their unreality or unnaturalness has little meaning.

If, on the other hand, the complaint about the "unreality" of EBC is intended as an assertion that what one experiences through artificial stimulation of the body or the brain is *illusory,* the criteria of proof or disproof are much more difficult to stipulate. When Nelson Adler attacks "the psychedelic hoax," he is not really commenting on the feelings, visions, or states subjectively experienced by certain drug users; on the contrary, he is expressing disapproval of the fact that they attach a great deal of *significance* to their experiences. At the risk of identifying my position with a view of the possibilities for transcendence through EBC that is not really mine (but of which I am tolerant, and always feel mildly uneasy about being *merely* tolerant

of!), I should like to cite Aldous Huxley's eloquent and thought-provoking comment on the alleged "unreality" of drug experiences. In
Huxley's comparatively little-known novel, *Island*, he offers a point of
view on the possible value of drugs that is altogether different from
his satirical portrait of "soma" in *Brave New World:*

> "You're assuming," said Dr. Robert, "that the brain *produces* con-
> sciousness. I'm assuming that it transmits consciousness. And my ex-
> planation is no more far-fetched than yours.... You say that the
> moksha-medicine [the psychotropic drug used in the utopian society of
> *Island*] does something to the silent areas of the brain which causes
> them to produce a set of subjective events to which people have given
> the name 'mystical experience.' I say that the moksha-medicine does
> something to the silent areas of the brain which opens some kind of
> neurological sluice and so allows a larger volume of Mind with a large
> 'M' to follow into your mind with a small 'm'. You can't demonstrate
> the truth of your hypothesis, and I can't demonstrate the truth of mine.
> And even if you could prove that I'm wrong, would it make any prac-
> tical difference? ... "
>
> "You're like that mynah [bird]," said Dr. Robert. "Trained to repeat
> words you don't understand or know the reason for, '*It isn't real.* It isn't
> real.' But if you'd experienced what Lakshmi and I went through yester-
> day [after taking the *moksha*-medicine] you'd know better. You'd know
> it was much more real than what you call reality."[19]

The same point is made by Marilyn Ferguson, author of *The
Aquarian Conspiracy*, in her discussion of why so many people are
afraid of transcendence, or even of careful use of drugs as an entry
point to transcendent modes of awareness:

> Some hesitate because they don't know where to turn next. Fear of
> criticism stops others. They might look foolish, pretentious, even crazy,
> to family, friends, co-workers. They worry that the journey inward will
> seem narcissistic or escapist. Indeed those who proceed past the entry
> point have to overcome a pervasive culture bias against introspection.
> The search for self-knowledge is often equated with self-importance,
> with a concern for one's own psyche at the expense of social responsi-
> bility. The popular criticism of psychotechnologies is typified by the
> term "the new narcissism."[20]

However, declares Ferguson (in a footnote quoting philosopher William Bartley), "There is nothing narcissistic about attempting to transcend those things in life that lead people to narcissism."

*It Would be Irresistible.* No one wants to be like Professor Olds' rats, interested in nothing but continual activation of the electrode implanted in the pleasure center of the brain. But how substantial is the danger that human beings will find any imaginable version of "Intensity" that compelling? People are not rats, and—assuming that their humanness has even half a chance to emerge—it is farfetched to assume that they will settle for nothing but pleasure when they can realistically hope for happiness and fulfillment as well.

Yet the mere assertion of the dictum—that people are not rats— settles nothing and the serious anxieties at stake here cannot be dismissed by just pooh-poohing them. The reassurance I hope to offer on this point is based on four separate arguments, ranging from the physiological to the sociological to the philosophical to the rhetorical. But first, it must be admitted that there is a significant element of truth in the fear—and a remedy must be devised.

Judging from the fact that a disturbingly large number of persons do use drugs (as well as TV, sports, and consumerism) as an escape from what we usually think of as the "normal" responsibilities and opportunities of life, it is plausible to suspect that some people will turn to EBC for the same purpose. But just as we do not enforce prohibition of alcohol, spectator entertainment, or installment buying because lots of people abuse their availability, the possibility of abuse should also not be used as grounds for wholesale disapproval and rejection of EBC, either. Most of the unfortunate people who fall into the escapist form of anomie are especially vulnerable, handicapped, or in some sense unfree to be fully human—and the way to prevent them from escapism is to do the best job possible of creating a psycho-social environment in which they develop a stronger sense of self-worth, greater self-confidence, better skills, and so on. Even this imperfect solution to a problem that can never be entirely eradicated will require educational, political, and economic measures the American voters have never yet been willing to commit themselves to, so if one believes that the many who can enjoy something without difficulty should refrain from doing so if there are any fellow humans who will inevitably come to disaster by doing likewise, then perhaps it follows that EBC should be forbidden. But the same logic would condemn most of what we do each day, and the attitudes that lead us to tolerate the inequalities, inhumanities, and human miseries with which we habitually live and the same appeal to "reality" that justifies these, can also be used to justify EBC. (Questions concerning the economic and political measures that are necessary to make EBC morally legitimate will be taken up in Chapter 6.)

One argument that can be offered in refutation to the charge that EBC-induced pleasure will be irresistible is physiological in nature. In the first place, according to neurosurgeon Eliot Valenstein, much of the talk about "pleasure centers" in the brain assumes a good deal more than it can prove. If laboratory animals repeat a given behavior because of EBC, it may be reasonable to hypothesize that they are enjoying pleasurable sensations and therefore the part of the brain being stimulated is a center of such sensations. But that is nothing more than a hypothesis—and it is certainly no proof that the much more complex brain of a human being is similarly structured or that human beings would respond in the same way (especially with the same monomorphic regularity). Valenstein says quite directly, "There are no reports of pleasure by patients receiving brain stimulation that suggest that the experience was so irresistible that they could be compelled to 'sell their souls' for more of the same."[21]

The second argument against fears of "hopeless addiction" is based on sociological analysis of the phenomenon of drug abuse. As the highly regarded *Encyclopedia of Bioethics* makes clear, there is a very significant distinction to be made between "frequent use" (or even "dependence") and *addiction* or drug abuse.[22] Many persons take certain drugs daily and are in fact dependent upon doing so for their health and their ability to function each day in their work (e.g., diabetics who have to inject themselves with insulin every day)—but they do so under the care of a physician and there is no reasonable sense in which they can be viewed as addicts. Furthermore, some students of "addiction" insist that the word should be used as a technical term in the literature of the social sciences, one that implies membership in a subculture that is virtually obsessed with the getting and taking of drugs as its central life interest. Thus, not all drug abusers are addicts in the full sense of the word—and those who are worried about the irresistibility of EBC should be comforted to know that abuse of drugs is neither so prevalent nor so long lasting as the popular misconceptions regarding, say, "getting hooked on tranquilizers" would have it.

Opponents of artificial happiness should be encouraged to reflect on the implication of research that suggests that *social* variables are critical in defining addiction:

(1) the extent to which a drug user has a circle of friends much broader than other drug users (that is, a number of other friends who are not drug users and with whom he or she enjoys doing things other than taking drugs); and

(2) the extent to which he has a stable routine of daily activities which lead him to identify only *certain* occasions as appropriate for drug use; and

(3) the extent to which society isolates and stigmatizes drug users as *objectionable* deviants.

These factors may be thought of as the "pull" and "push" toward addiction: 1 and 2 imply that unless a person has a multidimensional life that includes many interests and gratifications other than drugs, the drugs will exert a compelling pull toward that one satisfying dimension of living; 3 asserts that the unfortunate mental, emotional, and behavioral consequences of drug use can be augmented by a society that pushes the addict away by declaring him unworthy.

Stanton Peele explains the significance of the "pull" factor in a manner that is of particular significance for those who are worried about EBC. In the first place, he denies that studies of laboratory animals or infants born to mothers who are addicts have any relevance for the way that mature human beings will react to ESB or CSB. A rat or a monkey may continue to press a button that stimulates the pleasure center of its brain precisely because it is a creature that does not have available to it the full range of adult human experiences. (In our terms, it settles for sensory pleasure because it is incapable of happiness and fulfillment.) The same is true of an infant "addict," who is capable only of very primitive satisfactions, one of them being a "drug habit" inherited from the mother. Second, Peele defines an addict as someone who doesn't any longer get real pleasure from drugs, but uses them only to obliterate from consciousness the lack of genuine human satisfactions that is so painful to him—and who, in fact, has no real friendships in his circle of drug-using associates, but merely uses them as adjuncts to his habit.[23] Erich Fromm agrees with this second point when he states that the quest for orgiastic experience through drugs is a pathetic attempt to heal the terrible sense of aloneness that the addict feels.[24]

To speak of "aloneness" is to get at the "push" toward addiction that may be exerted by a disapproving and ostracizing society. As Jellinek has noted in his work on *The Disease Concept of Alcoholism*, there is a great difference between the "Gamma alcoholism" of America and the "Delta alcoholism" of France. In the latter country, consumption of large quantities of alcohol (sufficient to constitute "tissue alcoholism") is so common ("i.e., it is normal psychotropic behavior") that "no deviant role compounded of intense psychological misery and social rejection occurs." In America, the misery of the alcoholic—and dependence on alcohol—may be intensified by stigmatization in the humiliating social role of "the alcoholic."[25]

The significance of the sociological aspects of addiction is nicely summarized by David Richards:

> Careful empirical studies of the causes of drug devotion or abuse demonstrate the importance, not of physiological dependence, but of social and psychological factors. As of 1968 a very large proportion of new heroin addicts in the United States, for example, were young, psychologically dependent in their personality structures, occupationally unskilled, socially deracinated, poor, and disadvantaged. Many engaged in crime before they were addicted; after becoming addicted they turned to different kinds of crime more suited to maintain their habits. Many perceptive social analysts have observed that such disadvantaged and alienated young people find in heroin a kind of socially confirmed identity. Drug use may afford them an organizing focus. It generates its own social tasks and standards of successful achievement, its own forms of status and respect, and its own larger meaning, centering on the perceived qualities that the drug brings to the users' personal experiences, such as relief of anxiety and, sometimes, euphoric peace. They may value the very danger of drug use, seeing it as a challenge to the dominant culture and an affirmation of their own values.[26]

But even if particular spots can be located in the brains of particular individuals who receive ineffable sensory pleasure from having those spots set atingle, why is there any reason to suppose that they would be satisfied with living a life that consisted of nothing more than enjoying these sensations over and over again, to the exclusion of all the other activities they find rewarding (and, in various senses, *need* to engage in)? As J. R. Nuttin points out, most human beings will not be satisfied by "stimulation pleasure" alone, nor will they settle for just this level of satisfaction. They need, want, and will seek "causality pleasure"—that is, the kind of happiness that is a function of activities that lead to something (a richer feeling state, if not tangible achievements) beyond the intrinsic rewards of engaging in these activities.[27]

After reviewing all the facts concerning the physiology of pleasure, the use of tranquilizers, and addiction, I cannot help but conclude that little credence is to be given to the charge that EBC-induced pleasure would be *irresistible*. I believe it is more plausible to regard charges of this kind as exaggerated expressions of the suspicion that more than a little submission to a force as potent as pleasure is a threat to proper human performance and that EBC would make this submission *excessive* to an alarming degree.

*Artificial Pleasure Would Be an Ignominious Cop-Out.* This complaint is related to an exaggerated reverence for passive heroism, as the following passage from *The Tranquilizing of America* reveals:

[In analyzing] the tranquilizing of America, we have seen the individual —the "me" in all of us—get swept aside in a heedless rush for the quick and easy chemical way out. We have seen how each generation of new psychoactive drugs—Valium replacing Miltown, Miltown replacing phenobarbital—is heralded as safer, faster, and more effective than its predecessor. Poorly trained in the content and effects of drugs and heavily dependent on acquiring knowledge about drugs from the manufacturers, doctors embrace the new psychoactive wonders with abandon, and patients welcome the promised relief and presumed safety. As a new drug replaces an old one, eliminating the apparent harmful effects, the broader questions of their use do not get asked or answered. If science can eliminate the addiction potential from tranquilizers, society does not need to confront the problems of stress. If science can give us a new and better "smart pill," society does not need to do anything about the social problems confronting a disadvantaged child at home, in his neighborhood, and in his world. If science can provide a powerful sedative that eliminates the Parkinson-like shakes, society does not have to worry about the ethical questions of warehousing the mentally ill. If science can bring us a pill that will happily sedate the elderly without making them sleep all day, we don't have to worry about our own mortality, and society does not have to concern itself with finding a productive use for senior citizens.

In simple terms, if drugs can do everything for us, we do not need to do anything for ourselves, and we need not take any responsibility for ourselves or our society.

> As we approach the day of a drug for every mood, thought, feeling, and deed, we need to ask ourselves whether we want to take the risk of a continual dwarfing of the human spirit by making the "me" the drug in me.[28]

The cry of alarm voiced in this rather remarkable passage summarizes two of the most critical fears of the opponents of EBC. It assumes that use of drugs to allay anxiety or enhance intelligence is a "quick and easy way out" that somehow puts an end to society's interest in "broader questions" of social responsibility and our collective efforts to find a solution for social problems. It also assumes that drugs somehow destroy and/or take the place of the human spirit in persons who make use of them.

But these fears are ludicrous exaggerations. There is such a thing as drug abuse and it is a problem that must be taken seriously; indeed, I have acknowledged the problem and offered suggestions about how it may be dealt with. (More is said on the subject in Chapter 6.) The overwhelming majority of the people who use mood control drugs do not lose their souls by so doing; in fact, their motives for occasional use are to increase their overall efficiency as functioning members of the various institutions in which they participate (from family to workplace).[29] And those who advocate the use of EBC as a means to upgrading the performance of disadvantaged children or mitigating some of the unfortunate consequences of aging are under no illusions about the ability of chemical agents to solve complex social problems: EBC is seen as merely one part of a number of steps that need to be undertaken to overcome the worst aspects of these problems.

The fact that we sometimes use such things as mindless entertainment, superficial social contacts, and drugs to get a necessary respite from the rigors of the daily grind is nothing to be ashamed of and the prospect of finding new forms of EBC to perform this function in our lives is nothing to get particularly alarmed about. Far better to revise some of our pretentious notions about character and heroism than to stigmatize the use of "artificial" agents that can help us find a practical balance between optimal exercise of strength and realistic acknowledgment of our legitimate needs.

## Philosophical and Psychological Perspectives

Classical philosophy and modern psychoanalytical thought seem to agree on one salient point: The will-to-pleasure in human beings is a ferocious force that must be tamed or contained, lest it run away with the person in whom it resides. In Plato, the drives associated with the senses are likened to an unruly horse that has to be reined in very tightly and roughly. The Epicureans and the Stoics recommended a form of refined hedonism that placed great emphasis on the avoidance of excess and the style of life they preferred was really rather austere in its avoidance of strong drink, rich foods, troublesome enthusiasms, and, in short, anything that might disturb the inner composure of the wise soul. Even the often-maligned utilitarianism of Bentham counted prudence as the supreme virtue in its calculations of propinquity, certainty, fecundity, and the other practical criteria by means of which the relative merits of various pleasures might be judged. And Mill is famous for his distinction between lower and higher pleasures, and for his dictum that it is better to be Socrates dissatisfied than a pig satisfied.[30]

According to Thomas Szasz, "the psychoanalytic bias" lays a great deal of stress on the desirability of experiencing "all affects in moderation."[31] In Fenichel's words,

> The healthy ego experiences affects, knows them, discharges them and uses them for its own purposes. Of course, there is no such thing as the 'normal' person having no affects. But he is the master of his affects, whereas the weak ego is mastered by his affects.[32]

This warning that happiness as well as pleasure must be defined in terms of moderation is related to a curious emphasis on *release from anxiety* as a central element in natural pleasure itself:

> When the child discovers that he is now able to overcome without fear a situation that formerly would have overwhelmed him with anxiety, he experiences a certain kind of *pleasure*. The pleasure has the character of "I need not feel anxiety any more." It makes the child's play evolve from mere attempts at discharge to *mastery* of the external world by means of repeated practice. "Functional pleasure" is pleasure in the fact that the exercise of a function is now possible without anxiety, rather than the gratification of one specific type of instinct.[33]

From this point of view, says Szasz (following Fairbairn), "explicit pleasure-seeking represents a deterioration of behavior," for *object-seeking* represents a higher position in the "hierarchical development of pleasure" than "physiological need reduction."[34]

The point, for our purposes, is this: Both philosophy and psychology tend to attach a great deal of importance to the *avoidance of pain* in their notion of happiness and *even in their definition of rational pleasure*. Now, there is certainly a good deal of wisdom in this, for some pleasures are undeniably contaminated by unpleasant consequences or side effects. These unintended consequences sometimes outweigh the positive value of the sought-after pleasures in the mind of one who aspires to fulfillment in a well-balanced human life instead of *nothing but* the "discharges" that result from "explicit pleasure-seeking." What I find suspect in this account of real human experience—what I see as a plain, out and out *prejudice* in it—is the assumption that really intense pleasure (being temporarily "taken out of oneself" in ecstasy) is so dangerous that a wise person will avoid it as much as possible. I see no reason to assume (as does Fenichel) that "excitement is a sign of imminent trouble." One can appreciate the truth of Rollo May's caveat concerning the need for *eros* to be guided by will without abandoning the lust for *abandon* of Zorba.[35]

One way to sort out this rather intricate and subtle set of considerations is to examine Dan Brock's essay on "The Use of Drugs for Pleasure." In a report commissioned by the Hastings Center, Brock sketches two basic philosophical approaches to the topic and goes on to argue that a proper understanding of happiness and fulfillment makes it difficult to justify extensive use of EBC for artificial pleasure. The "preference theory" of pleasure is superior to the "property of conscious experience theory" because it recognizes that pleasure is not a *thing* (a property, a quality, an ideal essence) that can be separated from the activities that produce it: One does not play golf (an activity) in order to get something called pleasure out of the activity: instead, one enjoys (gets pleasure from) playing golf. What a golfer wants is not "pleasure," it is *playing golf*: and the full experience of this activity cannot be produced by EBC.[36]

I would argue that this entire analysis can be translated into an affirmation I am also disposed to make—namely, that the happiness and fulfillment human beings seek cannot be supplied by ESB or CSB and that even the pleasure derived from *certain* activities can be obtained in no other way. The pleasurable sensations obtained by ingesting a drug like "Intensity" will not be identical with the pleasurable happiness provided by a day on a beautiful golf course, nor, with the very special pleasure of hitting a few shots exactly right —and any golfer will certainly be aware of the difference and will sometimes prefer a round of golf to the pleasure available through EBC (or any other pleasure, for that matter). But this does not mean it is nonsensical to speak of "pleasure" (whether or not you call it a "property") as something to be sought and obtained through the activity of activating an electrical apparatus or taking a pill. Nor does it mean that the five objections to EBC given by Brock constitute a compelling argument against *occasional* utilization of EBC, for *some* pleasures can be *solitary, nonintellectual, neutral in regard to one's relations to other persons, and passive* without being intrinsically evil, and they can be just as much an expression of the autonomous "capacity to act in the manner that on reflection one values or most want to act" as any other form of enjoyable activity.

One could even admit that EBC-derived pleasure is "lower" than the "higher" pleasures stressed by the preference theory without considering the former unworthy of human beings or in any other sense illegitimate, provided it can be shown that the opponent of EBC is incorrect in assuming that one's interest in higher pleasures and one's capacity to appreciate and enjoy them are damaged by EBC. One may agree with Brock's assertion that "any rational basis for [opposition] must lie in arguments that the consequences of the use of drugs for pleasure are such that they interfere with or inhibit realization of other important aspects of a person's good."[37] As Brock himself appears to realize, this is a judgment that can only be made empirically (on the basis of knowledge about EBC technologies and about the specific human individuals who are potential users) and for each individual the decision about using or not using EBC is one of acceptable risk.

It might very well be that the happiness and fulfillment associated with EBC-stimulated pleasure are uniquely valuable in themselves: Masturbation or a self-cooked meal might be lower on a given person's overall preference hierarchy than making love to or eating (a better meal!) with one's spouse, but it might be the best option available on a given occasion. And the satisfaction that comes from being able to manage one's own experience satisfactorily (from having the *power* to do so, and being free from the *anxiety* of not being able to do so, if you want to put it that way) might be very substantial indeed. When the overall pattern of one's experience is considered in the context of one's rational life-plan, indulgence in EBC might be counted an important part of being fulfilled as a being capable of *creating*, not merely understanding, oneself.

This point is articulated nicely by David Richards in his book, *Sex, Drugs, Death and the Law*. Richards points out that the prejudice against artificial pleasure through drugs is part and parcel of a more general prejudice against lapses in self-mastery that emerges in Western culture in the thought of Augustine. Just as sexual pleasure apart from its appropriate metaphysical expression in procreation involved "a degrading loss of self-control," frequent use of euphoria-inducing drugs is regarded as a lowering of oneself to a subhuman level. Because

> Augustine's procreational model for sexuality was part of an emerging philosophy of self-mastery, marked by its concern to subordinate and, where necessary, to deny otherwise natural aspects of the self in the service of the stipulated moral conception, ... there is an inner unity in the belief that both natural and sexual impulses and drug experiences are degraded.[38]

But the truth of the matter is entirely to the contrary: People use drugs for many diverse purposes and they "consciously choose among these purposes" in accordance with unique personal notions of what they want to be and do with their lives:

> In so doing, they express self-respect by regulating the quality and versatility of their experiences in life to include greater control of mood and, sometimes, increased freedom and flexibility of imagination. For many, such drug use does not constitute fear-ridden anarchy, but promotes the rational self-control of those ingredients fundamental to the design of a fulfilled life.[39]

In any event, Dan Brock is certainly correct in concluding his analysis of pleasure enhancement through drugs by asserting that an empirical assessment of their presumed self-destructiveness would "show that the popular image is vastly oversimplified and probably largely false," and that "rational controversy must largely turn (on empirical research) and not on philosophical differences about the intrinsic value or disvalue of the use of drugs for pleasure."[40]

## The Irony of Resistance

In regard to the overwhelming majority of Americans, the fear of "besotted hedonism" or any other type of degeneration into a sub-human state is groundless; what's more, it is wonderfully ironic in its wrongheadedness. For the fact is, EBC is only one example of a pro-nounced cultural trend toward greater *individual awareness and choice* in the determination of one's identity and one's life. Critics may deplore this trend, of course, and it may be deplored on either psychological grounds (as "information overload" and "overchoice" that are more than the fragile organism can bear) or moral grounds (as an overemphasis on self-determination and, really, a self-indul-gence that constitutes a departure from the wisdom of traditional norms). But the trend exists, and most people seem to like it even when they have trouble adjusting to it. If "being fully human" means having a great deal of freedom to choose the kind of person you want to be, the kind of life you want to have and the kinds of goals you want to strive for—plus *having to take responsibility for the choices you make* (instead of being able to blame your lot in life on God, fate, or your mother and father), then EBC is a step in the direction of mature humanity, not a fall into dehumanization.

Two illustrations should suffice to explain this generalization. Con-sider, first, the woman who reads about a behavior modification workshop in *assertiveness training*. Just to realize that it is possible for her to change her whole style of interpersonal interaction instead of simply accepting the one she grew up with is a noteworthy event in itself. Assuming that she believes there really is some very substantial value in having good manners or concern for others' feelings, being cooperative (and, upon occasion, being self-sacrificing when some crucial benefit for another person is at stake), she has to weigh all of these important aspects of civilized life against the probability that she has been *oversold* on them—that she has, in fact, to some extent been victimized by a patriarchal culture that found it convenient to socialize women to be relatively submissive. (This patriarchal culture was quite willing to praise women for being more virtuous than men, so long as the men had most of the political and economic power and could browbeat women into submission in head-to-head combat by making them feel guilty if they were not "feminine," meaning "properly submissive.") She has to decide just *how* assertive she wants to become, and the limits she decides to put on the aggressiveness and manipulativeness she hopes to cultivate will have to be determined not only on *ethical* grounds ("Where's the line between being justifiably insistent on my own rights and, on the other hand, pushing other people around unfairly?") but also on grounds of *prudence* or enlightened self-interest ("How far can I carry the *quid pro quo* mode of interpersonal relationships in a nonutilitarian relationship—in love or deep friendship—without compromising the covenant intangibles or the ritual refinements that are themselves a part of the warmth and richness most people want in love and friendship?")

To be confronted with such a choice, to make it, and then to live with the consequences of the path you have chosen (which will almost inevitably be difficult enough to make you wonder if you might have been better off to take some other path!), is a profoundly human experience. And although the construction of elaborate role-structures and of the ritualized actions that implement them is also an impressive human achievement, many social analysts would argue that the freedom enjoyed and the responsibility borne by the self-determining modern person is somehow more fitting for human beings than conformity to traditional roles and rituals (and the lack of awareness that is often a comfortable corollary of conformity).

Consider, second, the choices one makes about the personal mix of pleasurable activities one wants. To say that EBC is a "flexibility mechanism" is to say that it gives people a greater range of possibilities from which to choose and thus contributes to autonomy by making them less dependent upon just a few possible avenues to gratification. The charge that EBC may tend to make people antisocial or excessively isolated, for example, may rest on a sort of romanticism about human interaction that is altogether dubious.

We like to make a virtue out of familiarity as well as necessity, so it is hardly surprising if we find ourselves saying that one "ought" to seek pleasure from company with other persons, not from solitary stimulation of sensory receptors by artificial means, and that it is unhealthy to do the latter instead of the former. But this sounds very much like what we used to say about the nuclear family and romantic love. Yet both of these institutional forms of human interaction are bolstered by destructive illusions and can be miserably oppressive. In recent years they have been convincingly debunked and although considerable strain and no little heartache have resulted, most young people (and quite a few of their elders) feel that they are better off having dispensed with the illusions and gotten out from under the oppression. They still fall in love and live in love with one or more intimates and they still commit themselves to the formidable responsibilities of family life—but with their eyes wide open (and therefore, one hopes, with fewer disappointments and, perhaps, a more tranquil state of realistic satisfaction).

The same process of readjustment may now take place in regard to the quest for pleasure and happiness. It may be a healthy step in the right direction for us to abandon the notion that solitary pleasure is inferior; it may be wise for us to acknowledge that human relationships are so difficult and *draining* that we cannot get ourselves up for them with infallible consistency, nor should we feel that we ought to try, and that we are inadquate when we fail or rotten not to try! We can loosen the suffocating hold of the demand for gregariousness without swinging all the way over to the opposite extreme of exclusive reliance on the "masturbatory" pursuit of solitary pleasure. And it is good to have a range of choices open to us so that we can pick different avenues at different times and seasons, according to our different needs and moods.

In commenting on the irony of the complaints that EBC dehumanizes by reducing humans to the status of rats who cannot help pushing the pleasure button, I have already begun to touch on a theme that will be developed at some length in the final chapter. It is the fascinating question, "But why is resistance to EBC so *ferocious*?" All that needs to be said on that score at this juncture is that something must be touching a terribly tender nerve. The arguments of the critics certainly must not be dismissed too quickly and cheaply through counterarguments that amount to nothing more than psychological reductionism (i.e., an indefensible refusal to consider an opponent's position because of aspersions cast upon his motives for adopting that position). Proponents of EBC must make every effort to meet the opposition head-on by taking their qualms seriously and weighing the evidence they adduce honestly. When an extremely polemical critic goes on a rampage against the evils of "the psychedelic hoax and the pharmacological fallacy," one may discount his rhetoric without doubting the sincerity of his concern: He is alarmed because he thinks far too many rather naive people expect certain drugs to give them sublime visions of Truth, Goodness, and Beauty and far too many others who are hedonistic in a more prosaic sense have an erroneous "magic bullet" image of the sensations they can get (and always count on getting) from particular substances.[41]

It is quite proper, nevertheless, to ask about the possible distortions introduced into the thinking of some of the critics by ideological bias. When Herman Kahn deplores the loss of entrepreneurial vigor that threatens to diminish the dynamism of our economy, he begs the questions that have been central in the minds of those who question the work-orientation that Kahn admires so much. When Irving Kristol and other neoconservatives deplore the upsurge of interest in sex and the apparently more permissive moral norms that now govern American sexual behavior, one wonders if their indignation is fueled by a petty resentment against people who refuse to put business before pleasure as rigorously as they should. As Robert Veatch points out, some of the animus against taking drugs for pleasure is resentment against those who "cheat" by getting pleasurable sensations without earning them (or paying for them!) in the accustomed ways.[42] One wonders, too, if some of the skepticism that many "practical" people (including the author) feel about altered states of consciousness and other "transcendent" experiences (whether EBC-induced or not) is a kind of defensiveness that protects us against the disquieting thought that other people may be getting something (something really important, something *wonderful*) that we are not getting out of life.

## THE REALISTIC PROSPECTS
## FOR ARTIFICIAL HAPPINESS

In Chapters 6 and 7, I shall deal with the political safeguards and the kinds of philosophical values needed to promote optimal use of EBC. In this chapter I have attempted only to establish the technological *feasibility* and the moral *legitimacy* of using various kinds of experience control to enhance personal happiness.

As I indicated in Chapter 1, there is no way to predict with absolute certainty that drugs with the precise characteristics of "intensity" will be available for over-the-counter purchase in the next five years. I have admitted that ESB may never be widely used except for therapeutic purposes. Yet I have cited the research that appears to be creating the capability for ever more precise and effective experience control. I have quoted expert opinion to the effect that we are moving rapidly in that direction and I have discussed currently available techniques that can have much broader nontherapeutic application.

I have argued that the kind and degree of pain relief possible through EBC is cause for rejoicing; indeed, when I recall what pain does to my own personality and my overall ability to function, I regard our new ability to manage pain as one of the greatest manifestations of human progress conceivable. To be able to grow old without having to be afraid of living in constant pain for months or years, to be able to recover from severe depression without having one's brain sliced or jolted into a subhuman condition, to be able to make crucial decisions without the distorting pressures of anxiety, or habits of mind that one no longer affirms when one is "at one's best"— these are among the finest fruits ever offered by scientific endeavor. 'Twould be folly indeed to allow a ridiculous romanticism about suffering, or the passive heroism supposedly demonstrated by enduring it, to keep us from seeking deliverance from needless pain.

I have also argued that EBC can be used to produce pleasurable sensations and moods without turning people into subhuman creatures who spend their lives doing nothing but wallowing in sensory delight. I have argued, in fact—and will do so at greater length in the final chapter—that the pursuit of "artificial" pleasure through EBC is a flexibility mechanism which can be utilized in a balanced way along with more common (but not necessarily more wholesome) "natural" means to pleasure or happiness, and that it is in certain respects *more* humanly fulfilling than the "pursuit of happiness" through consumerism that is practiced with such dubious results by so many Americans.

To be sure, there will doubtless be some individuals who cannot handle these possibilities constructively. For those who fall into a pattern of drug abuse, there are several possible safeguards and remedies (see Chapter 6), the most important of which is improvement of the positive life possibilities for those who see their resources and opportunities as woefully limited. In any case, the possibility of abuse by a relatively small number of persons should not prevent use on the part of the much larger number of persons whose lives will be enormously enriched by EBC. As Jonathan Glover observes in his recent book entitled *What Kind of People Should There Be?* "The implications of self-modification would ... vary for different people. But for those with a reasonably coherent dominant outlook, the new techniques would help rather than hinder self-creation over a lifetime."[43]

But the ethical sensitivity which prompts concern for those who may not use experience control properly is an essential ingredient in a morally defensible appropriation of the benefits of EBC. It leads to eager affirmation of the possibilities for artificial *goodness* through systematic behavior control—and it is to a treatment of this topic that we now turn.

## NOTES

1. Richard A. Shaffer, "Mastering the Mind," *The Wall Street Journal*, Vol. 97, No. 30 (Aug. 12, 1977), p. 18.
2. Vance Packard, *The People Shapers*, p. 59.
3. John G. Taylor, *The Shape of Minds to Come*, p. 181; cf. p. 264.
4. *Ibid.*, p. 42.
5. *Ibid.*
6. Personal conversation with Jose Delgado, Madrid, June 1982.
7. Taylor, *Shape*, p. 186.
8. *Ibid.*, pp. 62-63.
9. *Ibid.*, p. 68.
10. Robert Veatch, "Competing Drug Ethics," *Hastings Center Studies*, Vol. II, No. 1 (1974), pp. 68-80.
11. Charles Cochrane, *Christianity and Classical Culture*, pp. 446-455.
12. For an explanation of the special importance of the Calvinistic version of "the Protestant Ethic," see Max Weber, *The Protestant Ethic and the Spirit of Capitalism*.
13. Charles Trinkhaus, *Adversity's Noblemen*.
14. Donald B. Louria, "The Future of the Drug Scene," *The Futurist* (June 1978), p. 151.
15. Royal Commission into the Non-Medical Use of Drugs of South Australia, *The Social Control of Drug Use*, p. 20.
16. The transcript of conference highlights from which this quote is taken does not identify the speaker.
17. The source of this wry comment is a diplomat who must remain nameless.
18. Perry London, observations made at a conference on "The Ethics of Experience and Behavior Control" at the University of Southern California, Feb. 12, 1976.
19. Aldous Huxley, *Island*, pp. 144-145.
20. Marilyn Ferguson, *The Acquarian Conspiracy*, p. 90.
21. Eliot Valenstein, *Brain Control*, p. 72.
22. Robert Neville and Sidney Cohen, "Drug Use," *Encyclopedia of Bioethics*, pp. 326ff.
23. Stanton Peele, *Love and Addiction*, p. 66.
24. Erich, Fromm, *The Anatomy of Human Destructiveness*, p. 81.
25. Jack Young, *The Drugtakers: The Social Meaning of Drug Use*, pp. 94-95.

26. David Richards, *Sex, Drugs, Death and the Law,* p. 175.

27. J. R. Nuttin, "Pleasure and Reward in Human Motivation and Learning," in Berlyne and Madsen, *Pleasure, Reward and Deference,* p. 273f.

28. Richard Hughes and Robert Brewin, *The Tranquilizing of America,* p. 296-297.

29. Glover, *What Kind of People Should There Be?*

30. John Stuart Mill, *Utilitarianism,* pp. 18-19.

31. Thomas Szasz, *Pain and Pleasure,* p. 254.

32. Otto Fenichel, "The Ego and the Affects," *Psycoanalytical Review,* Vol. 28 (1941), p. 47, as quoted in Szasz, *Pain,* p. 254.

33. Otto Fenichel, *The Psychoanalytical Theory of Neurosis,* p. 54.

34. Szasz, *Pain,* p. 192.

35. Rollo May, *Love and Will,* pp. 123-129.

36. Dan W. Brock, "The Use of Drugs for Pleasure," pp. 15ff. An abridged version of this study document of the Institute of Society, Ethics and the Life Sciences has recently been published as "Can Pleasure Be Bad for You?" *Hastings Report,* Vol. XII, No. 4 (August, 1983), pp. 30-34.

37. *Ibid.,* p. 34.

38. Richards, *Sex, Drugs,* p. 169.

39. *Ibid.,* p. 170.

40. Brock, "Use," p. 16.

41. Nathan Adler, *The Underground Stream,* pp. 6ff.

42. Robert Veatch, "Competing," pp. 78-80.

43. Glover, *People,* p. 89.

# Chapter 4

# ARTIFICIAL GOODNESS

When we envision artificial goodness through EBC, we are thinking of a twofold possibility: the extinction of specific behaviors regarded as morally undesirable and the generation of broader behavior patterns and supportive attitudes regarded as ethically desirable by the person concerned. A review of the technical capabilities suggests that agents and processes such as "Congruity" and "Commitment" are already feasible, and ethical analysis indicates that they would be not only legitimate but desirable.

## GLORIA: A VIGNETTE

Gloria is a 30-year-old woman whose upbringing in and allegiance to the Episcopal Church are extremely important to her. Most of her closest friends are political activists whose interest in various worthy causes is motivated by religious conviction of one sort or another, and her social life is for the most part a spillover from the topical study groups and action committees in which she is continually involved.

The study group on EBC in which she had been a participant for three months more than two years ago was unusually significant in its impact on her thinking and on that of some of her close friends. Three of them had joined her in a successful antismoking clinic that had liberated all four of them from enslavement to the noxious weed. Two others had benefitted from a similar program in weight control. One who felt guilty about his extramarital sexual adventures had eliminated them—on the other hand, a woman who was exasperated by her sexual inhibitions had gone through a program of cognitive restructuring that had enabled her to live in accordance with her philosophical belief in free love by enjoying multiple concurrent love relationships without guilt. One person who had formerly been through terrible bouts of depression because of inner conflict over his homosexual inclinations became completely heterosexual; and another had succeeded in adopting a bisexual life style without the persistent sense of shame that used to dog her whenever she felt drawn to a lesbian liaison. Gloria admired the authenticity that manifested itself in the decisions that led these different individuals to make such choices, and she enjoyed the forthrightness and the tolerance that characterized her relationship with this network of friends.

She was fascinated and morally exhilarated by the seriousness of purpose that characterized the discussion carried out by her friends on the subject of how to find new ways of implementing their own deepest value commitments by shaping their behavior in both general and particular ways. A couple of behavior therapists who had earned the trust of certain members of the group by designing special programs for them and who had, as a result of this contact, developed a special sense of involvement with the group, offered free consulting services to any individual interested in investigating the feasibility of controlling offensive behavior scientifically. Plans were afoot to design programs to help one person overcome his tendency to kleptomania, to enable another to control her penchant for reckless driving, and to assist others to solve various family problems ranging from wife beating and child abuse to "simple" nagging. A compulsive gambler was ready to submit himself to a program of behavior therapy that would transfer his attention from Las Vegas to a substitute activity with fewer drawbacks. The most striking consequence of the successful experience participants in the group had already had with EBC was that they all tended now to think of behavior problem areas that could probably be *solved* effectively, and they viewed the search for effective means to accomplish these objectives as a necessary logical implication of their professed values.

Gloria herself was troubled about two situations that had a bearing on her sense of vocation. She was under some pressure to go back to Iowa and take care of her recently widowed mother whose health was very poor and whose death would probably occur within five years. She was also worried about waiting too long to have the two babies she wanted to have before the odds on problem-free pregnancies began to lengthen. Her husband, who was also from Iowa, would not have objected to a move back home, and Gloria had no worries about being able to find satisfactory employment there. But she felt that her political work in Denver was really her primary calling at the moment and that it would bear rich fruit if only she could continue to devote a great deal of time to it for the next several years.

What Gloria was most concerned about was what prominent leaders of her denomination called "the world food and population problem." She was fed up with being in a church where people continuously talked about their responsibility to share generously with the hungry and about their own personal obligation to change their life style but never did anything beyond giving token contributions of money. She was prepared, with the support of an impressive number of local religious leaders, to take the lead in launching an ambitious ecumenical life-style change campaign in Denver. The text of a speech she was scheduled to make at next month's meeting of the Denver Interfaith Council included the following appeal:

It's time to quit talking and start reshaping our behavior. Here is a partial list of the changes that need to be made:

(1) Since the grain required to fatten livestock to provide meat for two persons could feed ten, we ought to eliminate altogether or cut back drastically on our consumption of meat.

(2) Since our reckless consumption of petroleum endangers world peace and contributes mightily to economic instability and injustice, we ought to switch from self-indulgent reliance on our private cars to some combination of car pooling, bus riding, and getting about on bicycles.

(3) Since it is wrong for the haves to own private yachts and seldom-used ski lodges or summer homes when millions are starving, we ought to give all or most of the money we make in excess of the national average to benefit the poor (economically, culturally, or politically).

The crucial element in the action we propose is this: Any or all of these possible life-style changes can be effected almost immediately in the lives of those who choose to adopt them. There are behavior control techniques for enabling any individual who feels that such changes would be right to bring them about promptly. If you say to yourself, "I'd like to, but I can't," you are lying. If you say, "I will do it if only someone will show me how to get started," you don't have to wait any longer: We'll show you how, and we'll get you started—right now.

There is only one question you have to answer: Do I really mean it when I say that I believe in sharing the world's resources justly? And am I willing to make use of the demonstrably efficacious means for making myself live that way?" In answering these questions, there's just one portion of Scripture you need to remember: "If one of you sees a brother in need, yet closes his heart against him, how does God's love abide in him?" (I John 3:17.)

The document prepared for distribution at the time when the speech was to be delivered included thumbnail descriptions of several operant conditioning programs designed to eradicate a number of "consumer hoaxes," as they were called, that were regarded as especially pernicious: the desire for a pleasure boat or a luxury car, a craving for high fashion clothing, and the yen for exorbitant vacations in sucker-seducing resorts were among the items listed.

The machinery was all set to carry out this plan. It could certainly be done under someone else's leadership, and if it worked, she could do something similar in Iowa, perhaps. But she wasn't sure anyone else would get the job done in Denver quite as energetically and, finally, as successfully as she would.

Gloria wasn't sure which path she would take. But one thing she was sure about: She would make a decisive choice promptly, and she would use EBC to help her implement that choice. She wouldn't waste any time or energy in an agonized paralysis of indecision, complaining to others that she just couldn't figure out what she ought to do—or that having decided what should be done, "she just couldn't get herself to do it."

## EXTINCTION

Behavior modification is the technique that has the most to offer in connection with both kinds of artificial goodness, but before analyzing its capabilities in detail we ought to take note of the fact that several other kinds of EBC are also applicable here. CSB has been used to "cure" the "problem" of "hyperactive" children and it can be used to carry out "chemical castration" on those who suffer from "hypersexuality." (In case anyone is interested, cyproterone acetate, the drug that can annihilate sexual desire, can be obtained—by prescription—under the trade name of Sinevir.) But we ought to resist the temptation to be sarcastic about this usage, because it is not impossible to imagine circumstances in which one would voluntarily choose to do away with the distraction of sexual interest for a limited period of time, so that one could pour every ounce of one's energy into some extraordinarily important and demanding project. Drugs like Ritalin are probably more controversial when used to "help school children concentrate better." But the potential abuse of drugs like this under similar circumstances is very great; the dangers will be discussed in Chapter 6. We must note in passing that opponents of Ritalin are worried not only about its misuse, but also about the technical features of the drug, notably its unreliability (i.e., its tendency to have opposite effect on different individuals and its possible long-range side effects.)[1]

Psychosurgery has often been used to wipe out troublesome behaviors, and although procedures as crude as lobotomies are no longer in favor, surgery is still being recommended and used as a cure for specific problems. A man with an uncontrollable passion for gambling was ordered to submit to an operation to rid him of this passion by a judge in England (who was swiftly reversed by a higher court upon appeal).[2] Much speculation has also centered on psychosurgery as an approach to the control of violence and a significant breakthrough in this area has recently occurred in the form of a "brain pacemaker" that is apparently helpful to some epileptics, schizophrenics, and other victims of periodic seizures. This combination of surgery and ESB has been remarkably successful in treatment of "episodic dyscontrol" by Dr. Robert Heath of the Tulane University Medical School:

> The first patient to undergo the operation was a 19-year-old boy, slightly retarded from birth, who had repeatedly tried to kill himself or relatives. He was confined to a Louisiana state mental hospital....
>
> The pacemaker consists of 20 tiny platinum disc electrodes placed on the surface of the cerebellum, the hind part of the brain at the lower back of the head. These are attached to a receiver about the size of a quarter in the left side of the chest.... None of this is visible from outside.

An antenna, which can be removed for bathing or swimming, is strapped over the receiver. Its battery-powered transmitter is carried in a pocket. Eventually, Heath hopes for a completely implantable unit with a long-lasting power source. At present, the batteries must be changed every week or 10 days and so must be carried outside the body....

"From the day the pacemaker was activated the patient's outbursts of violence ceased," Heath said. "His tardive dyskenesia gradually diminished. His behavior has continued to improve. He is now a pleasant and sociable young man. He was enlisted in a vocational rehabilitation course and he is now ready for job placement....

"Clinically, the patient has had a complete remission. He copes adequately with the vicissitudes of everyday life. He is receiving no medication. It was necessary for him to visit the state hospital where he had last been a patient before the physicians and nursing staff could believe that it was possible for him to live outside an institution. . . .

Heath's procedure carries a low risk, does not involve slicing deep into the brain itself, and, unlike the old lobotomies, does not interfere with the person's capacity to experience anger, albeit "a controlled anger." Feelings of pleasure are increased, while those of rage and violence are decreased, but the person still has a full range of emotions. Nor does the operation erase memory.

"It does not affect the patient's bank of memories," Heath said. Rather, it alters awareness, emotional state and perception, making it possible for the person to perceive differently, and only through this gradually modifies behavioral patterns based on background memories.[3]

But the mode of EBC that holds the greatest promise for artificial goodness is behavior therapy. As experts in this field never tire of asserting, "Specificity is the hallmark of behavior therapy," therefore, it is impossible to formulate sweeping a priori generalizations about the technical feasibility of particular behavior shaping programs for particular individuals. Nevertheless, as Rachman and Wilson conclude at the end of their meticulous evaluation of The Effects of Psychological Therapy,

It can safely be said that there are well-established methods for reducing anxieties and fears of various sorts, good progress has been made in establishing an equally powerful method for dealing with obsessions and compulsions, and significant advances have been made in dealing with some sexual dysfunctions. Some useful if slow progress had been made in improving the deficient social skills of people with interpersonal problems, at least a degree of progress has been made in shaping up rehabilitation programmes for people with chronic and disabling disorders, and even where progress has been disappointing (e.g., the treatment of smoking) there are a number of fresh and enlivening ideas under consideration.[4]

In the case of psychotherapy, one continues to ask *if* the method works; in the case of behavior therapy, one asks *why* it works. Even when the goal is the relatively simple one of extinguishing a specific behavior, although the question of effectiveness cannot be regarded as settled, once and for all. The success of behavior therapy in overcoming phobias, compulsions, and certain childhood disorders or sexual difficulties is outstanding, but its record in stamping out addiction is more spotty. As late as 1975, O'Leary and Wilson described the antismoking programs evaluated in their study as "uniformly unimpressive," and an early statement on the success rate of weight control programs by one of the leaders in that area was pessimistic in the extreme: "Most obese persons will not stay in treatment for obesity. Of those who stay in treatment, most will not lose weight, and of those who do lose weight, most will regain it."[5]

Progress, however, is often rapid in fledgling specializations, and recent findings are more encouraging. Three studies of antismoking programs conducted since 1975 indicate that the addition of a technique called "rapid smoking" or satiation results in abstinence rates of 60%, 62%, and 76%.[6] The 1978 report on the "controlled drinking" program described in Chapter 2 found that chronic drinkers *formerly hospitalized* for alcoholism "functioned well" 89.61% of all days in the second year of a follow-up study.[7] Another report on similar subjects whose treatment included a community reinforcement maintenance feature relapsed into problem drinking only 2% of the time during a two-year follow-up and had to be hospitalized only .1% of that time.[8] There is even some evidence that weight control programs can achieve significant results: One behavioral treatment group showed a weight loss of about 75% after one year, and Kingsley and Wilson found that although *individual* therapy was followed by a high rate of relapse, "a comparable *group* treatment produced satisfactory maintenance of weight loss over a 1-year follow-up." Although "use of booster sessions has yielded disappointing results of the whole," bringing in the obese person's spouse as an active participant "appears to be a particularly promis-

ing means" to greater success.[9] Thus, Rachman and Wilson's op-
timism regarding "multi-faceted, sophisticated" obesity treatment
seems to be applicable to specifically targeted extinction programs in
general:

> Behavioral procedures for the treatment of obesity have proven to be
> easily disseminable, efficient, and relatively cost-effective.... Treatment
> effects have been replicable across a broad range of different therapists,
> overweight populations and situations. Behavior therapy for obesity has
> been shown to be effective without appearing to produce adverse side
> effects.[10]

"Symptom-substitution" has been notably absent.

Because "symptom substitution" is so often cited as a powerful
argument against behavior therapy, considerable attention will be
devoted to an investigation of the claims concerning it in the second
half of this chapter. For the moment, all that needs to be said on the
subject is to define the term and repeat the conclusions regarding its
dangers reached by Rachman and Wilson. The term refers to the
possibility that the eradication of one unwanted behavior (a phobia,
let us say) may lead to another unwanted "symptom" (say, migraine
headaches). Fear of symptom-substitution is based on the theory that
symptoms have underlying causes (e.g., an unresolved Oedipal conflict), and that unless the *cause* of emotional or behavioral problems
is dealt with, this "root" of the problem will keep producing new
symptoms in place of those that are successfully treated. The fact is,
however, the evaulation studies reveal no confirmation whatsoever
for the fear that new symptoms will arise when problems are dealt
with directly through behavior therapy without reference to presumed "underlying causes." Rachman and Wilson's summary statement on the matter is this: "*No evidence of symptom substitution
following behavior therapy was obtained*, even in studies explicitly
designed to uncover negative side effects" [italics in the original].[11]
They support this generalization with the following citation from an
important study by Sloane et al.:

> Not a single patient whose original problem had substantially improved
> reported new symptoms cropping up. On the contrary, assessors had
> the informal impression that when a patient's primary symptoms im-
> proved, he often spontaneously reported improvement of minor diffi-
> culties.[12]

Erwin's concluding comment on symptom-substitution carries the same import: He reports that studies designed to "discern the appearance of new maladaptive characteristics ... have found that the phenomenon sometimes occurs, but not usually."[13]

In summary, there are a number of fundamental principles that seem to be operative in the kind of specifically targeted behavior therapy that any normal, healthy, intelligent person might use to eradicate an unwanted behavior:

(1) The program is entirely voluntary, the behavior therapist acting simply as a consultant who listens to the client describe the problem as he or she perceives it and who then prescribes a specific remedy that is enacted only after both the therapist and the client feel that the requirements of informed consent have been satisfied.

(2) The program leads to and in some measure usually depends on increased understanding on the part of the client, who learns a great deal about what occasions the unwanted behaviors, their effect on body and mind, and reasons why he or she does not have to be "stuck" with them:

   (a) Careful *record-keeping* is usually an important feature of the program. It not only provides immediate reinforcement by showing the person concerned that progress is being made; it also sets up "stimulus control."

   (b) By identifying those situations in which one is most likely to be tempted to engage in the unwanted behavior, one learns *stimulus control*: By avoiding these situations, one avoids temptation and thus, reduces the incidence of the behavior.

   (c) In addition, one learns to practice *substitution*: whenever one feels the urge to do X (the behavior one wants to get rid of), one does Y (a substitute action) instead.

(3) The program frequently adds a new dimension to the experience of the client (who learns, for example, the satisfaction of taking deep breaths or sipping from a glass of cold water instead of smoking) and perhaps also the scope and variety of his or her social interactions. This is particularly true if substitute gratifications introduce a person to novel pursuits and to new people who also engage in them.

As Davison and Wilson point out,

Behavior therapy is far from being inconsistent with a humanistic philosophy. On the contrary, it is probably the most effective means of promoting personal freedom and individualism because it enhances the individual's freedom of choice.[14]

## POSITIVE BEHAVIOR CONTROL

The avoidance of evil or self-destructive behavior is only one part of ethics and probably the least important part, at that. Far more significant is the cultivation of good behavior; indeed, the formation of virtue as a habitual inclination toward good behavior is a prominent aspect of the traditional notion of goodness. The possibilities can be thought of as points on the continuum that appears in Figure 3. An explanation of each category and of the relations among them follows.

*Imprinting* is a concept that comes from ethology. It refers to the instinctual responses with which some species are born as a protective element in their genetic heritage.

> Animals rely a great deal on ancestral memories, on so-called instincts that have been engraved in their brains by some genetic mechanism. A young squirrel taken away from its mother at birth and raised in isolation on concrete floors will still dig an imaginary hole in which to hide the first nutlike object it ever encounters. And even after twenty generations of breeding in laboratory cages, rats will revert to digging burrows in the ground at the first opportunity.[15]

Such responses can be channelled illogically, as Konrad Lorenz has shown: By presenting himself (in a waddling, ducklike posture) to a group of just-hatched ducklings, he got them to treat him exactly as they would have treated a mother duck. So the fact that human infants can be decisively influenced by experiences they have between the ages of six weeks and six months has led some psychologists to wonder if certain characteristics can be imprinted on small children. If this can be done, a whole new field of child care might develop, that of the professional imprinter. The leading exponent of this intriguing plan is Eleanor B. Luckey, a child psychologist who "has accepted the concept of imprinting as a development that occurs when the child is extraordinarily impressionable." Assuming the "periods of maximum impressionability [could] be pinpointed for various characteristics," professional imprinters might serve as visiting consultants in the homes where small children were growing up:

> If, for example, it is established that personality fixing proceeds most rapidly between the eighth and tenth month, an imprinter specializing

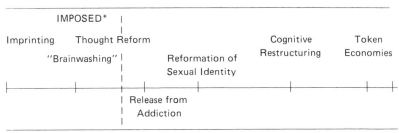

**Figure 3   Positive Behavior Control**

in personality might be on hand several hours a week during that period to help optimize the traits particularly desired by the family.[16]

(Readers of Aldous Huxley's *Brave New World* will remember that prebirth imprinting was carried out on the fetuses of that dystopian society. Babies emerged from the incubator destined to be content with their preprogrammed identity as manual workers, clerks or leaders. Some scientists are of the opinion that prenatal imprinting of a sort can be carried out with human embryos inside the womb, because certain inclinations and/or capacities can be heightened or rendered more probable by chemical injections made before birth.)[17]

*Brainwashing* is a loaded term, one that Robert Jay Lifton rejects in his book on *Thought Reform in China*. Call it what you will, the reshaping of minds, personalities, and actions described in Lifton's work is amazingly extensive and deep. To the average "bourgeois individualist" of our society, in fact, Chinese thought reform amounts to a terrifying violation of human selfhood. The process moves through these stages.

(1) The subject is placed in a social unit made up exclusively of— or at least dominated by—true believers. He or she is usually bound or shackled, and imposed physical discomfort is a part of the pressure that soon drives him or her to care about only one thing: "What do they want me to say?"

(2) "What they want to hear" is self-condemnation, a confession of past crimes and sins that is coupled with emotional expressions of

repentance and evidence of a sound comprehension of the New Gospel one is now going to believe in and follow wholeheartedly.

—Initial articulations of the desired verbal formulae are met (quite appropriately) with angry skepticism. After being told, "You're just saying that to get untied; you don't really mean it!" several times, the victim becomes desperate enough to give at least one convincing confession and vow of repentance. For this he is rewarded ... and is thus encouraged mightily to come up with some more convincing confessions as soon as possible.

—One of the true believers comes to him "secretly" to give words of comfort and advice. "I am your friend," he declares. "I know what you are going through, because I had to go through the same thing myself not long ago. I understand how much it hurts to have to admit that you were terribly, terribly wrong, that your family was wicked for generations, etc., etc. But you must dig deeper and deeper, and you must be genuinely convicted of sin in your own heart—that is the only path to salvation."

(3) So the poor reformee does dig deeper. He accuses himself, his family, and his old friends of new evils; he sees new light; he commits himself to new modes of regeneration. He may *think* he is merely conning his tormentors—but the more he says what they want to hear (and thinks in the manner he has to in order to *devise* those little speeches and *display* the appropriate emotions), the more he himself begins to believe what he's saying and feel what he tries to *appear* to feel. Thus are his mind and his emotions actually re-formed.

(4) He succeeds, finally, in convincing himself as well as the newly significant others upon whom he is now dependent that the new ways of thinking and acting are *right* and that he *wants* to accept and live up to the new standards. Similar to the obedient son who internalizes the superego fashioned by his parents, he now carries around an inner policeman to keep his behavior in line. Like the unfortunate protagonist of *1984*, he not only *says* he sees five fingers when his torturer only holds up four, he *really does* see five! And he weeps tears of *genuine* gratitude when he sees the visage of Big Brother and thinks how much Big Brother loves him and has done to make his life blessed.[18]

Unequivocally successful *rehabilitation programs for drug addicts* are not easy to find. Even if they make use of substitute chemical agents (such as methadone), the best programs usually include a social dimension that provides emotional reinforcement and a new set of understanding friends. The similarities with the Chinese model are sometimes striking. Synanon subjects all newcomers to a "haircut"—that is, an ordeal of public humiliation in which old members of the group surround the initiate and try to destroy her old sense of self-worth so that it can be rebuilt without reliance on drugs. Social isolation and group discipline are also common features of the Health, Education and Welfare (HEW) program for youthful addicts in Florida called "Seedlings":

> The youths ... pressed into this program were isolated from family, friends and the outside world. They were stripped of all identification and thrust at a low position into a precise social structure. Then they were subjected to carefully managed, intense, peer-group pressure from fellow Seedlings already in the program. A Seedling could advance upward in the structure only by rigid right-thinking. There was a good deal of talk about goodness and love but there was also a deliberate effort to smash the new Seedling's psychological defenses and make him feel totally dependent on the group. He was instilled with the urgency of being constantly aware of the group's wishes. One Seedling reported that Seedlings slept in the same room with him; they accompanied him whenever he traveled by car and even when he went to the bathroom.

> "When they return (testified a guidance counselor at a Miami high school who had encountered many returned Seedlings), they are 'straight,' namely quiet, well dressed, with short hair, and not under the influence of drugs compared to their previous appearance of being stoned most of the time. However, they seem to be living in a robotlike atmosphere, and they won't speak to anyone outside their own group. They sit in a class together and the classes become divided [with] Seedlings opposing non-Seedlings. ... Seedlings seems to have an informing system on each other and on others that is similar to Nazi Germany. They run in to use the telephone daily, to report against each other to the Seed."[19]

It would be instructive to compare this program—that sounds as though its apparent effectiveness is bought at a high price—with a Massachusetts program described by Barbara Brown in which 1,800 youthful drug abusers were "weaned away" from drugs through their being given instruction in Transcendental Meditation. No doubt the "Hawthorne Effect" of being part of a group involved in a special experimental program was operative in both programs, but the one in Massachusetts accentuated the positive rather than imposing rigid disciplines: its "nearly 90 percent" effectiveness was "greatly enhanced *by providing the user with an experience which is more meaningful, useful and inner-directing than that of the drug experience*" (italics in original).[20]

Thought reform can sometimes be carried out on an individual basis, as it often has been (or used to be until the American Psychological Association reversed its position on the matter and withdrew its endorsement) to repress homosexuality in gays who want to become heterosexual. When aversive therapy is employed, a male client may receive a slight electric shock when the picture of a nude man is presented. He can avoid repetition of the shock by pressing a button that substitutes a picture of a sexually provocative woman. "The hope is that the homosexual stimulus will be associated with, and hence inhibited by, the painful shock, while the heterosexual stimulus will be rewardingly associated with the pleasurable cessation of the pain."[21] But aversive therapy is not essential. One of Robert Heath's patients, for instance, became interested in women for the first time in his life when he saw a stag film after being put into a state of euphoria through ESB. While watching the film (he had previously found disgusting, before having the pleasure center of his brain stimulated),

> he became sexually aroused and masturbated to orgasm. During the following week his interest in women continued, and his counselors ... answered his questions about sexual techniques. (He had never in his life had a heterosexual experience). Stimulation of the septal pleasure center continued periodically and he eventually expressed a desire for a heterosexual relationship.... A sympathetic, cooperative young prostitute ... seduced him as they lay side by side in a private room and he reported experiencing intercourse climaxed by orgasm. During the following year ... he developed a close sexual attachment to another girl, and reported that he had become heterosexually oriented.[22]

Most appropriate and most successful as a means to active goodness is what practitioners call *cognitive restructuring*. Rachman and Wilson's summary of this approach distinguishes four major variants, all of which are somewhat difficult to evaluate for effectiveness, but are considered to have "considerable promise." The theory of behavior therapy should acknowledge, say Rachman and Wilson, that many of its most highly regarded techniques are really forms of cognitive restructuring, or at least include an element of this approach. "Modelling," for example, depends upon vicarious learning, in which one alters preconceptions and expectations in accordance with what others are seen to do or what one imagines oneself doing. "Flooding" works because events and experiences once viewed as threatening are recreated until one gradually comes to see them as tolerable and conceive of them as acceptable. Even desensitization, the brightest star in the behavioral galaxy, is effective because it introduces new concepts of what one is capable of handling in daily life. Thus,

> Bandura has proposed that systematic desensitization and other fear-reduction methods, such as flooding and modelling, work because they provide sources of information that alter self-efficacy expectations. If one accepted this interpretation then systematic desensitization would be classified as a "cognitive behavior modification" technique.[23]

The oldest type of cognitive restructuring is Ellis's "rational emotive therapy" (RET). It usually includes—although it is not always limited to—five procedures:

(1) verbal persuasion aimed at convincing the client of the philosophical tenets of RET;
(2) identification of irrational thoughts through client self-monitoring and the therapist's feedback;
(3) the therapist directly challenges irrational ideas and models rational interpretations of disturbing events;
(4) repeated cognitive rehearsal aimed at substituting rational self-statement for previously irrational interpretation;
(5) behavioral tasks designed to develop rational reactions.[24]

Among the irrational thoughts that the therapist aggressively attacks as silly and tries to get the client to abandon are the notion that "everybody must love me" and "I must be perfect in everything that I do." A second type of cognitive restructuring is "systematic rational restructuring" as practiced by Goldfried and Davison, which differs from the foregoing only in that "a Socratic approach is adopted in contrast to the direct challenging of clients' irrational cognitions that is the hallmark of Ellis's RET."[25]

Meichenbaum's "self-instructional training" (SIT) is a third type of cognitive restructuring. It was "derived, in part, from Ellis's RET," so it is not surprising that its procedures reveal many similarities in step-by-step approach:

(1) training the client to identify and become aware of maladaptive thoughts (self-statements);
(2) the therapist models appropriate behavior while verbalizing effective action strategies; these verbalizations include an appraisal of task requirements, self-instructions that guide graded performance, self-statements that stress personal adequacy and counteract worry over failure, and covert self-reinforcement for successful performance;
(3) the client then performs the target behavior while verbalizing aloud the appropriate self-instructions and later by covertly rehearsing them; therapist feedback during this phase assists in ensuring that constructive problem-solving self-talk replaces previously anxiety-inducing cognitions associated with that behavior.[26]

There are, however, important differences. Mahoney and Arnkoff summarize them as follows:

Both RET and SIT deemphasize the importance of self-statements and thought patterns in adaptive and maladaptive behavior. However, there are important differences in technique and focus. Where Ellis tends to focus on his set of ''core rational ideas,'' Meichenbaum et al. have seemed to be more interested in idiosyncratic thought patterns. The latter have also devoted more attention to the role of graduated practice in their cognitive training package. In addition, self-instructional training presents a somewhat more heterogeneous package which contains elements of desensitization, modelling, and behavior rehearsal. Of particular note is the fact that this approach emphasizes practical coping skills for dealing with problematic situations. While the major emphasis of RET is the *destruction* of maladaptive beliefs, self-instructional training supplants this with a *constructive* phase of skills development. Where RET highlights the rationality of a thought—believing that rationality is synonymous with adaptiveness—self-instructional training places more emphasis on its adaptiveness and its constructive alternatives. Thus, while RET posits differences in the thoughts of normal and distressed persons, a self-instructional therapist would place more emphasis on an individual's methods of coping with those thoughts.... In other words, it is not the content or incidence of irrational beliefs that differentiates normal and distressed persons—it is their learned means of coping with these beliefs.[27]

Meichenbaum also differs from Ellis in utilizing the Socratic mode "in which therapy is structured so that clients discover for themselves the inaccuracies and distortions in their thinking ... [and are] helped to identify and alter automatic thoughts through a more gentle and strategic progression of therapeutic intervention."[28]

Finally, there is Beck's "cognitive therapy," which emphasizes four elements that can also be found in the other versions of cognitive restructuring:

(1) clients become aware of their thoughts;
(2) they learn to identify inaccurate or distorted thoughts;
(3) these inaccuracies are replaced by accurate, more objective cognitions; and
(4) the therapist provides feedback and reinforcement for cognitive and behavioral change.[29]

Beck lays particular stress on "distancing" and "decentering." In the former, the subject learns "the ability to view one's thoughts more objectively, to draw a distinction between 'I believe' (an opinion that is open to disconfirmation) and 'I know' (an 'irrefutable' fact)." In the latter, clients are taught to "separate themselves from vicariously experiencing the adversities of others."[30]

Rachman and Wilson analyze all major outcome evaluations of the kinds of cognitive restructuring listed above. They declare that the efficacy of Beck's approach cannot be conclusively judged on the basis of existing studies but that "initial results are encouraging." RET is adjudged to be "too global and imprecise" to allow definitive evaluation (especially in such features as the "irrational beliefs" cited above); indeed, Rachman and Wilson fear that recent elaborations of the difference between "general or inelegant RET" and "elegant RET" penned by Ellis "threaten to make RET untestable." Nevertheless, they conclude that "the evidence suggests that RET is more effective than no-treatment or placebo influences on some measures, in most studies." They view SIT as "scientifically superior to control conditions in most studies," and they claim that SIT equalled or outperformed comparison treatments in others."[31]

A *token economy* is a program that makes use of some kind of "token"—poker chips, play money, or the like—as a medium of exchange in the therapeutic setting. Subjects earn tokens by exhibiting desired target behaviors; they lose tokens when they fail to do assigned tasks or violate rules. This can, of course, be done on a strictly voluntary basis by people who desire to shape their own behavior and the exchange of tokens can be carried out simply by keeping an on-paper record of behavior. Keith Miller of the University of Kansas has been very successful in setting up student residence communities where participants save money and gain various study-related benefits by contributing time and skills to the community.[32] At Twin Oaks, the intentional community in Virginia that is patterned after the "scientific utopia" described in B. F. Skinner's *Walden II*, one person who wanted to be sure to brush his teeth simply entered into a contract with his roommate: At the beginning of the week, he gave him seven dollars; each day, he got a dollar back if he remembered to do his teeth and reported this to the monitoring roommate.[33]

Token economies lie on the extreme end of the continuum of positive behavior control possibilities because their use does not necessarily attempt to induce or speculate about "thought reform" (which therapists committed to behaviorism as a philosophical stance would consider an obscurantist category, anyhow).[34] Despite complaints about evaluation study research design and resulting ambiguity in the findings, Rachman and Wilson stipulate that token economies "can effect widespread changes across different responses in institutionalized psychiatric patients."[35] It is ironic, then, that recent court decisions have tended to make it illegal for hospital or prison staffs to reshape inmate behavior by making them earn certain daily comforts and privileges through displaying a consistent pattern of constructive behavior, or by rewarding them for contributing to the maintenance of the institution.[36]

## ANALYSIS OF PHILOSOPHICAL
## AND ETHICAL ISSUES

As in Chapter 3, there are a few important general observations to make before commencing an analysis of the philosophical and ethical issues raised by the possibilities for artificial goodness. To begin with, all that has been said earlier about the limited place of EBC in the balanced life led by the freely choosing individual applies here as well. So does what was said in the preceding chapter about the enhancement of human stature because of an increase in the range of choice available, awareness of the need to choose, and implications of being responsible for the consequences of the choices made.

The latter point is true to a special degree and in a very special sense where choices pertaining to good or bad behavior are concerned. If one is genuinely troubled by the uncertainty and the ambivalence of an equivocal moral situation—for example, a well-established pattern of giving into homosexual temptations that one really feels bad about and does not want to be involved, then knowing that there is, in fact, a way to put an end to the troublesome behavior and the guilt it occasions is in itself a salient psychospiritual datum. If you know you *can* put a stop to a condition that you *claim* to be troubled about, then there is no point in beating your breast because of the cruelty of fate in burdening you with such an affliction. You either eliminate the condition, or you admit that (because of the gratifications you enjoy, which are evidently more rewarding than the tension you experience is disturbing) you are not sure you want to—and in either case you can cease complaining about your sufferings and (however indirectly or subtly) boasting about your passive heroism in bearing up under them. The availability of EBC, in other words, promotes—and even demands—good faith: It makes it more difficult for you to kid yourself about the values you really believe in and the strength or weakness of your commitment to them.

What EBC does not and cannot do, however, is to simplify the outlines of the situation of moral choice: You, the moral agent in question, still have to go through the process of moral reflection that forces you to ask, "What is the source of my discomfort?" and "What are my reasons for wanting to alter the conditions which produce it?" One may feel apprehensive about adulterous or homosexual impulses, for example, for more reasons than one: You can believe that they are really wrong in some ethically normative sense (because they violate the will of God, the intentions of Nature, or your own sense of what is fitting for the kind of person you want to be), or you can merely be embarrassed by them in the sense that they are imprudent because other people whose opinions matter to you would disapprove and might punish you in some way that you want to avoid). If prudence is high on your list of virtues—because, for instance, the good opinion of rather conservative people is vital to your keeping the job that enables you to perform what you consider a significant vocation and thus make your contribution to the world, then the removal of this potential cause for embarrassment might be a perfect-ly valid, even a commendable, motivating factor. If, on the other hand, you feel that renouncing homosexuality would constitute a violation of your integrity or a loss of something essential in your very being, the risk of discovery and embarrassment might be one you would have to take—and in that case, the kind of EBC you sign up for might be a program to reduce anxiety, not one to alter behavior. If you feel very strongly about the rightness of your homosexuality and about the shamefulness of not being open about it, you might want a program that could give you the courage to come out of the closet.

These three options represent a set of ethical choices. EBC can help you implement the choice you make; it cannot make the choice for you.

Because educators, moralists, parents, and law enforcement of-ficials seem to devote endless amounts of energy to the task of promoting good behavior, one might suppose that they would wel-come the advent of the new technologies of behavior control. But many of those who are fully satisfied that artificial goodness is tech-nically possible are unsure about the philosophical or moral proprie-ty of creating it by the means we have described. Why is this the case? What are they worried about, actually?

Ultimately, they may be worried about what was referred to in the introductory chapter as a "Fourth Copernican Revolution." For those who are enamored of the Classical Christian view of human-kind, it was bad enough when Copernicus discovered that the whole universe did not move around the earth. Darwin stirred up a comparable fuss when he suggested that humanity had descended from lower animals instead of being the unique product of divine creation portrayed in the early chapters of Genesis. Another shock came with Freud's attack on the sovereignty of the rational mind. Now comes B. F. Skinner with the claim that behaviorism renders obsolete the notions of freedom and dignity most of us have always believed in—and there is something about the prospect of gener-ating desired behaviors by operant conditioning that seems at first glance to be a kind of final insult to our self-understanding as creatures fashioned in the image of God. The fears of many tradi-tionalists would attain a special frenzy in the light of Jose Delgado's dictum (cited in Chapter 1) that it is no longer enough to follow the ancient adage, "Know thyself," because today it would be more to the point to say, "Create an improved version of thyself."[37]

I like to think of EBC as a development of decisive importance, a constellation of scientific discoveries and technological applications that can make a crucial difference in the way we perceive ourselves and manage our lives in the future. The analogy of the Fourth Copernican Revolution also appeals to me, because it is a good reminder of how extreme the initial reaction of traditionalists has often been and how the implications of a new discovery or idea—often exaggerated or misunderstood at first—have been assimilated into our subsequent understanding of human nature without fatal complications. Copernicus, Darwin, and Freud did not deliver a death blow to our conception of human beings as creatures of intelligence and moral sensibility who have a potential for grandeur as well as misery, and neither will EBC. Delgado's comment need not be seen as the epitome of hubris. But the objections of those who entertain fears of this kind must be considered carefully and answered satisfactorily and that is what the remainder of this chapter is intended to do.

## Objections

There are at least five major objections to artificial goodness:

(1) It isn't *necessary*.
(2) It wouldn't be *effective* in the long run.
(3) It wouldn't be *genuine goodness*.
(4) It would, in fact, be *dehumanizing*.
(5) Even if one grants a certain limited validity to procedures such as "Congruity" or "Commitment," the results achieved by these means would constitute *a good that is enemy of the best*. Better results could be achieved by familiar methods.

If all these objections are heard from the mouth of one speaker, who represents the most thoughtful and well-intentioned skeptic, the resulting statement might sound something like this:

You insult my intelligence and my strength of character when you suggest that I *need* operant conditioning, chemicals, or any other kind of artificial assistance in order to do anything important I want to do, or feel I ought to do, or in order to avoid doing something I believe I ought not to do. If I seem to lack willpower in regard to certain negative injunctions or positive exhortations, that's misleading. I certainly don't need "Congruity" or "Commitment"; all I need is a little more time to think things through. When my mind has finished sorting things out, I'll take appropriate action.

Besides, I'm still not convinced that EBC *works*. Oh, I've listened to your arguments about the unlikelihood of unwanted secondary effects that can't be easily counteracted and I suppose there's good evidence to support the claims to safety, precision, reliability, and so on. But I'm sure something is wrong somewhere, because merely erasing one symptom can't be very satisfying for very long if the underlying cause is left untouched. Even to talk about it this way bothers me, because when I say EBC won't work I mean something that goes beyond clinical observation of symptoms, side effects, etc. I mean that "quenching the behavioral artifact" may leave the poor client worse off than before— because that may simply cover up problems he needs to be aware of and the *apparent* success of EBC may lead him to avoid this necessary awareness and postpone developing those insights or character resources he needs to develop in order to deal adequately with the root problem.

Furthermore, I don't regard the kind of artificially stimulated behavior you're talking about as *genuine goodness*, not at all. A moral action is more than a "behavioral output"; it is a complex unity of perception, interpretation, motivation, decision, and act in which mind, conscience, will, and character all play an indispensable part. Taking a short cut to the act, or leaving out in whatever way or for whatever reason some of the other elements in the *Gestalt* simply won't do. Good fruits can only grow on good trees; if they are fabricated in some other way, they are fakes.

The more I think about it, the more upset I become. The whole idea of *artificial goodness is dehumanizing*. We do something terrible to ourselves if we fool around with this gimmickry; we lose our nature as human beings and become something we are not meant to be when we treat ourselves as objects to be manipulated, mechanical entities from which "behaviors" are to be elicited, the way we teach a dog to do tricks.

And even if I could be shown that all those complaints were invalid, I'd still say it's *better* to produce goodness in the old-fashioned way. Not only do good acts have to be the expression of good character in a good person, good persons have to be a part of a moral community where people with similar values love, nurture, and rebuke one another all the time. *Solitary* goodness is morally and spiritually inferior to the goodness of a self-in-community whose goodness is an expression of the community and of the covenant binding all its members together. To produce seemingly good actions in any other way is not only artificial, it's below par—and thus, actions produced through EBC are illusory goods that are enemies of the *best* anyone is capable of in the right kind of human community.

Each of these objections deserves closer examination. After the thrust and the logic of each one has been analyzed, an answer to each will be given and a constructive statement explaining the moral reasoning underlying a positive view of artificial goodness will be presented.

*(1) It Isn't Necessary.* The world is full of smokers who will assure you that they can quit anytime they want to. If you were to suggest that they take advantage of a program such as "Congruity" to assist them, they would inhale deeply, smile, and say, "Who needs it? Whenever I decide I really want to stop, I have the will power to do it. I know, because I've done it plenty of times in the past."

It's hard to contend with anyone who takes that line of argument. You can't prove he's wrong: Maybe he can stop whenever he really wants to. But if you could get him to put some money on it (providing the sum was not sufficiently large to activate that will power decisively and provided the length of time covered by the bet was long enough), the odds would definitely be in your favor. In theory, he doesn't need help; he can use his will power to take the desired action "any time." In actuality, he probably will *not* stop smoking unless (a) something dramatic happens to intensify his desire to quit or (b) he gets a better "handle" on the situation in the form of a *technique* that will enable him to stop *without* the special motivation provided by some dramatic change in attitude (e.g., being told by his physician that he will probably have a heart attack within two years if he doesn't change his habits).

The analogy is far from trivial. It reveals how easy it is to dupe ourselves when it comes to the question of what is "necessary" to get us to do something we are always telling ourselves we want to do. If "necessary" is a word that is to be allowed only in situations where the act in question simply cannot be accomplished without the intervention being considered, then necessity is almost impossible to prove. If the word can be used in situations in which there is a demonstrably low *probability* of the action's occurring without an intervention of the kind under consideration, then it isn't so hard. And if necessity is measured in terms of probability, then "Congruity" and "Commitment" are statistically "necessary" in the situations we have hypothesized. That is, in plain language, there are many situations of moral choice when the persons concerned are not very likely to make *what they themselves would say* is the right choice unless they get "help." To make the same point in a slightly different way, the availability of the effective handle makes implementation of the decision so easy to carry out that not to use that handle would be paradoxical.

So let's not try to show "necessity"; let's content ourselves with demonstrating "advisability," or "compelling appropriateness," or something like that which means, speaking plainly, "Given the facts as they stand, it certainly would be curious if you didn't use X, which is readily available and effective, to get Y, which you say you want." My argument, then, would run as follows: "If Y is as important to you as you have said it is, you must be terribly distressed because your efforts to get it by means of Z have been so unsuccessful for so long. Now that X has been shown to be so effective in enabling its users to get Y swiftly and surely, you will doubtless want to make use of X yourself."

Opponents can still say that people *ought* not to need EBC because they ought to be strong enough to do what they ought to do without crutches, shortcuts or anything else of that kind. But when that argument is put alongside the facts concerning the efficacy of known EBC techniques, it doesn't look very impressive.

What that boils down to is this: EBC may not be "necessary" in theory or in logic, for any given individual is perfectly free (in theory) to decide at any given moment that *now,* after intending it for a long time but not doing it, he *will* stop doing P or start doing G. But the longer those intentions have existed only in the mind, or in talk about them, the longer an outside observer may be pardoned for doubting that the frequently announced intentions will be acted on (except erratically, spasmodically, and very partially).

Eugene O'Neill satirized the frailty of good intentions in the *The Iceman Cometh*, which tells the story of an unsavory crowd of drunkards, whores, and pimps who do little but sit around a New York bar, striving to maintain a few vestiges of self-respect by talking about the wonderful deeds they will do someday (at some point in the future, when conditions are right, when they're ready, when the time has come, etc.). The action of the play hinges on the arrival of an outside character who forces them to begin *that very day* to actualize their various "pipe dreams"—and then forces them to acknowledge that they had been kidding themselves all along. They are forced to admit the hollowness of their good intentions because each of them returns, in defeat, having been unable even to make a decent start at doing whatever they had always said they were going to do someday. By the time the play ends, the outside character has been dispensed with and all of the barflies have either resurrected their patently dishonest illusions (or else been driven to suicide by their acknowledgment of their inability to do so).

Fortunately, there's no need to be as cynical as O'Neill: Human beings are seldom completely beyond redemption, and a group of persons with more resources to draw on than the characters in *Iceman* might have a higher batting average in their response to some dramatic event that broke the spell of inertia and set them in motion. But one might profit from O'Neill's realism about the propensity of most people, including sober and respectable types, to substitute pipe dreams for action. And one ought to be realistic enough to admit that it's rather stupid to sit around and wait for some earth-shaking event to set you in motion at last. Why wait to be shaken out of your apathy by startling news when you know you can get a handle on the situation and turn it your way through EBC? You may not "need it"—but you might be a fool not to use it.

*(2) It Isn't Effective.* The question about efficacy is fundamentally a technical question and every effort has been made to answer it in technical terms in the first part of this chapter. Further uneasiness based on the rather vague suspicion that "there must be something wrong with treating symptoms apart from underlying causes" seems to be based on a couple of misunderstandings that can be straightened out without too much difficulty.

Amitai Etzioni once wrote a thought-provoking essay in which he dealt with the "symptoms/roots" debate as it arose in connection with the social problem of street crime. He told of a particular urban neighborhood that did not have enough money to attack the underlying causes of crime by improving housing, schools, community recreational facilities, job opportunities, and so on. So it used its limited funds to provide plenty of street lights throughout the neighborhood. Opponents of this use of funds complained that it was only a "bandaid" designed to create an illusion that the real problem had been dealt with, when as a matter of fact it would hardly be touched.

But the street lights were installed, and they were replaced immediately whenever one was put out ... and crime in that neighborhood
dropped precipitously, almost to the vanishing point.

The point of Etzioni's study, and of reporting it here, is not that all
problems can easily be solved, cheaply and quickly, by a direct approach. The social pathologies that drive some people to crime were
still in existence, and still demanded remedial measures much more
far-reaching and costly than street lights; moreover, the crimes that
no longer occurred in that particular neighborhood may have been
displaced to other neighborhoods not blessed with good lighting.
The story does serve to remind us, though, that specific ills (parts of
larger problems, if you insist) can be cured by specifically targeted
tactics—and that the best way to solve many large-scale problems
may be to attack specific aspects of those problems with measures intended precisely for them. It reminds us that one important measure
of success is a given remedial action's effect on those special aspects
of the problem for which it was designed.

The moral of the story, then, is this: It is unfair to expect an
operant conditioning program intended to extinguish one particular
behavior to do more than that, and it is unreasonable to require a
program intended to induce one attitude or behavior pattern to
reshape a person's whole personality. If the particular behavior in
question is successfully wiped out or generated, then EBC will have
done its job, or rather, the job assigned on this particular go-around.
Other jobs will necessitate the design and execution of other programs (or the use of other approaches) targeted on other specific
aspects of the problem. Thus a "Congruity" program that "works"
to eliminate A should not be blamed for allowing B and C to be
maintained; nor should its achievement be counted for naught by
the accusation that it in some vague way reinforces the System
abcdef because it removes A without touching bcdef. And a "Commitment" program that increases philanthropic giving 500% should
not be criticized in regard to effectiveness because the donor still
drinks champagne every weekend: If the donor sees that as a
problem, she can tackle it next (and those who deplore champagne
in a world where many children lack milk can urge her to do so).

In actuality, there is ample reason to believe that the person who
wants to alter larger patterns of behavior will be far more encouraged
to keep working away at it by specific, limited successes than exhortations to change dramatically all in one fell swoop. So if "effective-

ness" means "resulting in specific changes in behavior and leading to a subsequent personal history in which many other desired changes in behavior are systematically sought and achieved," EBC has uncommonly good claims to the honor.

*(3) It Isn't Genuine Goodness.* For many of the opponents of EBC —especially those whose thinking is informed by theology—this is the cardinal objection. Their qualms need to be taken with the utmost seriousness and their conception of the shortcomings of EBC needs to be understood as fully as possible.

It might be instructive to get a firm grasp on this line of thought by examining the work of Bernard Häring, one of the foremost Roman Catholic theologians of our day. His book on *The Ethics of Manipulation* begins by asserting that "manipulation, as such, is not ... a sin at all," and the chapter on behavior modification goes on to praise the behavioral sciences because they "enable and oblige us to make a more conscious and systematic approach to responsibility for the world in which we live."[38] Yet, Häring declares that "a mere therapy of external behavior is unthinkable for Christians, since they "do not believe that one can make good the fruits without making the tree good."[39] After commenting on "the immense difference between the morality of the beatitudes and any form of eudaemonistic ethics," he concludes,

> The more Skinnerian psychologists are blind to the spiritual experience ... and blind to the experience of goodness in itself, the sharper should be our consciousness of the difference between a simple system of reinforcers and the gospel of divine love and its ethics of the beatitudes....
>
> Real behavior therapy needs a qualitative change in persons according to the gospel message. Only then can mankind conquer the tremendous threats posed by the behavior managers who have in their hands —and will have even more so in the future—a weapon more threatening to human dignity than the atom bomb.[40]

Religious moral philosophers could write volumes if they wanted to unpack those few sentences completely, but the crucial features of the position are suggested by the reference to "the good tree," "the experience of goodness in itself," "qualitative change in persons," and "the difference between a simple system of reinforcers and the gospel of divine love."

The point of view represented by Häring is articulated with greater clarity and force in Martin Luther, the pioneer of the Protestant Reformation. Luther, whose chief polemic was against the insolent notion that vile sinners could earn their salvation by good works, was emphatic in his insistence that

> good works do not make a good man, but a good man does good works; evil works do not make a wicked man, but a wicked man does evil works; so that it is always necessary that the 'substance' or person itself be good before there can be any good works, and that good follow and proceed from the good person, as Christ also says, 'A corrupt tree does not bring forth good fruit, a good tree does not bring forth evil fruit.[41]

Given this assumption, one cannot admit that "good behaviors" (which would have to be put in quotation marks to indicate their status as so-called, phony good works) are really good, and this would be especially true of "good behaviors" resulting from the manipulation of the reinforcements (that appeal, after all, to one's pleasure/pain calculus, and therefore spring from unworthy motivations). Thus, "artificial goodness" is a contradiction in itself: goodness cannot be contrived, it must flow naturally out of a soul that is already good. As Luther put it, "Good works ... follow spontaneously [from the goodness of the redeemed soul] and not under the compulsion of the law."[42]

Any secular person—particularly, no doubt, a down-to-earth, practical, thoroughly utilitarian twentieth-century American—may be bewildered by this line of thought. But anyone familiar with the Christian tradition, especially the Reformation, will understand. For what is at stake here is the holiness and majesty of God. If all goodness and all power to generate goodness must be attributed to God (lest worshippers be guilty of pride), then human goodness apart from God is impossible and the very aspiration toward goodness apart from faith and religious redemption is blasphemous. Kierkegaard captured the essence of this mode of thinking in his famous aphorism, "The opposite of sin is not virtue; it is faith."[43] In this brand of theology, the horizontal dimension of the religious life (i.e., ethics) is secondary; what really counts is the vertical dimension (i.e., faith in God and obedience to his commands).

The objection to EBC raised by this school of thought is so basic that it must be answered in some detail. The two main points that I shall try to establish in my counterargument are these: (1) the most important consideration in ethics is *the consequences of behavior* for those affected by it, and (2) "contrived" goodness through EBC offers the same kind of reliability and consistency of behavior promised by old-fashioned notions of character and conscience (but with greater speed and a higher degree of certainty.)

Preoccupation with the righteousness of the soul of the moral agent at the expense of attention to the consequences of behavior is a holdover from earlier notions of religion that conceived of God as an arbitrary patriarch who would punish disobedience with eternal hellfire and damnation. The logic of belief in a God of love ought to lead inescapably to an emphasis upon the well-being of those whom God loves rather than on the soul and its fate in another world, but older obsessions with the majesty of a Heavenly King die hard. The primacy of consequences ought to be clear, though, if we look at ethics from the standpoint of those who are victims of injustice and misfortune. As *The Family of Man*'s eloquent photograph of starving people in Calcutta proclaims, "Nothing is real to us but hunger"— and nothing about ethics concerns them except the *deeds* of those who claim to have compassion for them. Their question is, "Who is actually giving us food?" not "What are their motives?" or "What faith undergirds their concern?" or anything of that sort. And the only thing that will save them is good behavior in the form of food actually delivered, not holy hearts or pious intentions. The same point is clear in the research on what used to be called "race relations" in the United States. So long as the focus of attention was on "prejudice" (attitudes in the mind), little progress was made in the struggle for racial justice. It was only when attention shifted to "discrimination" (behavior), and to the laws and administrative actions necessary to alter behavioral patterns directly, that the treatment of blacks changed noticeably. As soon as behavior changed, so did attitudes—because the continued repetition of discriminatory behavior patterns reinforces prejudice, whereas nondiscriminatory behavior undermines the attitudes on which discrimination is based.

So the first error of the theological position we are attacking here is its failure to recognize the prime importance of behavior and of the consequences of behavior in ethics. Its preoccupation with such secondary matters as the soul of the moral agent (its state of grace vis-à-vis the Deity, its purity of motivation, etc.) is counterproductive, for it all too often creates a boomerang effect in the mind and the behavior of the believer. In terms of the New Testament parable of the two sons and the vineyard, the vertically-oriented believer spends so much time saying "Yes" to the "Ol' Massa" at the Big House, he never gets around to doing the work in the vineyard. The son who is not hung up on saying "yes" is free to concentrate on getting the job done in the vineyard—and is also free to use all the tools, including EBC, that will enable him to get the job done most efficiently and effectively.

Ironically then, the concern with motivation that characterizes theological thought turns out to be self-defeating. This suggests that the best motive (best in terms of the consequences produced, which is the prime criterion) is concern with the well-being of the neighbors served by one's actions, not the God who is honored thereby. Concentrate on honoring God and you produce less in the way of good consequences for your neighbors; concentrate on the neighbors and you produce more of the consequences that are presumably pleasing to a loving God. One is tempted to conclude that the only good motive, finally, is a desire to produce the greatest quantity of beneficial consequences for human beings in need—and that any other motive is inferior precisely because it produces fewer such consequences.

But what about *character*, *conscience*, and *virtue*? Even if stress laid upon these prominent items of traditional ethics can be shown to diminish the production of good consequences for persons through the production of good behavior in moral agents, surely it cannot be said that they are irrelevant to the moral life. To be forced to that conclusion would be a supreme irony, as the practical effect of the cultivation of virtuous character and of the formation of conscience has always been claimed to be a life of *consistent* goodness (virtue being by definition the "habit" of doing what is right). It is just this concern for habitual good behavior, for a conscience that more or less automatically inclines one to choose rightly instead of wrongly that ought to make EBC spectacularly attractive to exponents of traditional moral theology. For in EBC we have a kind of "exercise" (analogous to the "spiritual exercises" by means of which monastics, mystics, and saints have sought to cultivate faith and virtue) that produces consistent good behavior more reliably than anything but the most phenomenally successful processes of character development according to the old model could achieve—and produces it far more speedily than the traditional mode of character formation and conscience development could. EBC doesn't keep you waiting as long as the painstaking molding of conscience does. (Where would southern blacks have been today if they had been forced to wait until the *hearts* of white people had changed?) Moreover, EBC yields consistency of performance that outstrips that of most people who have acquired virtue in traditional ways. Only an exponent of extreme existentialism who feels that real goodness must be shown in *de novo* decisions in each situation of moral choice, without dependence upon either character or law, really has compelling grounds for rejecting artificial goodness through EBC.

(4) *It Would Be Dehumanizing.* The charge that artificial goodness is not real goodness is fairly specific compared to the sweeping allegation that it is somehow dehumanizing. Often this charge is based on intuitive insights that are not explained in rational argumentation (and may not be explicable by such argumentation). When this occurs, there is little to be said in refutation except to point out that unexplained and undocumented intuitions have little persuasive power for others who are not already convinced.

But now and then one comes across a concise statement of the dehumanization complaint, such as the summary highlights of a Harvard Conference on Behavior Control Technologies in 1967. A number of well-known educators, notably Jacques Barzun, contributed to the following appraisal of EBC:[44]

(a) It is *deliberate* in an area of human experience (moral sensibility and striving) when too much *system* or *technique* is a detriment rather than an asset. Barzun, who is primarily a literary scholar, contends that "the saving grace about my methods is that they are fitful and uncertain and in one important sense not deliberate." Citing his distaste for "erotic technique" as an illustration, Barzun confesses his fear of the "side effects which come not from the technique, but from the deliberateness of the technique."

It is certainly not impossible to take the position that ethics is better conceived and practiced as an art rather than as a science, and many philosophers have preferred intuition (or "moral sentiment," as it was called in the eighteenth-century Enlightenment in England) to reason or ecclesiastically defined revelation as the key source of ethical wisdom. But exponents of these convictions need to offer some justification for their preferences; otherwise, they are bound to seem arbitrary. Barzun's distaste for "deliberateness" smacks of sheer superstition, as if there were something spooky about simply being *careful* or rationally *aware* in one's efforts to accomplish some purpose. One recognizes here the prejudice against modernity that is typically present in aristocratic critics of mass society, especially writers such as Jacques Ellul, whose extended polemic against "the technological society" and its emphasis of *la technique* is more of an obfuscation than it is a stimulus to constructive thought.[45]

(b) It breathes the aroma of *coercion*. What Barzun and several other conference participants fasten on here is not the danger of political abuses, but the possible *irresistibility* of EBC. For academic intellectuals, the supremely sacred value in life is choice based on wise understanding; therefore, they are wary of a system of behavior management that seems to involve surrender of critical judgment after an initial step (in this case, submission to the process of operant conditioning) has been taken. But a counterargument similar to the one regarding irresistibility in the preceding chapter may also be advanced here: What is the qualitative difference between the "coercion" (actually, the effective implementation of intent) of EBC and the shaping of behavior carried out by families, churches, corporations, and schools in the "normal" socialization process? What humanists favor is character, conscience, and virtue when formed in traditional ways—yet if these cultural artifacts have been successfully fashioned, they will have an effect upon perceptions, conceptions, and acts of will that could be called "coercive" to a rather substantial degree, and are in fact called "compulsive" by some.

Of course, the coercion attributed to EBC is not a flaw that I am disposed to eliminate but rather a strength I celebrate. The decision to enter into a program of "Congruity" or "Commitment" is just as free as an adult decision to join the Methodist Church, get married in a public ceremony that constitutes a rite of passage and seals a new identity for the participants, or become a member of the Republican Party. And the precision, reliability, and added certainty offered by EBC strikes me as an asset, not a liability.

(c) It is *irreversible*. This is another version of b, and against it we may cite the contention of EBC experts such as Ulrich and Delgado that alterations wrought by these means are in many cases *more easily reversed,* should one decide to reverse them, than are the deeply ingrained patterns resulting from conventional socialization.

(d) It is an assault upon the Western view of humanity. Deploring what might be called the mechanistic fallacy of breaking the human self into separate components, Barzun argues that "man is a whole which cannot be viewed as divided and subdivided behaviors." Even the rise of EBC and the behaviorism on which it is based signifies "the total disappearance of any model of man," our culture's loss of its historic conception "of what a man should be."

But this kind of rhetoric is a mystification. As I endeavor to show in the final chapter, it is not impossible to reconcile the use of EBC with many of the most important aspects of the concept of humanity that derives from the Judeo-Christian and the Greco-Roman traditions. One can still believe in soul, mind, free will, heroism, and infamy; one can still make use of perennial notions of good and evil in utilizing EBC to optimize the human potential for realizing the former and overcoming the latter. It may be wise to revise or discard some of our familiar ideas about human nature and destiny, but the historical view of homo sapiens as being formed in the image of God is compatible with use of EBC.

(e) It is too *extensive*. Quoting with approval a legal scholar who observes that society should not "prevent all things which would be punished if they occurred," Barzun laments the scope and force of EBC. "Sometimes," he declares, "the use of ineffectual mechanisms in an area as delicate as this one [i.e., human choice and behavior] is a virtue."

If this is a caveat concerning the need to be extremely careful about unintended side effects or latent functions of EBC, it is a valid objection (one that I have tried to deal with in Chapter 2). But if it is a complaint about the very effectiveness of EBC in accomplishing what it is designed to accomplish, it has little merit. Or, recalling that the only kind of EBC advocated here is that which is purely voluntary, the counterargument might be simply stated in this way: Let each person who utilizes EBC decide for him/herself exactly what behaviors are to be manipulated and how "extensive" these manipulations are to be.

Edwin Erwin confronts the charge of dehumanization forthrightly in his *Behavior Therapy: Scientific, Philosophical and Moral Foundations*. Erwin, a philosopher by training, makes a good deal of the distinction between behavior therapy as a paradigm and as a kind of clinical technique, and he cites aversive therapy to alter homosexuality as an illustration of the significance of the distinction. He declares,

The complaint [that behavior therapy is dehumanizing because it treats man as if he were a mere physical object instead of a person] may have some force if directed at the paradigm accepted by *some* behavioral therapists. Someone who is a behaviorist may hold that we can reasonably ignore a subject's mental state and view him as if he were not a person; but a behavior therapist need not, and should not, accept this view.... It *might* be that a case could be made that a particular use of a certain type of behavior therapy, such as the use of electric shock in modifying homosexual behavior, is dehumanizing ... because the procedure is so mechanical and because it is directed at something so deeply personal as one's sexuality.... But it is not clear that the charge would be justified even in this case; it is not true that the patient's mental states are ignored; it is not *obvious* that the client is "not treated as a person." ... It may be that in some sense it is "dehumanizing" to have to undergo any sort of therapy for certain types of very private problems; but in exactly what respect is it true that systematic desensitization, modelling, assertive training, cognitive restructuring and self-control procedures are "dehumanizing" in a way that nonbehavior therapies are not?[46]

Illogical gut reactions are often evident, too, in the sentiments voiced by students who are introduced to the subject of EBC for the first time in a medical ethics course. On one such occasion, the visiting lecturer showed a videotape of an EBC program that had been used to solve a seriously disruptive family dispute, one between a mother and daughter over the latter's tendency to "forget" to set the table for dinner by the appointed six o'clock hour because she was involved in a lengthy telephone conversation with a schoolmate. The procedure was delightfully simple; it required nothing more than identification of the actions that caused distress on each side, agreement on a quid pro quo contract that called upon each party to desist and subsequent alteration of the behavior exhibited by both parties. The program worked. It was easy to see how it worked and why; indeed, one could easily see how similar programs could be designed to overcome many kinds of interpersonal conflict. But the class refused to acknowledge the success of the program or the cogency of the theory on which it was based. They pointed out all kinds of intangibles—such as the mother's sense of parental authority, or the daughter's need to establish her independence, or both parties' feeling that "if she really loved me I wouldn't have to explain, because she would just *know* how I feel about this"—which had not been touched. What they had difficulty in seeing, apparently, is that *dealing with the specifics of a problem is often the best way to deal with its intangibles.* "Parental authority" should not be interpreted as the right to dominance, and a wise parent who cares about her child's well-being will understand that an intelligent conception of authority must encompass calm negotiation processes that will become increasingly significant as the adolescent grows to adulthood. The daughter must realize the importance of negotiating skills, too, for if her sense of independence is defined as "doing exactly what I feel like doing" at any given moment, regardless of earlier promises or commitments or role-duties, she is going to be in a whole lot of trouble the rest of her life. EBC programs such as the one described are anything but "dehumanizing"; on the contrary, they make a crucial contribution to the humanization of the persons concerned, for such programs help their beneficiaries live in peace and justice with their neighbors.

(5) *It's a Good That Is Enemy of the Best.* Some critics who are willing to agree that consequences are the most important aspect of ethics, and to concede that contrived improvements in behavior are genuine goodness, are still unenthusiastic about EBC because they view it as a kind of cop-out. Their ethical ideal demands that goodness be rooted in the life of a community of dedicated persons who provide for one another a kind and degree of insight, incentives to improved performance levels, and reinforcement that chemicals, electrodes, and operant conditioning could never do. From this point of view, artifically created goodness is *minimal* goodness; it is substituting a few bandaids for the radical replacement of organs or limbs that is "really needed."

I have no quarrel with the premise of this argument. I concur in thinking that the "natural" goodness of a community of like-minded folk, acting singly and collectively to educate, exhort, and support each other in concerted ethical action is superior to piecemeal reformation of particular behaviors of individuals who are acting more or less in isolation from a sustaining moral community and who are using EBC to accomplish this end. Their *ideal* of the wellsprings of social ethics is the same as mine.

But striving to attain this ideal is a gamble. I prefer the readily attainable half-loaf of artificial goodness to the rare and on the whole improbable whole-loaf of sectarian goodness. (I say "sectarian" goodness, because the model being looked to here is that of the religious sect, in which a relatively small group of persons have come together precisely because of their wholehearted devotion to ideals that do not fit very well in everyday life or in large ecclesiastical communities.) Whenever sectarian morality can flourish (as, for example, in the Movement for a New Society), more power to the members of the sect, who are evidently so imbued with the Holy Spirit that they have no need of EBC! But saints are few and far between and the vast majority of people—those of us who are not moral heroes—need the pedestrian techniques of EBC.

Incidentally, there is no need to postulate an either/or choice in this regard. There is no reason at all why those who believe in EBC should not form intentional communities of their own to reinforce their zeal and to extend their applications of EBC to more and more areas of behavior that can profit from it. (Consider the vignette on Gloria at the beginning of this chapter.)

## The Roots of Resistance

All but one of the five objections to artificial goodness just considered seem to be based in one way or another on Challenge/Response assumptions—only this time it's not passive heroism in the face of pain or suffering that comes to the fore; rather, it is the active heroism of unremitting effort in the face of insuperable odds. As the discussion of this motif in the preceding chapter makes clear, adversity sometimes does bring out the best in people and believing that "sudden the worst turns the best for the brave," as that representative Victorian poet, Robert Browning put it, can be instrumental in helping one to maintain a high level of courage and endeavor.

But just as one can go too far in forcing oneself to endure unnecessary pain or crippling anguish, one can also go too far in imitating Sisyphus. When determination to act heroically becomes a pointless refusal to relinquish some impossible dream—when it becomes, for example, an absurd glorification of refusal to abandon ridiculous utopian pretensions, as in *Man of La Mancha*'s astounding distortion of Don Quixote, one has become a victim of what might be called (paraphrasing Toynbee) "the idolization of an ephemeral image." Insisting that everybody ought to seek goodness in only one approved way (or, in any case, that nobody ought to sink to the ignominy of *contrived* good behavior through EBC) is going too far. It's Don Quixote tilting at windmills; it's Archie Bunker protesting high inheritance taxes because he doesn't want to have his incentive to become a millionaire taken away! We are forced once again to ask why it is that allegiance to the ideal of heroic struggle is so undiscriminating and so unyielding.

Some of the resistance to behavior modification is both concrete and forthright. Many intelligent people of good will are simply horrified at what they regard as the cruel excesses of certain techniques—for example, aversive therapy or physical restraint of autistic children. Their horror is understandable, but it may be misplaced. Which is better (better for the autistic *child* concerned), to allow a young person to scratch her head continually until the entire scalp has become a bloody pulp on which no hair will grow or to put her arms in loose bonds with the clear indication that the bonds will be removed if the patient can avoid scratching her head? If the expression "being cruel to be kind" ever has a persuasive meaning, it applies here. Not only is the child being benevolently protected from self-inflicted damage, but the protection is being provided in the context of a long and difficult therapeutic program that may in time cure a grievously debilitating symptom. On the face of it, there's much to be gained by using restraints and nothing tangible to lose (except a destructively employed "freedom of movement")—and one may be pardoned for looking upon objections to this form of treatment as stupidly sentimental and scandalously counterproductive.

Some resistance to EBC seems to be not only unwise but also dubious in its origins and its motivations. When you come right down to it, some of the opposition to artificial goodness seems to be based on ambivalence verging on hypocrisy.

Allan Dyer, a perceptive psychologist whose keen insights may be due in no small measure to his theological training, analyzes some of the resistance as follows.[47] People would not rush out in hordes to enroll in a "Commitment" program because they aren't really sure on Monday morning that the enthusiasm they felt for sharing with the poor on Sunday is as powerful as they thought. They are capable of being roused to heights of compassion and that feeling is altogether genuine when it arises (as it may, for example, in the "collective effervescence" of a religious service) and as long as it lasts. In that moment, they can be made to feel terribly guilty about their hardness of heart in sharing so little with the wretched of the earth, and they might be amenable to the suggestion that they sign up for "Commitment." They might even write their names on the dotted line of a pledge card and plunk down a deposit for the costs of the program. But on Monday their consciousness has become attuned to other messages (say, the messages of the advertisements that tell them they simply must have commodity X in order to be happy, and they really owe it to themselves to purchase experience Y in order to hold their heads up as members of such and such a status group). Their consciences come into conflict with a host of self-conceptions, aspirations, and assumptions about personal worth that bestir in them acute feelings of anxiety about their financial condition—and then they can only think about ways to make more and more for themselves instead of sharing.

The ambivalence is clear. Whether it is compounded by hypocrisy is another matter and one that would be hard to prove. But one can hardly avoid raising the question, for if you say, over and over again, with great moral and religious fervor, that you believe in sharing, and that you know you ought to share more generously, and that you *intend* to (after you've finished paying for X or enjoying Y), but you haven't *done* it yet ... and then you are made aware of a safe and effective means to get yourself to live up to the values you profess, *but refuse to do so*—isn't there bound to be some doubt about the depth and sincerity of your commitment to those values? Because this is such an uncomfortable line of reasoning, it is not surprising that one finds great psychological comfort in being able to believe that artificial goodness is not genuine, or that it is dehumanizing, or that it is not really very effective after all.

There is an ironic parallel here between the notion of morality under analysis and the medieval idea of Courtly Love. As numerous scholars have demonstrated, the real focus of Courtly Love was *the spiritual edification of the lover*. The love was not supposed to be consummated; it was merely meant to be *experienced* by the lover. And in the thrills, torments, and physical sickness brought on by unfulfilled love, the lover's soul would be refined, enobled, and elevated to a higher plane.[48]

Isn't that what some opponents of EBC seem to cherish in the old view of character formation and the spiritual conception of what goodness is? They seem to be less interested in the consummation of altruistic sentiments in actual deeds of loving kindness that are of tangible benefit to real persons than they are in the righteousness that will accrue in their own souls as a result of their having *felt* compassion, obedience to God, or whatever holy sentiments they glory in. But this is a disgustingly hollow posture. There is no better answer to be given to it than the one given many centuries ago by the author of the Epistle of James: "If a brother or sister is ill-clad and in lack of daily food, and one of you says to them, 'Go in peace, be warmed and filled' without giving them the things needed for the body, what does it profit? So faith by itself, if it has no works, is dead."

To put it with extreme bluntness: It seems to me that there is something shamefully self-indulgent and therefore unethical about a moral philosophy that places the presumed inward growth of the moral agent above the demonstrable safety, welfare, and happiness of all the other citizens affected by what the agent actually does or does not do. Surely the common good, as measured by objective indices such as the number of persons living in poverty or deprivation, ought to be given priority over the vague ideal of inner perfection. And a steadfast desire to promote the common good by the most effective means available should be acknowledged as the best motive a moral agent can have.

The implications of this line of thinking ought to be self-evident, but they are so important they must be made explicit. Assuming that the technological and political qualms about EBC can be satisfactorily resolved, then the philosophical objections ought to be set aside for the purposes of public policy. The objections are unconvincing on the following grounds:

(1) The desirable consequences attainable through EBC are so concrete, and so important as a boon to humankind, that only compelling evidence establishing beyond reasonable doubt the high probability of extremely significant negative side effects should be allowed to deter use of EBC by those who voluntarily choose to make use of it.

(2) Philosophical objections to EBC are based on a view of human nature and destiny that (no matter how venerable, and how *inspiring*, when all its assumptions and pretensions are granted) is highly dubious—far too dubious to justify its perpetuation at the expense of losing the many tangible goods available through EBC. Whatever is truly noble in the traditional view of man may be salvaged (indeed, allowed to flourish as never before) in a refined conception that provides for greater goodness and happiness through EBC.

(3) The argument being advanced here can be put in terms of a set of paired concepts familiar to all students of ethics. To focus on inner growth is to espouse an ethic of redemption, one which makes

sense only if one is *so sure* about the reality of the soul as a metaphysical entity and about what it needs to be perfected, that one is
willing to say (along with the Stoic sage on the rack) "nothing else
really matters." From the standpoint of an ethic of responsibility,
however, such prosaic "external" matters as human freedom, welfare, justice, peace, and happiness in this life in this world are of
greater significance. To say to the potential beneficiary of EBC, who
has studied its impact and wants to utilize it to shape his or her own
behavior for moral ends, "Wait! You don't realize what you're doing;
think of the growth of your soul!" is worse than ridiculous. And it is
culpably cruel to say to the victims of the still hurtful behavior of the
still imperfect pilgrim, "Well, you have to keep on trusting in the old
methods of character formation, which will someday produce better
behavior—just be patient."

## REALISTIC PROSPECTS
## FOR ARTIFICIAL GOODNESS

In this chapter I have tried to establish the technical feasibility and
the moral legitimacy of using behavior control to achieve increased
goodness. Many examples of the ways in which undesirable behaviors can be eliminated or made less troublesome have been given
and the possibilities for inducing positive behavior control in the form
of attitudinal and behavior change have been analyzed.

I have contended that good behavior—behavior that is less harmful or more helpful in its consequences for those affected by it—is real
goodness and that using EBC to generate such behavior is a wise and
laudable moral action in itself. I have argued, furthermore, that implementing one's ethical will by these means is humanizing rather
than dehumanizing: It delivers the moral agent from the demoraliz-
ing impact of continually paying lip service to moral values that one
seldom realizes in deeds. I have pointed out that EBC is no substitute
for moral decisions about *ends*—for example, the affirmation of
justice and compassion as philosophical ideals and a desire to serve
these ideals by sharing more generously with the poor; it is "merely"
a more effective *means* for getting oneself actually to share instead of
just talking about it and intending to do so. But this improvement in
means will be decisive in enabling countless people to actualize the
good ends they are honestly committed to.

Of course, there will probably never be enough people of good will and never enough good behavior to overcome the world's injustice and misery. Thus, it is important not only to use our limited resources as effectively as possible, but also to increase those resources, both qualitatively and quantitatively. Chapter 5 treats these possibilities.

## NOTES

1. Peter Schrag and Diane Dworkin, *The Myth of the Hyperactive Child,* pp. 53, 85-95.

2. Vance Packard, *The People Shapers,* pp. 68-69.

3. Robert Heath, as quoted in Lois Timnick, "Brain Pacemaker Success Reported," *Los Angeles Times* (May 3, 1977), Part I, p. 31.

4. Stanley Rachman and G. T. Wilson, *The Effects of Psychological Therapy,* p. 261.

5. *Ibid.,* p. 179.

6. *Ibid.,* pp. 177-178.

7. *Ibid.,* pp. 174-175.

8. *Ibid.,* p. 176.

9. *Ibid.,* pp. 181-182.

10. *Ibid.,* p. 183.

11. *Ibid.,* p. 120.

12. *Ibid.*

13. Edward Erwin, *Behavior Therapy: Scientific, Philosophical and Moral Foundations,* p. 160.

14. Gerald Davison and G. T. Wilson, "A Road to Self-Control," *Psychology Today* (October, 1975), p. 60.

15. Packard, *Shapers,* p. 154.

16. *Ibid.,* p. 64.

17. *Ibid.,* pp. 64-65.

18. George Orwell, *1984,* pp. 206-213; 244-245.

19. Packard, *Shapers,* p. 182.

20. Barbara Brown, *New Mind, New Body,* pp. 380-381.

21. Morton M. Hunt, "A Neurosis if 'Just' a Bad Habit," *New York Times Magazine* (June 4, 1967), p. 38.

22. Maya Pines, *The Brain Changers,* p. 66.

23. Rachman and Wilson, *Effects,* p. 225.

24. *Ibid.,* pp. 196-198.

25. *Ibid.,* p. 198.

26. *Ibid.,* pp. 208ff.

27. *Ibid.,* pp. 208-209.

28. *Ibid.,* pp. 209.

29. *Ibid.,* p. 220.

30. *Ibid.*

31. *Ibid.*, p. 217.

32. Richard Feallock and L. Keith Miller, "Design and Evaluation of a Worksharing System for Experimental Group Living," *Journal of Applied Behavioral Analysis*, Vol. 9 (Fall 1976), pp. 277-288.

33. Kathleen Kinkade, *Twin Oaks: A Walden II Experiment*, pp. 148ff.

34. Erwin, *Therapy*, pp. 185-187ff.

35. Rachman and Wilson, *Effects*, pp. 185-187.

36. David B. Wexler, "Token and Taboo: Behavior Modification, Token Economies and the Law," *California Law Review*, Vol. 61, No. 8 (1973), p. 93.

37. See note 3 of Chapter 1.

38. Bernard Häring, *Ethics of Manipulation*, pp. 11, 123.

39. *Ibid.*, p. 123.

40. *Ibid.*, pp. 128-129.

41. George Forrell, *Faith Active in Love*, pp. 84f.

42. *Ibid.*, p. 87.

43. Soren Kierkegaard, *Fear and Trembling*, pp. 78-91.

44. Everett Mendelsohn et al. [eds.] *Human Aspects of Biomedical Innovation*, pp. 120ff.

45. Jacques Ellul, *The Technological Society, passim.*

46. Erwin, *Therapy*, p. 182.

47. Personal conversation with Alan Dyer, Duke University, June 1975. Dyer is a psychiatrist at Duke who has a doctorate in both medicine and theological ethics.

48. John Stevens, *Medieval Romance*, Chapter 4.

# Chapter 5

# ARTIFICIALLY INCREASED CAPACITY

Quantitative and qualitative upgrading of human capacity will presumably enable lots of people to achieve greater happiness and will undoubtedly enable them to increase the amount of goodness that they contribute to the world. But the possibilities for increased capacity are treated as a separate category here because of the fact that (in comparison with the possibilities analyzed in the two preceding chapters) they raise relatively few philosophical and ethical questions. This chapter does explore two important normative issues, but the bulk of it is devoted to an examination of the prospects for improved *efficiency, effectiveness,* and *versatility* of performance through EBC.

One additonal prefatory comment is in order. Any therapy that restores a lost "normal" capacity by bringing health to an impaired person is of obvious importance. But such therapies will not be discussed in this chapter, nor will matters normally considered under the rubric of "health care," because the main focus of interest is on dramatically new manifestations of the human potential opened up by scientific knowledge and technological ingenuity.

## WALTER: A VIGNETTE

Walt Driscoll was a systems analyst by profession, so calculations of efficient time and resource utilization came naturally to him. What he preached in organizational life, on the job, he also practiced in his personal life, so he was a regular client of the Boston Rev Up Center. Over the years, he had taken advantage of almost every program the Boston Center offered on memory enhancement, speed sleeping, and sleep learning. He had used his revved up capacities to learn five foreign languages, including Chinese, and his ability to prepare thoroughly for a lengthy meeting and remember details pertinent to the matters being discussed was almost legendary in his company and in the several civic associations and social reform organizations to which he often contributed his services free of charge. He was especially valuable to the electronics firm for which he worked because of his ability as a trouble shooter: He had the reputation of being able to work around the clock, maintaining high levels of concentration and proficiency, longer and better than anyone in the whole metropolitan area. By judicious use of the techniques and the pharmaceutical aids that he had become acquainted with through Rev Up, Walt was able to accomplish more in a given number of hours or days on the job than anyone else at his educational level with comparable years of experience in the field. His professional colleagues admired especially—and envied—his ability to keep up with the latest advances in state of the art knowledge in systems analysis.

What he believed in for himself he also believed in and tried to obtain for his one child, a 15-year-old daughter named Pamela. Ever since her birth, Walt had made it his business to keep up with the latest research in chemical enrichment of the brain, and from early childhood on Pamela had followed a nutritional/chemical supplement program designed to heighten brain size and power, including probable ability to learn certain specific skills and bodies of knowledge of interest to her. She had taken part in MIT's first postexperimental program in upgrading right brain functions in elementary school children, and she was also involved in a leisurely but long-term effort to augment creativity by focusing and expanding the content of her dreams.

Walt's wife Louise was especially interested in altered states of consciousness. She had spent a good deal of time in biofeedback training, learning not only elementary stress reduction and deep relaxation in general, but particularly the art of immersing herself in a state in which her brain produced nothing but alpha waves, so as to be able to practice religious meditation more effectively. She had experimented once or twice with chemical substances designed to intensify mystical consciousness, but she was dedicated to the proposition that natural powers of the mind and spirit could provide deeper knowledge of cosmic synchronicity than any drug could provide, and she hardly ever used drugs except for therapeutic purposes. She occasionally joined Walt and Pamela in taking a small dose of Intensity when they went down to the coast to watch a sunrise, or a storm at sea, or when they made their annual pilgrimage through New England to see the fall foliage at its brightest, but she always contended that Intensity only made such experiences especially vivid in a different, not in a *better* way. On the whole, she preferred to rely on the extraordinary powers of perception and awareness she had cultivated over the years—but she did not consider herself spiritually superior to those who chose to make use of the "short cut" furnished by Intensity and she made no effort to persuade her husband and her daughter that they ought to do it her way.

## EFFICIENCY

Several technologies of EBC promise greater efficiency in human performance through quantitative increases in energy, the amount of time available for productive work, and so on. The ability to lapse into *deep relaxation*, whether this is accomplished through time-honored techniques of religious meditation or through the new-fangled gadgetry of biofeedback, offers multiple benefits. As a means to stress reduction, it contributes to health in the short run, and there is now some evidence that it may actually add years to one's life span. A physiologist who compared a group of persons who had been meditating at least twice a day for more than five years to a group that had not practiced meditation reports,

> When compared on the basis of blood pressure, hearing, vision, cardio-vascular fitness and vital capacity (respiration efficiency), people who have been meditating ... are physiologically 12 to 15 years younger than a non-meditating control group.[1]

Moreover, as noted in the previous chapter, the ability to enter a relaxed state is a crucial asset in some behavior modification programs.

Besides bringing about control of tension, heartbeat, and migraine headaches, EBC is bringing us closer to *sleep control*. Victims of chronic insomnia may soon find that they have nothing to worry about:

> The insomnia problem ... appears to be chemical. Reports from laboratories in France indicate that cats begin to doze when the neurotransmitter serotonin puts the brakes on another part of the brain that is responsible for alertness. Applying these findings in man, psychiatrists at Boston State Hospital have demonstrated that insomniacs fall asleep twice as fast when given small doses of L-tryptophan, the chemical from which the body makes serotonin, and they awaken the next morning without the drugged, groggy feeling that sleeping pills often cause.[2]

Hard-working people may be able to increase their alertness during the day or cut down on the number of hours they need to sleep at night by implementing Barbara Brown's suggestion that we learn how to get more reinvigoration out of "such sleep substitutes as rest, cat-napping and momentary relaxation."[3] Or "the need for sleep can be reduced by monoamine oxidase inhibitors" to the point that "three and a half hours may be plenty."[4] (If this estimate startles, consider the historical fact noted by Nathan S. Kline: Moghul cavalrymen conquered a good part of the Asian world on a travel schedule that allowed no more sleep than this.)[5] Kline, coauthor of *Psychotropic Drugs in the Year 2000*, ventures to assert, "We may conceivably be able to simulate or induce the bioelectric biochemical activity required" to enable human beings to function without actually having to lie down and sleep.[6] John Taylor reaches a similar conclusion:

> If the chemical processes underlying sleep are properly understood, it may even be possible in the future to avoid sleep altogether by speeding up or altering such processes. This may result in a "sleep pill" which does away with sleep; it would give each human being the bonus of an extra twenty years of life.[7]

Not everyone would want to live a sleepless life, and not everyone will even be able to conceive of such a possibility. But one does not have to accept either the desirability or the likelihood of a development this seemingly incredulous to grasp the main point: People who want to sleep more (and who want to be able to sleep at times when they now find difficulty in doing so) will almost certainly be able to enjoy restful sleep when they need it and anyone who wants to be able to sleep less *for a certain length of time, now and then, on demand,* will probably be able to do so. And both forms of sleep control will be exercised much more surely and safely than ever before.

## EFFECTIVENESS

Equally exciting are the possibilities for increased effectiveness in the utilization of the ordinary capabilities of mind and body. The use of hypnosis or drugs to promote greater physical strength or vitality is a fascinating story in itself: Anabolic steroids can be used to push the prowess of athletes to unprecedented limits,[8] and hypnosis may sharpen the will to win or "get the mind out of the way" so that patterns of skilled muscle coordination work more smoothly; sexual vitality is augmented by L-dopa; a special burst of needed energy may be supplied in a crisis by judicious use of amphetamines. The part of the story that has to do with physical performance is of less interest than the new possibilities for enhanced memory, intelligence, and creativity offered by EBC.

Memory research has shown that both short-term and long-term recall (which are located in different areas of the brain) can be either sharpened or dulled by CSB. The difficulties of learning in the young and the sorrows of senility in the aged can both be alleviated by memory-intensifying drugs. Adults who need to do "crash course" learning at various times in their lives may be able to do so through EBC. Biofeedback will enable them to heighten their powers of concentration, and drugs such as Metrazol (which has improved certain problem-solving abilities up to 400% in animals) will help them assimilate remarkable quantities of new material in an astonishingly short period of time.[9]

As the last two examples reveal, memory and learning ability are hard to separate even for analytical purposes, and such a separation may be entirely unnecessary for an understanding of the practical possibilities and implications of "supermind." Brain size itself (and, therefore, one may presume, brain power) has been increased to a spectacular degree in rats injected with acetylcholine and given an "enriched environment" in the form of increased opportunities to exercise their brains in work and play (i.e., in task performance, on treadmills, in the learning of simple skills, etc.).David Krech, the Berkeley neuroscientist who conducted the famous experiments with "smart rats," has predicted the imminent availability of "regimens combining psychological and chemical measures which will permit us to exercise a significant degree of control over development of man's intellectual capacities."[10] Krech believes it will be feasible to produce "special abilities, or clusters of abilities—e.g., verbal abilities, arithmetical reasoning abilities, or artistic abilities at will," and he sees particular capacity-enhancement of this kind as more probable than large undifferentiated rises in IQ in general.[11] The picture that emerges is one in which a wide range of fairly specific improvements of mind will be open to individuals, parents, educators, therapists, or institutional leaders (corporation heads, government officials, military leaders) who want to see various intellectual capacities "revved up." If you have only five weeks to qualify yourself (in a minimal way, at least) for a diplomatic post in a country about which you know virtually nothing, you may be able to pull it off. If you wish to give your children an extra fast start in life, you can step up their ability to learn many types of information at one of several "critical development phases" through which they pass. And you don't necessarily have to resign yourself to devastating loss of memory or (greater-than-usual) absentmindedness as you grow older.[12]

Most exhilarating of all, perhaps, is the astounding possibility of what Krech calls "psychoneurobiochemeducation." Given the fact that brain activity is to such a large degree chemical, researchers have been intrigued with the notion that certain "bits" of knowledge—or, more precisely, or more probably, an upgraded capacity to learn or remember certain kinds of knowledge—can be transmitted chemically. This "chemical trace" theory of knowledge transmission was tested in a celebrated series of experiments with large flatworms called planarians conducted by Dr. James McConnell of the University of Michigan. After training a group of planarians to react in an unusual way to light, McConnell cut them in half—and discovered that the lower half, which had to grow a new brain, "remembered" how to react to light as well as the upper half. He "concluded that specific memories were stored chemically within individual cells,

not only in the brain, but throughout the animal's body." He then
fed the chopped-up bodies of planarians that had been trained to
find their way through a maze of untrained planarians, and found
that

> the cannibals that had eaten educated victims did significantly better
> (right from the very first trial) than did cannibals that had eaten un-
> trained victims. We had achieved the first interanimal transfer of infor-
> mation.[13]

(As one university administrator quipped, "If these experiments
really mean what they seem to, we have found a solution to one of
our most vexing problems: Now we know what to do with all our old
professors!")

McConnell's theory became clouded in controversy after many
other researchers who tried to duplicate his findings were unable to
do so (even though more than twenty laboratories all over the world
*did* replicate the experiments). Admitting that higher animals cannot
"swallow" knowledge in the same way that planarians can—"because their digestive systems would break down the food so thoroughly that the memories would be lost," McConnell began testing
the transfer of *propensities* to learn specific tasks in rats. He had some
encouraging results, but "he could not shake off the controversies
surrounding his work," and he finally got so sick and tired of all the
arguments about details of his experimental procedures that he shut
down his lab, convinced that "the field simply wasn't ready for the
discovery of memory transfer."[14]

George Ungar has performed similar experiments with goldfish
and rats and has demonstrated that rodents injected with extracts
from the brains of fellow creatures that had been taught to fear the
dark (something unheard of in rats) also "began to shun the dark
almost as often as the trained animals." The substance contained in
these extracts was dubbed "scotophobin" because of its power to in-
still a phobia for the dark and has subsequently been synthesized in
the laboratory (and even marketed by a German drug company).
Laboratory-produced scotophobin creates the same behavior in
animals injected with it—but the theory of the chemical transfer of
learning is still greeted with skepticism in scholarly circles.[15]

So the day has not yet arrived when college freshmen can take
Math 101 by injection instead of enrolling in a course. But who
knows—the day may not be far off when millions of young men and

women learn the same body of knowledge a lot sooner and/or a lot quicker because their brains have been chemically enriched. At the very least (whether psychoneurobiochemeducation becomes a reality or not), Krech's experiments suggest that better nutrition can greatly increase the intellectual stature of undernourished children and that human intelligence can be augmented substantially by imaginative use of EBC.

There is, finally, the path to increased effectiveness by means of enhanced imagination and creativity. Artists and poets as well as persons in psychotherapy may benefit from being able to increase both the clarity and the frequency of elaborate dreams, especially if they are able to influence the content of these dreams. A recent article in the British journal, New Scientist, reports the contriving of a "portable 'dream machine' . . . which detects REM sleep and automatically gives electrical impulses so as to 'trigger' lucidity [in dreaming]." The author claims that "several subjects have successfully undergone 'lucid dream induction' in the laboratory," and describes the benefits of this process as follows:

> In lucid dreams, conscious insight emerges within the dream state. It is like being awake, having "free will" and possessing "critical faculties," but being in a totally artificial "other" world, and at the same time knowing so.[16]

If Theodore Roszak is even halfway right about the one-sidedness of the "objective consciousness" into which we snap ourselves each morning by drinking coffee or tea (drugs that came into widespread usage at the time of the Industrial Revolution and were particularly useful in adjusting people to its requirements),[17] then stimulating a fuller and richer dream life may be among the most important goals we could set for ourselves—and this might be especially true for people with artistic talent. The affective, manual, and intuitive strengths of the right hemisphere of the brain will become more accessible through split-brain research, and if we can also learn to coordinate the special proclivities of each hemisphere, both cognitive and aesthetic powers may be magnified significantly in countless individuals. Robert Ornstein and David Galin of the Langley Porter Neuropsychiatric Institute of San Francisco put it this way:

> Eventually, ... people will learn to activate the left or right hemisphere voluntarily. This has already been tried in the lab. With electrodes on

their scalp to record changes in their brains' electrical activity, and earphones to inform them instantly of how they are doing, half a dozen volunteers have attempted to increase the asymmetry between their two half-brains. So far the results appear promising: nearly all the volunteers have managed to activate one hemisphere more than the other, through feedback.[18]

Hypnosis, including self-hypnosis, can be used not only to anesthetize pain, speed up recall in psychiatric patients, affect bodily functions, hype up athletic skills or promote relaxation, but also to stimulate aesthetic fancy. Perry London believes that hypnotism is a technique that can be used to provide a "booster effect" on almost any kind of self-resolve or instructions given to a willing subject.[19] And there are some grounds for hypothesizing that biofeedback can engender artistic creativity as well as keener problem-solving ability through the learned capability of generating theta brain waves.[20]

Perhaps the most arresting example of an extraordinary stimulus to creativity is the kind reported by Jean Houston of the Foundation for Mind Research:

> A songwriter in a trance is told to wander into an imaginary cafe in a distant city where she will hear an imaginary singer singing songs she has never heard before. She does so, in accelerated time. When she is out of trance, we ask her what happened—and, as part of her account, she spends 15 minutes singing a pleasant and original number and portions of two others. We are not suggesting that she was teleported to some strange other world to hear these new songs—only that her creative capacities had been somewhat enhanced so the process could take place.[21]

## VERSATILITY

"Versatility" is used here as a category under which to discuss very briefly all those possibilities for increasing human capacity that are apt to strike the average person as mind-boggling. Some of the items in this category are clearly desirable, but seem too exotic, technically difficult, or expensive to be practical (as yet) on a large scale. Assuming that the visual area of the brain is healthy, the blind can be made to "see," by implanting hundreds of electrodes there and then connecting them to a television apparatus that can transmit appropriate stimuli to the brain.[22] Clairvoyance and mental telepathy are possible, but it's hard to imagine a world in which large numbers of people have such powers of mind, and telekenesis strains the credulity of ordinary folks. As for the micro-miniaturized "memory-enhancing computer" that could be placed in the skull (along with the myriad electrodes needed to get it "tuned in to the brain's own electrochemical language")[23]—well, most of us would look upon that as too bizarre to consider it a real option for personal implementation.

Yet, the history of science if full of surprises. It is surely a mistake to limit research to only those possibilities that are easy to conceive as an immediately realizable actuality for practically everyone. Thus, polysensibility may someday be routine, and an intriguing mode of classroom instruction known as "suggestology" may at some future time be the rule rather than the exception. Suggestology claims to be able to treble or quadruple the learning rate of pupils by making them pretend to be real or imagined persons of great knowledge and/or skill, to think the way these persons would think, make the decisions they would be called upon to make, and so on.[24] And we may soon become acquainted with all kinds of altered states of consciousness or accelerated mental processes such as the following remarkable occurrence that also took place at the Foundation for Mind Research.

A pianist is put into a light trance state by simple verbal suggestion. As she goes deeper into trance, she is instructed to practice a sonata that she must soon perform at a concert. It is a piece she knows well but has not played in a long while. She is now told to take all the time she needs for perfecting the piece. Upon emerging from trance, she says she feels much more confident after an intensive hour of rehearsal. Then she sits down at the piano and demonstrates how much her playing of the sonata has indeed improved.

Two remarkable things have happened. The improvement took place even though the pianist only *imagined* the rehearsal session. Yet the exercise had done her as much good as if she had actually practiced on a real piano. The other, and perhaps more remarkable, aspect of the experiment: though she subjectively had a good hour's practice, in fact only one minute of "real" clock time had passed![25]

No one yet understands exactly what happens in an experience of this kind. But both aspects of it are empirically familiar and have been cultivated or known by many individuals in various parts of the world at various times. If an action is already "known" to the body and is stored in the muscle memory of a person (such as a pianist or an athlete), it can be practiced by an act of imagining that "somehow signals the involved muscles to respond, albeit imperceptibly." And of course "the 'imagining' must transcend our usual lazy imagining; it must be concentrated and powerfully evocative—a total *mind-body visualization of the act*."[26] As for the bypassing of purely linear time, it is a form of accelerated mental process (AMP) that has been documented many times, strikingly in the reports of mountain climbers who, falling suddenly and believing their death was imminent, underwent the experience of having their whole life unfold before them in an instant.[27]

## TWO CRUCIAL PHILOSOPHICAL ISSUES

Philosophers and theologians with widely divergent views of science and technology worry about two opposite aspects of increased human capacity. Those who tend to see Nature as something more or less fixed (and sacred in its givenness) fear that dramatic extensions of the human organism's capabilities might involve "playing God" and they argue that we ought to observe certain fairly strict rules about drawing the line short of that impious point. Those who embrace the dynamism of technological innovation ask a different question: Because we can increase our resources greatly, they reason, why should we be content with drawing any lines short of *maximum* increase, and why should we obey any rule except that of *maximum* productivity? The first point of view poses the question of "Artificiality versus Naturalness;" the second, that of "Technological Calvinism."

### Artificial versus Natural

Virtually all cultures have a number of universally known stories whose main point is to warn against the dire hazard of *hubris* (cosmic pride). The word comes into our language through Greek drama, where those who are guilty of hubris meet the nemesis of divine retribution as punishment for their presumption. Its most memorable manifestation is in the first act of *Agamemnon,* when the king, returning victorious from the wars, allows his vengeful wife to persuade him to walk on a purple carpet as he makes his way from ship to throne. In so doing, he accepts more glory than any mortal man is entitled to receive, thus exhibiting a tragic flaw that justifies his subsequent downfall.

The jealousy of the gods, who do not want mere mortals to aspire to their status or usurp their prerogatives, is also a major element in the story of Prometheus and its latter-day counterpart (which Spengler regarded as the quintessential expression of modern Western culture), the story of *Faust*.[28] Students of the Bible find the hubris theme in the story of the Tower of Babel and it is also apparent in the story of the Garden of Eden (where the tree of "the knowledge of good and evil" is touted by the serpent as a means to divine status) as well as in other Near Eastern legends, notably the Gilgamesh Epic. These stories usually show admiration for the valor of the heroes who aspire to greatness for themselves or seek to bring some great benefit to the human race—but the message is, "Don't fly too high or the gods will melt your wings and send you plunging to destruction."

How is the ubiquity of the warning against hubris to be explained? A disciple of Freud might argue that it expresses a fundamental fact of the psychological life of humankind: To gain powers inappropriate to a dependent child is to threaten usurpation of the father's dominant position and is thus to risk losing his favor and incurring his punishment. So the acquisition of new powers arouses apprehension as well as satisfaction. A philosopher or a theologian might contend that our enjoyment of position, power, or wealth is always rendered (appropriately) uncomfortable by our awareness of the deprivations of those who are less fortunate. Those who are relatively well off are always aware (usually only in some dim corner of the mind where unpalatable truths are stored) that they do not really deserve their superior privileges and that they ought to do more than they usually do to rectify inequalities and establish genuine community in their city or country. Perhaps a historian of culture would simply merge these two interpretations in the very general observation that departure from tradition always awakens guilty misgivings because it seems to involve rejection of our forebears along with the ways of looking at or doing things that they established. Maybe they were right, after all (we think)—they always told us so!—and maybe we will suffer some as yet unforeseeable retribution for our failure to trust them completely and keep the faith that they bequeathed unto us.

Be that as it may, exuberant independence of tradition is a characteristic of modern Western civilization that was surely chosen confidently and fixed firmly at the time of the Renaissance. The rediscovery of the world and the individual that took place in fifteenth-century Italy, and soon thereafter in most parts of Europe, meant rebellion against the otherworldliness on which medieval life was based. Something decisive happened in the Renaissance to Western man's self-perception and to the ideal of self-fulfillment to which men and women in our culture aspire: People began to see themselves as active agents in history, not as passive souls born merely to endure whatever the fates might decree. From the Renaissance on, the *virtù* developed by thinking, choosing, upwardly striving individuals is seen as more important than the *fortuna* to which they are subjected. To be sure, *fortuna* is a factor of enormous significance; it still sets limits, places obstacles in one's path (or provides lucky opportunities that one could not have expected but must be adroit in seizing!) and, in short, determines to a substantial degree the destiny that awaits each person. But attention is now centered on the degree to which, and the ways in which, the plucky individual can evade limits, overcome obstacles, and take advantage of unanticipated opportunities. For the fifteenth-century humanist, Poggio, the contingencies of *fortuna* have only a very partial and time-bound power over the individual:

> The dangers threatening man from without (the forces of destiny) are strongest so long as man's true self has not yet been formed, i.e., so long as he is still in childhood and early youth. They retreat as soon as this self is awakened, and as soon as it is developed to full efficiency through the energy of moral and intellectual effort. Thus, it is *virtus* and *studium* that finally defeat all the inimical forces of the heavens.[29]

The dominant image in which these verities are conveyed changes significantly:

> In the medieval doctrine of two worlds, and in all the dualisms derived from it, man simply stands apart from the forces that are fighting over him; he is, in a sense, at their mercy. Though he experiences the conflict of these forces, he takes no active part in it. He is the stage of this great drama of the world, but he has not yet become a truly independent antagonist. In the Renaissance a different image emerges ever more clearly. The old image of Fortune with a wheel, seizing men and

dragging them along, sometimes raising them, sometimes throwing them down into the abyss, now gives way to the depiction of Fortune with a *sailboat*. And this bark is not controlled by Fortune alone—man himself is steering it.[30]

One of the excellencies most honored and diligently cultivated by the young Renaissance man on the make was the technical ability that could equip him to make use of and contribute to the scientific, economic, military, and artistic innovations of the age. To be especially adept in the skills of artifice by means of which engineering, commerce, warfare, and art flourished was to be hailed as a man of exceptional *virtù*, as (in the best sense, without any of the modern connotations of "mere" dexterity or soullessness) a virtuoso. Art historians of the nineteenth and twentieth centuries have taught us to prefer the profundity of Early and High Renaissance artists over the comparative shallowness of "mannerist" virtuosity, but late Renaissance connoisseurs had only the highest praise for the technical perfection of artists who displayed a mastery of the skills of *maniera*, and their ability to give delight (including their ability to create illusion) was highly prized and generously rewarded by patrons of that time.[31]

The point, for our purposes, is this: The ability to improve on Nature and mold Fortune to our own aspirations by our arts (our crafts, our skills) is one of the most coveted forms of human excellence in our culture. To be clever in devising artifice—to be effective in achieving desired results artificially—is one of the finest manifestations of *virtù* there is. In the words of Joseph Fletcher, "It is precisely artificiality which is man's hallmark." So the word "artificial" is not the antonym of "natural"; indeed, "whatever can happen, with or without human control, is natural." To identify naturalness exclusively with "that which will happen in the absence of rationally calculated human intervention" is an unacceptably one-sided definition of the concept. To lessen the tyranny of chance by increasing the degree of human control over life is a kind of behavior that is eminently *natural*—and especially appropriate—for Homo sapiens (fated as we are, "by brain and thumb," to be a problem-solving, meaning-seeking animal). Where the skills of artifice are directed toward the promotion of human welfare, there is a sense in which "being artificial is supremely human—humanly motivated and humanly manipulated."[32]

Defending artificiality is most emphatically not the same as baptizing every aspect of modern technology and everything done in its name or by its power. Many of its works are evil and ought to be denounced as such; furthermore, even its benefits do not always match costs. But undesirable applications of technological expertise should be judged and ruled out or restrained on the basis of pragmatic assessment of specific costs and benefits, not on the basis of vague anxieties about "playing God." Western civilization is committed to a view of the legitimacy and significance of energetic human activity, and the arts of EBC cannot be condemned simply on the grounds that their use in creating happiness, goodness, and increased capacity is "artificial." One may argue, of course, that stress-reduction through meditation is in some sense "better" than stress-reduction through drugs—but if one elects to take this position, it must be justified by reference to palpable advantages (e.g., lower cost, fewer noxious side effects, etc.), *not* by an appeal to a dubiously skewed notion of "naturalness."

*Ernest Becker's Thesis on the Irony of Evil.* The fact is, many of the protests against the artificiality of modern technology in general and EBC in particular are really expressions of fear concerning the will-to-power of human beings rather than fear concerning science per se. From this perspective, *all* human efforts to create a better life— through economic endeavor, through politics, or through even the most benevolently intended social reform movements—are permeated with danger and destined for tragedy. The key problem (and the supreme irony) of the human condition, according to Ernest Becker, is humanity's "dread of insignificance;" it is this form of hubris that accounts for the ever-recurring triumph of evil in human affairs.[33] Becker declares that the stupidity and evil in which the human animal is constantly enmeshed cannot be blamed, *pace* Rousseau and Marx, on social institutions or economic arrangements. On the contrary, inequality, tyranny, and war are caused by, and can only be comprehended in terms of, man's deep psychic frailty. (The language of patriarchalism is entirely appropriate in the following section, for we are talking about an ideology elaborated by power-obsessed *males*.)

We are, contends Becker, a species that is driven to desperation by its awareness of finitude and fear of death. Only a deeply rooted sense of terror because of our smallness, weakness, and guilt can explain the excesses of which we are capable (and that we exhibit again and again). This assumption does a lot to illuminate the irrationalities of both the debased and the pathetic models of the misguided pursuit of "happiness" that are analyzed in Chapter 7. As Norman O. Brown has pointed out, money may have been minted in the form of round coins made of shiny metals because it was seen as partaking of the durable brightness of the sun and the moon and as containing the life-giving potency of Nature.[34] (It was not merely an instinct for ribaldry that inspired the artists of Pompeii to compare the *élan vital* of sexuality to that of money in their representations of the penis being weighed in a scale against sacks of gold.) Money has come to represent "the cosmological unification of visible and invisible powers" that enables humans to transcend finitude; it is the latest "immortality ideology" of our culture. We cannot bear the thought of economic equality because having more money than others is a source of the reassurance we must always have (but can never get enough of) that the gods are with us and that therefore we will not (cannot!) die. We cling to our money and to our "right" to amass more of it than others, because "man dies when his little symbols of specialness die."[35]

But there isn't enough money in the world (or in any given society) to satisfy the insatiable appetite for reassurance of the entire population, so tyranny and war are the expedients we usually end up resorting to. There is nothing quite so invigorating, says Becker, as *physical* triumph over others: Canetti was profoundly correct when he defined man as the creature who raises his head above a field strewn with corpses, feels the sun shining on his face, smiles and proclaims that life is good![36] Thus, men tend always to indulge themselves in the great ritual gratifications of war and to submit to tyrants who promise ever greater conquests. Even the hardships and injustices imposed by tyrants are welcomed as a form of expiation of the guilt we feel because of our insignificance and our frantic efforts to overcome it by standing on the bodies of those we have vanquished.[37] Economic activity can also be seen as expiatory, and conspicuous consumption is a form of religious devotion—but nothing can relieve us of the need for fresh reassurance or deliver us from the evils we commit to generate it.[38]

And the saddest fact of human experience, writes Becker, is this: Even our finest sentiments and our noblest strivings are infected with the virus of death-denial. The most terrible paradox of all is that "*evil comes from man's urge to heroic victory over evil"* (italics in original). As Arthur Koestler observes, the worst evils in history result from "unselfish devotion" to pretentious causes and/or leaders, because such devotion all too readily becomes a "hyperdependence cum suggestibility" that can be exploited by demagogues.[39] Both crowds and tyrants *magnify* our propensity to wreak havoc in the name of ideals, but its *cause* is within each person, put there by the exigencies of a childhood in which we are "baffled from within and transcended from without," and from which we emerge with a crushing sense of guilt, inadequacy, and insecurity. We grow up with a need to lie, even (or especially) to ourselves, and we therefore develop a positive desire to be mystified. "Man is a frightened animal who must lie to live"; indeed, as Otto Rank maintained, even (each person's concept of his or her own) "character is a vital lie." Every society, then, becomes a "hero system which promises victory over evil and death," and every society is "a hopeful mystification of a determined lie."[40]

Strong medicine. One response to this gloomy doctrine is to relapse into a reactionary obscurantism such as that of Jacques Ellul and other opponents of modernity who aver that humanity should hope for very little in this fallen world and that above all one should avoid placing any hope in the state or in science and technology. I would argue, however, for a less hysterical response, one that accepts the significant profundities of Becker's vision without being swept away by it to his somber conclusions (or to those conclusions thinkers like Ellul arrive at).

Surely it is an inescapable part of wisdom to acknowledge the depth and persistence of humankind's capacity for evil. The problem is not one that can be *entirely* solved by a rearrangement of social institutions nor is it something that scientific rationality can easily overcome by bringing illumination that ignores the desperate anxieties and the ontological guilt of the human situation. As twentieth-century theologians such as Reinhold Niebuhr and Paul Tillich have shown, and as philosophically sophisticated psychologists such as Rollo May have confirmed, there is a substantial measure of truth in a properly reinterpreted version of the venerable Christian teaching of original sin.[41]

But it is possible to benefit from this insight and to govern all of one's expectations in light of it (as well as discounting all one's own pretensions to *rightness* in accordance with it) without conceding that the impulse to build the good city, or at least to devote a portion of one's energies to the achievement of realistic projects that lead in that direction, is bound to become "an all-consuming activity to make the world conform to our desires."[42] We *can* do more than retreat to the Olympian heights of a Stoic posture that reduces the constructive role of a modern Promethean to nothing more than debunking all the delusions and lies spawned by an undisciplined will-to-meaning. We can strive meaningfully *and successfully* to improve the lives of this segment of humanity by 8% in such and such an area of their experience and of that segment by 11% in some other area—and these tasks are worth undertaking. The rock may roll back down the hill every time Sisyphus pushes it to the top—but if it can be kept from rolling *all the way back* each time it rolls down again, so that a few inches of ground are won with every performance of the never-ending task, then we can imagine Sisyphus happy and we can know that his labors are not in vain.

Those who are impressed (or depressed) by Becker's thesis should be especially favorable toward EBC. One of the advantages of technologically contrived happiness and goodness would be the fact that one would not need, or be able, to spin out far-reaching myths of self-importance in relation to them. No great credit can be claimed for something that involves little heroic effort beyond the original decision to generate a given experience or produce a certain behavior through the artifice of technology. So the perils of an inflated sense of personal glory, and the evils it could lead to, are minimized by reliance on EBC. In this case, then, technology contributes to culture by pushing us toward the more chastened and in that sense less dangerous view of human grandeur adumbrated in Chapter 7.

## Technological Calvinism

The second main philosophical issue raised by capacity-enlargement is that of "technological Calvinism." The term is used as a way of emphasizing the affinity between possibilities in this area and the austere work orientation of the so-called Protestant ethic (or, as it is often called in America, the "Puritan ethic"). The key point at stake in the employment of the term is this: Given the highly secularized, but nonetheless still quasi-religious reverence for maximum productivity in many technologically advanced societies today (especially in the USA), EBC-enhanced capabilities may be welcomed as a form of self-development that one is *morally obligated* to undertake.[43] To the general moral imperative of the technological society—"If it can be done, it will be done!"—is added a special normative twist: "If one's productive energies can be augmented, they ought to be (and anyone who refuses to develop him/herself to the fullest extent possible is a wicked person)."

Scholarly debate about the import and the validity of Max Weber's famous thesis concerning *The Protestant Ethic and the Spirit of Capitalism* is endless, and disagreement about its details will never be entirely resolved. Yet, the principal thrust of Weber's argument is clear: Just at the moment when the burgeoning economy of Europe needed a cultural ethos that reinforced vigorous activity in worldly pursuits such as science, navigation, engineering, and commerce, a religious movement whose teaching supplied this ethos sprang into being. In proclaiming that one could be just as good a Christian by serving God in some ordinary calling in the world as one could by taking cover in a monastic life, the Reformation allowed people to escape from the preoccupation with the realm of the spirit and the life hereafter that permeated early and medieval Christianity. In giving special endorsement to the virtues of "inner-worldly asceticism" —the habits of diligence, thrift, sobriety, and rigorous self-discipline that characterized the Calvinist ideal of "a godly, righteous and sober life"—the new religious movement helped people feel *right* about working hard, avoiding luxury, and ploughing the profits they accumulated back into investments that would bear fruit in ever greater capital ventures, each of which could be interpreted as an act of worship that glorified God and his Creation. And in replacing the relatively relaxed (shall we say, "humane"?) penitential system of the Roman Catholic Church with the demand for perfection paradoxically implied in the doctrine of predestination, Calvinism infused its notion of faithful service to God with a relentlessness that carried over into the secularized work ethic of the Industrial Revolution as hardness of heart toward the unproductive. Both the relentlessness and the hardness of heart became important ingredients in the technological society's demand for maximum production and its drive toward "the one best way" of rationalizing all energy in the most efficient manner possible.[44]

The heroic ideal of twentieth-century urban culture has incorporated a great deal of the Calvinistic stress on productive self-discipline. It could be argued, for example, that *courage* (although still very important) has been replaced as the prime virtue in the contemporary canon by *ingenuity*—or, more simply and more tellingly, the ability to *win* (and to be a "winner"). Likewise, the form of sacrificial love most esteemed in the modern world is not the strength of character that leads one to make the gesture of laying down one's life for the faith or for some sacred principle; it is, rather, *efficacious* self-sacrifice in the sense of total commitment to the firm, the party, or the cause. It should not be surprising, then, that some persons of the utmost moral earnestness will see in EBC, especially in its power to upgrade human capacity, a means of making themselves (and all right-thinking persons) more heroically productive than ever before. Just as Olympic athletes may be expected to ingest all kinds of muscle-building substances and make use of novel training techniques in order to maximize competitive success, those who imagine themselves to be moral or spiritual athletes may feel duty bound to use any reliable form of EBC that will help them become as intelligent, intuitive, persuasive, diligent, and in sum, *productive*, as they can conceivably be.

Moral evaluation of "revving up" one's capacities depends on the purposes toward which the effort is directed. If an ambitious business or professional person uses every imaginable means to increase her capacities in order to pursue spurious status or power goals, that is (from a normative perspective) hardly laudable. If a dedicated social reformer with nothing in mind but greater justice for the oppressed follows the same course of self-development, we may see it as praiseworthy. And we can be certain that zealots will arise who will proclaim that the most fruitful avenue toward maximum goodness lies not in the direction of behavior control that extinguishes specific unworthy acts or merely mobilizes one's existing talents, but rather in the expansion and extension of one's ability to serve the common good. Just as a dynamic economy that doubles the output of useful goods over a short period of time may benefit a populace more than one that simply redistributes a static GNP more equitably, the most noble servants of humanity may be (or may be said to be) those who rev themselves up to the limit and use their supranormal capacities altruistically.

Those who are a bit skeptical about EBC or about the stress on maximum production in technological Calvinism may want to point out the dangers of subjecting the human spirit to excessive rationalization. They may repeat the warnings of Ernest Becker, or they may point to the difficulties experienced by prodigies such as John Stuart Mill (who went through an anguished period of depression and low effectiveness in his adult life because of having been pushed so hard and fast toward maximum achievement by his father). Yet, it seems churlish not to grant that shaping oneself in the heroic mold of maximum productivity *in genuinely worthy endeavors* is commendable. What can we say to those who follow this calling except "More power to you!"?

But we have to acknowledge that most people, even most religious persons and most of those with an above-average quotient of moral earnestness, will probably look upon the heroism of super capacity development as a counsel of perfection that they do not feel called upon to emulate. Similar to Christian love in its supreme form (as interpreted by Reinhold Niebuhr), rigorous capacity-enhancement may be an "impossible possibility" that one is obligated to rise to in special circumstances but that one neither expects nor tries to achieve consistently. Thus, the philosophical issue arising from the attainability of higher capacities translates into the political issue of freedom versus coercion. Chapter 6 addresses this matter and a number of the other problems of the potential abuse of EBC.

## NOTES

1. Richard A. Shaffer, "Mastering the Mind," *The Wall Street Journal,* Vol. 92, No. 30 (August 12, 1977), p. 1.

2. *Ibid.*

3. Barbara Brown, *New Mind, New Body,* p. 373.

4. Vance Packard, *The People Shapers,* pp. 57-58.

5. *Ibid.*

6. Nathan S. Kline, "The Future of Drugs and Drugs of the Future," *Journal of Social Issues,* Vol. 27, No. 3 (1971), p. 82.

7. John G. Taylor, *The Shape of Minds to Come,* p. 155.

8. Again, abuse should not bar use: excessive or prolonged use of steroids violates the principle of acceptable risk and should not be engaged in or allowed by the rules governing athletic competition, but use within safe limits may be legitimate. Of course, enforcing these limits might prove to be such a problem that official prohibition might become necessary. And if upgrading performance in effect destroys the game being played, a pragmatic decision to rule out artificial performance enhancers might be agreed upon by all the competitors concerned. For a stern denunciation of "The Coercive Power of Drugs in Sports," see the article thus entitled by Thomas H. Murray in the *Hastings Center Report* 18, 4 (August 1983), pp. 24-30.

9. Packard, *Shapers,* pp. 98-101.

10. David Krech, Testimony given before the Congress of the United States, April 2, 1968, p. 7.

11. *Ibid.*

12. Packard, *Shapers,* pp. 106-107.

13. James McConnell, as quoted in Maya Pines, *The Brain Changers,* pp. 156-157.

14. *Ibid.,* pp. 158-159.

15. Gerald Jonas, "The Human Brain," *The New Yorker* (July 1, 1974), p. 60.

16. Jonathan Glover, *What Kind of People Should There Be?,* p. 91.

17. Theodore Roszak, *Where the Wasteland Ends,* pp. 77-78.

18. Pines, *Changers,* p. 141.

19. Packard, *Shapers,* pp. 171-172.

20. Brown, *New Mind,* pp. 346-347.

21. Jean Houston, "Putting the First Man on Earth," *Saturday Review* (Feb. 22, 1975), p. 28.

22. Pines, *Changers,* pp. 192-193.

23. Packard, *Shapers,* pp. 286-288.

24. Alex Ben Block, "The Sputnik of the Classrooms," *New West* (July 18, 1977), pp. 36-43.

25. Houston, "Putting," p. 28.

26. *Ibid.*

27. *Ibid.*

28. Oswald Spengler, *The Decline of the West,* pp. 183-216.

29. Ernst Cassirer, *The Individual and the Cosmos in Renaissance Philosophy,* p. 76.

30. *Ibid.*

31. John Shearman, *Mannerism,* pp. 16-22.

32. Joseph Fletcher, *The Ethics of Genetic Control,* pp. 35-36.

33. Becker highlights the term "dread of significance" in pp. 3-5 of *Evil,* but in a larger sense both of these books are an elaboration of the theme. See especially Chapter 1 of *Evil* (pp. 6-25).

34. Norman O. Brown, *Life Against Death,* p. 247.

35. Ernest Becker, *Escape from Evil,* pp. 81, 73ff., 85.

36. Elias Canetti, *Crowds and Power,* p. 448.

37. Becker, *Escape,* pp. 101f.

38. *Ibid.,* pp. 26ff.

39. Arthur Koestler, as quoted in *Ibid.,* p. 134.

40. Becker, *Ibid.,* pp. 136, 32ff., 153.

41. Reinhold Niebuhr, *The Nature and Destiny of Man.*

42. Becker, *Escape,* p. 122.

43. Gerald Klerman, "Psychotropic Drugs as Therapeutic Agents." *Hastings Center Studies,* Vol. II, No. 1 (1974), pp. 81-93.

44. Max Weber, *The Protestant Ethic and the Spirit of Capitalism;* cf. Jacques Ellul, *The Technological Society.*

# Chapter 6

# POLITICAL RAMIFICATIONS

The analysis thus far has been centered on questions of technical feasibility and moral/philosophical legitimacy. Some possibilities have been ruled out as improbable on technical grounds; others have been rejected as undesirable or illicit on ethical grounds. That leaves quite a large number of EBC applications that would seem to be altogether appropriate as means to "artificial" happiness, goodness, and increased capacity for those who choose to utilize them.

But there is another crucial area of analysis that must be carried out before we can say, realistically, that this "seems to be" is viable in actual practice. Because no matter how dazzling one's scenario of the *possible* or how inspiring one's dream of the *ought*, they may be irrelevant—or even dangerous—unless they can be enacted in the real world of imperfect institutions and the imperfect persons who run them. Unless an investigation of the politics of EBC yields reasonable assurance that the frightful abuses one easily imagines can be prevented, the beneficial uses that are theoretically viable may be too risky to undertake. (I am using the concept of "politics" and the term "political" in a very broad sense to refer to the complexities and difficulties of widespread use of EBC in a society in which the individual's choices regarding it will be so greatly in-

fluenced by the action of institutions seeking to promote—or prohibit—particular uses and when many institutions—or persons—will
seek to further their own interests by *imposing* use without due regard for the well-being or the wishes of freely choosing individuals.)

The material covered in this chapter is organized under two main
headings: guarding against oppression and ensuring access. In the
first part of the chapter, I shall attempt to answer the apprehensions
of those who fear that EBC will inevitably amount to the terrors of
*1984*-type state control (or the more subtle distortions of "the therapeutic state"). In the second part, I shall discuss the economic,
political, and cultural conditions that will be necessary to promote
tolerably equal and open access to the benefits of EBC on the part of
all citizens. In each case, the discussion must include consideration
of "the other side of the coin" being examined: In speaking of the
safeguards against excessive institutional control through EBC, we
shall need to say something about society's legitimate (and enormously vital) interest in controlling or preventing socially destructive
behavior and the role of EBC in effecting this purpose; in speaking of
the "right to be treated" (i.e., the right to avail oneself of the forms of
EBC one considers advantageous for oneself), we shall deal with consumer education, societal regulation of research on the marketing of
new drugs and therapies, and the problem of paternalism.

## THE PERILS OF OPPRESSION

George Orwell's celebrated novel, *1984*, depicts a grim totalitarian
society in which thought control of the most rigorous kind is practiced by methods that range from sloganeering through the rewriting
of history to torture. Every citizen is forced to live in the almost constant presence of huge (wall-size) two-way television screens that
serve a dual purpose: They can be used to transmit the propaganda
messages of the state with overwhelming intensity and frequency,
and they can also be used to verify the presence of each citizen in his
appointed location and to monitor his actions. A diabolical technique
of psychological manipulation called the "Two Minutes Hate"
creates a sense of dependence on the ruling regime and loyalty to it
by picturing deviants as depraved enemies of the common good and
by concentrating hatred on a former party leader named Goldstein
(read Trotsky):

The program of the Two Minutes Hate varied from day to day, but there was none in which Goldstein was not the principal figure. He was the primal traitor, the earliest defiler of the Party's purity. All subsequent crimes against the Party, all treacheries, acts of sabotage, heresies, deviations, sprang directly out of his teaching.

In its second minute the Hate rose to a frenzy. People were leaping up and down in their places and shouting at the tops of their voices in an effort to drown the maddening bleating voice that came from the screen. The little sandy-haired woman had turned bright pink, and her mouth was opening and shutting like that of a landed fish. Even O'Brien's heavy face was flushed. He was sitting very straight in his chair, his powerful chest swelling and quivering as though he were standing up to the assault of a wave. The dark-haired girl behind Winston had begun crying out "Swine! Swine!" and suddenly she picked up a heavy Newspeak dictionary and flung it at the screen. It struck Goldstein's nose and bounced off; the voice continued inexorably. In a lucid moment Winston found that he was shouting with the others and kicking his heel violently against the rung of his chair. The horrible thing about the Two Minutes Hate was not that one was obliged to act a part, but that it was impossible to avoid joining in. Within thirty seconds any pretense was always unnecessary. A hideous ecstasy of fear and vindictiveness, a desire to kill, to torture, to smash faces in with a sledge hammer, seemed to flow through the whole group of people like an electric current, turning one even against one's will into a grimacing, screaming lunatic.[1]

But the dictatorial regime of Big Brother in *1984* is not invincible. Its protagonist is able to preserve enough freedom of spirit to rebel, and he is only subdued in the end by an exquisitely contrived process of torture that is so irresistible that it makes him betray the woman he loves and reduces him to a sniffling blob of acquiescence who feels nothing but love and gratitude for Big Brother. The fear of those who regard EBC as too hot to handle is that it would provide techniques of oppression far more invincible and far more practicable—that is, cost effective—than the relatively crude tactics relied upon by the ruling elite of *1984*. They fear, for example,

—that ESB or posthypnotic suggestion can be used to produce robot behavior in human beings;
—that CSB or ESB can be used to provide incentives or disincentives so powerful as to be irresistible: pleasures so sweet that no one who has tasted them can escape their lure in the future and who therefore will

do anything he or she is told to do in order to obtain them once again; pains so excruciating that a person who has experienced them will do absolutely anything to avoid them;

—that behavior modification techniques can be made so successful and so precise that anyone subjected to them will end up doing what he or she is programmed to do (regardless of what the person thinks or feels about these actions, that "take place" independently of mind or will);

—that "remote control hypnosis" can be used to create apathy on the eve of a national crisis.[2]

The analysis of technical feasibility in Chapter 2 and in the beginning portions of Chapters 3 through 5 has already established my contention that the eventualities feared are simply not likely to occur, either because they are impossible or because they would cost more in time, money, and scarce expertise than they would be worth. Jose Delgado's emphatic denial regarding robot control has already been quoted and it can be amplified by his explanation of *why* this possibility is so remote:

Personal identity and reactivity depend on a large number of factors accumulated through many years of experience interacting with genetic trends within the complexity of neuronal networks. Language and culture are among the essential elements of individual structure. All these elements cannot be substituted for by the delivery of electricity to the brain. Memories can be recalled, emotions awakened, and conversations speeded up by ESB, but the patients always express themselves according to their background and experience. It is possible to disturb consciousness, to confuse sensory interpretations, or to elicit hallucinations during excitation of the brain. It is also possible to induce fear, pleasure, and changes in aggressive behavior, but these responses do not represent the creation of a new personality—only a change in emotionality or reactivity with the appearance of manifestations closely related to the previous history of the subject.

Delgado concludes,

ESB cannot substitute one personality for another because electricity cannot replicate or influence all the innumerable factors which integrate individual identity. Contrary to the stories of science fiction writers, we cannot modify political ideology, past history or national loyalties by electrical tickling of some secret areas of the brain. A complete change in personality is beyond the theoretical and practical potential of ESB.[3]

What Delgado says about the impracticability of widespread thought control through ESB is echoed by other authorities whose area of expertise is behavior modification through operant conditioning or CSB. As every behavior modifier from B. F. Skinner on has insisted, aversive controls are far less effective than positive reinforcement, and there are no techniques of this kind powerful enough to induce subjects to adopt far-ranging behavior patterns (of the sort that would be necessary for reliable political conformity) against their wills.

What remains, then, is "biomedical manipulations," which Frank Ervin looks upon as the "techniques of choice" for a "power structure ... really interested in modifying the social behavior, either of large numbers of people or of a single person, for a protracted period of time and covertly." Ervin conjures up the following scenario:

> Suppose a social control agency were to want to take a militant leader of dissent and to modify his behavior without removing him from the scene. If the usual techniques of bribery, murder, or cooptation did not work, it would be quite feasible to imbed secretly in his tissues a slow release capsule of LSD and put him on a permanent trip. He would not know what was happening. He would be moderately crazy looking and probably ineffectual. And the intervention would be undetectable unless somebody knew precisely what to look for. If the desire were to be even more effective, a single dose of one of the neurotransmitter antagonists, which destroy nerve endings selectively in the brain, probably would irreversibly wipe out complex, well-organized functions in the individual.[4]

Could such things really happen here? We know that agencies such as the CIA have experimented with possibilities of this kind, and we know that there are some people who would not hesitate to use EBC in this fashion if they thought it would work and they could get away with it.

But what are the odds on the widespread and repeated applications of techniques such as these (if indeed they could be perfected)? Even Ervin admits that none of the "shelf full of metabolic and biochemical procedures available ... can precisely control a fragment of the behavioral repertoire within individuals." He continues,

> There is no way in which one can uniquely make a given individual do a precise act. Even the most specific of the biopsychological agents only change global states.[5]

Ervin's considered conclusion is that "by far the most potent techniques for social control remain in the province of socio-technology
(i.e., mass media and group pressure, not CSB, ESB, clinical behavior
modification, or the like):

> Most of the fantasy about biological brainwashing techniques, for in-
> stance, are just that—fantasies. People can have their minds radically
> changed, but the way it is done is in groups of people and with environ-
> mental manipulation, not in general with drugs, surgery, hormonal or
> genetic manipulation.[6]

Moreover, how "unusual" could the speech or actions of a "militant
leader of dissent" (or anyone else whose thoughts and behavior were
sufficiently well known, let alone *subversive*, to make him or her a
target of covert countermeasures) be rendered without arousing suspicion on the part of friends and leading to the kinds of scrutiny that
would reveal that the person had been tampered with? Can pills or
injections be administered without *any* risk of detection? Can im-
plants be made without leaving *any* discernible traces?) And how
often could these tactics succeed after their use had been exposed to
public view even once?

A lot hinges, of course, on one's estimate of the political health of
our society. Are our news media free enough for us to trust in their
ability to expose abuses promptly? Are governing officials (in both
public and private institutions) sufficiently afraid of bad publicity and
responsive enough to public indignation to be wary of attempting
oppression through EBC?

My tentative conclusion regarding the perils of oppression through
EBC is as follows. The technologies of manipulation and control that
are the subject matter of this book offer nothing new or terribly
promising to would-be totalitarian rulers. The massive propaganda
tools and the ingenious tortures described in *1984* are still available
to oppressive states, and they will be used (and are in fact now being
used) in societies in which freedom of the press and a long-standing
tradition of civil rights and civil liberties do not flourish. The relatively
healthy pluralism of our relatively open American society could of
course degenerate into a mass or a totalitarian society—but if that
were to happen, it would not be because of EBC, nor would the technologies of EBC be of much use to the ruling elites.

Although it is true that drugs, shock treatments, and aversive therapies of all kinds *can* unquestionably be used in violation of human rights to elicit obedience, induce apathy, and, in short, damage the bodies and minds of nonconsenting inmates in nursing homes, mental hospitals, prisons, and even schools, it does not seem likely to me that such abuses could be carried out on a massive scale, or even on more than a very, *very* occasional basis, with people who are not institutionalized. It is incumbent upon all citizens to exercise civic concern by being on guard against abuses in the four kinds of institutions alluded to—but that is a special problem that lies on the periphery of the constellation of issues being dealt with in this book.

## The Therapeutic State

Insofar as the likelihood of oppression through EBC is to be seen as a serious possibility, it is only through the possibility of a greatly extended "therapeutic state." The rationale of such a state can be explained through the extension of the state's responsibilities under the concept of *parens patriae* (i.e., the parental role of a state in which the king is seen as "father of his country"). According to Nicholas Kittrie, the welfare state has already expanded the protective obligations of the state under *parens patriae* to include many obligations to provide for the economic and educational needs of the citizenry. It is just another step to include the regulation of the citizenry's physical and mental health as a concern of the therapeutic state.[7]

The insidious thing about this extension of the notion of the parental role of the state is that it allows forced submission to voluntary therapies to be rationalized in the name of compassion.

> If it is an injustice to punish an innocent person, it is no less an injustice, and a far more significant one in our day, to fail to promote as best we can through adequate facilities and medical care the treatment of those who are ill.... Society should be ... sensitive to the injustice of not bringing back to the community of persons those whom it is possible to bring back.[8]

In theory, nothing could be more benevolent. In practice, the abuses that may readily occur are hair-raising. Consider, for example, the case of Frederick C. Lynch, who was charged with passing bad checks in a District of Columbia court. Despite his insistence that he was mentally competent at the time his offenses were committed, Lynch was found not guilty by reason of insanity—and he was confined to a mental hospital in accordance with a legal philosophy that averred that "the only issue is whether the defendant will go to jail for punishment or to a hospital for treatment," and declared that "the length of his hospitalization must depend solely on his need (or lack of it) for further treatment."⁹ The ironically tragic outcome was that

> Frederick Lynch, on his bad check charge, could have been sentenced to a maximum of 12 months in jail. The more likely probability would have been probation. His commitment to a mental institution, on the other hand, was for an indeterminate period of time. Harassed, branded, and tired, Lynch committed suicide.¹⁰

In light of Lynch's unhappy fate, the ominous implications of Robert Michels's statement regarding the therapeutic state are all too apparent:

> By insisting upon full protection of a mental patient's rights, including the right of full consent, the state runs the risk ... of making "a liberty they [sic] cannot enjoy ... superior to a health that must sometimes be forced upon them."¹¹

One rational fear regarding the therapeutic state, then, concerns due process. Will an ostensibly benevolent regard for the rehabilitation (or "cure") of a sick person lead to qualitative and quantitative forms of treatment that violate rights that an accused criminal would otherwise have and result in terms of confinement far greater than a convicted criminal would have to endure? It is encouraging to know that the Supreme Court reversed the lower court decisions in the Lynch case, ruling that a person who does not resort to a plea of insanity or diminished capacity cannot be forced to undergo treatment in a mental institution. Yet, as late as 1975, several years after the Supreme Court's reversal of *Lynch*, a philosopher felt no compunction about declaring that if society can punish without consent (as our criminal code certainly presupposes), it can also give therapy without consent!¹²

An even greater concern, of course, has to do with the fear that health care institutions and the professionals who work in them will be less than fully devoted to the welfare of their patients. The extreme case of fraudulent "treatment," of course, is the use of hospitalization as a way of silencing dissidents in the Soviet Union. In a society in which "mental health" implies endorsement of the official doctrines of the state and cooperation with its directives, deviance can be labelled "sickness" and deviants can be involuntarily packed off to "treatment centers" to be "cured."[13] But the perils of the therapeutic state are not exclusively a function of political regimes that cynically eradicate deviance. They are also a factor to be reckoned with in any society where—as in ours—an idolatrous reverence for "science" causes people to suspend their ordinary common sense about what is being done to human beings.

Numerous horror stories come to mind in this connection. One is that of the now infamous experiments set up by Stanley Milgram at Yale; another is that of the forty-year study of untreated syphilitics in Macon County, Alabama. In the former, unsuspecting persons who had been told they were being hired to assist scientists in a pain tolerance study ignored the cries of apparent anguish and the feigned loss of consciousness of the presumed subjects of the study, who were supposedly being subjected to electrical shock. The real subjects of the research continued to increase the amount of electricity ostensibly being delivered so long as they were instructed to do so by the men in the white coats who were running the experiments.[14] In the latter, a host of health professionals, public health service bureaucrats, and leaders of the black community near the Tuskegee Institute cooperated for decades in denying treatment to a large number of poor black males who were known to have a potentially lethal disease that could have been cured.[15]

My contention is, however, that such aberrations will become increasingly rare as the public continues to learn how necessary it is to adopt an attitude of healthy skepticism toward the pretensions of professionals and as the current trend toward demanding ever greater accountability from government, professionals, and all large institutions keeps on manifesting itself. In any case, the possible abuses that may occasionally arise as a result of the excessive zeal or the callousness of a few practitioners of the therapeutic state should not be allowed to stand as a formidable argument against voluntary use of EBC for nontherapeutic purposes.

## Safeguards

Having examined the perils of the therapeutic state, we are now in a position to explain the logic of the safeguards that would afford protection against these perils and to enumerate a few specific safeguards that are especially important.

In the first place, there must be ironclad legal guarantees of due process. No citizen should be incarcerated or institutionalized against his or her will until and unless sufficient cause has been established in a tribunal that assumes innocence (or health) until guilt (or serious illness) has been proven by procedures that allow for fair scrutiny of evidence and cross-examination of witnesses or testifying experts.

Second, the kinds of therapy authorized must be limited. Kittrie suggests two principles that ought to apply in this connection: the *inviolability* of bodily and personal integrity and *proportionality*. On the first point, he argues that "if the Eighth Amendment's protections are withheld from the patient because he is now undergoing punishment, the final possible repository of the right to personality is the Ninth Amendment."[16] In *Griswold v. Connecticut*, the Supreme Court interpreted the "broad, sweeping and vague" language of that clause in such a way as to protect the privacy of the marital bed, an entitlement nowhere mentioned explicitly in the Constitution or the Bill of Rights. Surely, says Kittrie, "the right to remain as you are, ... free from bodily and psychological alteration," is a right the framers of the Constitution would have protected if they could have foreseen the power of contemporary medical science. In regard to the second principle, Kittrie urges the legal system to "outlaw certain surgical, chemical or psychological techniques altogether, or at least to insist that the measure of treatment be proportionate to the severity and hazard of social deviance."[17]

It is also necessary, no doubt, to establish legal and administrative restraints on what Virginia Held calls "coercive offers." (Any proposition made by one party to another is a coercive offer if the party being propositioned has reason to believe that refusal will result in punitive measures being initiated by the propositioner. It may also be coercive in a different sense if refusal will result in loss of an asset, actual or potential, that the party being propositioned deems especially valuable.) It is important, however, not to label *all* incentives and disincentives offered by governments or employers as coercive or to equate them with "friendly fascism." The fact is (whether we like it or not), Robert Heilbroner was right when he declared in *Reflections on the Human Prospect* that we will have to give up some freedoms in order to enjoy secure possession of others in the future. Thus, liberty-restricting measures that are necessary to protect everyone against the extreme mischief-making of terrorists are entirely legitimate and so are government-sponsored programs that seek to produce socially useful behavior through psychological and monetary incentives or disincentives. For example,

—It is silly to inveigh against the "oppressiveness" of laws such as the one requiring airline passengers to submit to an inspection of themselves and their baggage (or to pillory the "sheepish compliance" of those who willingly undergo the ritual of inspection in order to be able to fly in reasonable safety).[18] The clear and present danger of a terrorist bomb is so great and the potential for disaster so great that the inconvenience of an inspection gate is a very small price to pay.

—Tax incentives and disincentives are a perfectly reasonable instrument for pushing aggregate social behavior in some desired direction. Tax credits for home insulation to conserve energy and high taxes on private automobiles in large cities to encourage use of public transportation are commendable efforts to shape the life-style of the citizenry in the public interest.

—Sociopsychological incentives in the form of public interest citizen or consumer education programs are also a legitimate mechanism for collective behavior shaping. These programs may be branded as "propaganda"—but they are legitimate, so long as they are not untruthful or misleading and so long as opposing messages can be heard and seen.

## EBC AS AN ALTERNATIVE TO INCARCERATION

The progression of the argument in the first half of this chapter has now moved from a discussion of the dangers of oppression to the question of where the line of limitations on state power should be drawn so as to allow for appropriate uses of the state's influence on behalf of the common good. This matter cannot be settled here, but an answer can be given to a test case that is of great importance in connection with the democratic and humane utilization of EBC for important social purposes. The test case I have in mind is that of EBC as an alternative to imprisonment in a penal institution.

*Clockwork Orange*, this devastating cinematic *tour de force* that tells Anthony Burgess's tale of a vicious psychopath who is cured of his devotion to "ultraviolence" through behavior modification, has given a bad name to EBC as an alternative to incarceration. The protagonist is such a winning youth and the clinical techniques employed to "fix" him are so crude and unpalatable that a moviegoer tends to forget what evil had been wrought by the youth in the first twelve minutes of the film. Thus one is tempted to agree with Michael Shapiro's denunciation of "the coercive use of organic therapies" and with his judgment that the reformed protagonist's "conforming behavior was certainly not praiseworthy ... and probably not rehabilitation."[19]

In addition, the courts have gone to great lengths to protect prisoners against coercive offers. The Kaimowitz decision—in which a Michigan court ruled that an inmate could not elect to have psychosurgery as treatment for the pathological behavior that had put him in prison—is a landmark case in establishing the principle that inmates in total institutions are not really in a position to give genuinely voluntary informed consent to organic therapies. Acceptance of this claim

> is only empirical, not *a priori*. That is, it is not claimed to be logically impossible for a prisoner to consent voluntarily to anything at all, or to anything proposed to him by his jailers with effects they cannot fully control, that he cannot fully understand, and that involve physical intervention with his body. All that is insisted is that in the typical case, informed voluntary consent cannot be reliably given by persons under prison discipline to quasi-therapeutic methods of physical intervention.[20]

Denial of the inmate's right to elect treatment that he desires is based, in other words, on the fear that prisoners are too vulnerable to manipulation, intimidation, and downright persecution if they refuse to consent to some "treatment" the prison officials want them to undergo.

We may applaud the sentiments that prompt such concern for the welfare of the prison inmates without agreeing with the policy position advanced. For the fact is, according to many experienced analysts, that a very large number of prisoners would like to have the option of being released from incarceration through a behavior

modification program that would restrain them from committing
the kinds of crime that put them behind bars.[21] Furthermore, there
is every reason to believe that effective safeguards against coercive
therapeutic offers can be set up. It would be possible, for example, to
establish an ombudsman for each part of the penal system whose
special responsibility would be to ensure that the therapeutic options
were clearly and fully explained to all interested inmates and that no
manipulative pressures were used in persuading them to sign up. A
formal informed consent hearing under the supervision of the ombudsman would be required before treatment could be undertaken.
And if these procedures were combined with a right of speedy transfer to a different prison in disputed cases, the prisoner would have a
very substantial degree of protection. (Besides, why should prison
officials want to *force* inmates to submit to EBC? Their chances of
continued employment in the penal system are a function of the continuing existence of a large prison population!)

The real test case for our purposes arises when the proposal is
made to *compel* correctional institute inmates to submit to EBC so
that they may be set free. If criminals can be "fixed," and if doing so
will save the taxpayers a lot of money, we can be sure that some
political leaders will urge that prisoners be forced to receive the appropriate "organic therapy." But would such a policy be ethically
acceptable?

Adam Bedau, a psychologist who has done extensive studies on
the penal system, maintains that "these new [EBC] techniques are not
intended to be used in a purely incapacitative, retributive, socially
defensive way." Instead, they "have elements of rehabilitation and
therapy that are undeniable"—thus, *in some cases* a prisoner "may
be involuntarily subjected to physical interventions designed to make
him less dangerous to others."[22] But the argument he advances is
meant to apply to inmates whose conduct is deemed dangerous to
the well-being of other inmates. I believe that any prisoner who prefers continued confinement to an EBC process that might qualify him
for release should be allowed to exercise that preference, and I fear
that compromise on this principle would open a Pandora's box of
potential abuses.

Reluctance to use organic therapies as an alternative to incarceration are ultimately based on two questionable points of view. One is
the stern moralistic view articulated long ago by Durkheim, who
argued that the principal purpose of penal servitude is to reinforce

the law-abiding behavior of good people by letting them see that crime does not pay and that convicted criminals really suffer for their sins.[23] The other is an excessive concern for full psychological and ethical rehabilitation, as expressed, for instance, in Shapiro's comment on the inadequacies of the treatment given to the antihero in *Clockwork Orange* and as amplified in these words:

> Rehabilitation denotes not only the goal of volitional law-abiding behavior, generated more from a sense of rightness than from a fear of punishment, but suggests at least generally that the means used to effect rehabilitation do not involve direct psychotropic intervention into one's patterns of mentation, nor organic conditioning techniques.[24]

There it is again: the familiar complaint, so dear to the heart of traditional moralists, that good behavior achieved through "artificial" means is not true goodness.

My reply to Durkheim and Shapiro is as follows:

(1) We simply have to find a more humane *and more effective* way to protect law-abiding citizens from the ravages of criminal behavior. What Karl Menninger has dubbed "the crime of punishment" in our present penal system offers only an illusory and spurious comfort to decent folk, for all too often it merely embitters those who are imprisoned and serves as a school for instruction in more insidious criminal tactics. Quite apart from the dubious philosophical merit of revenge as a motive for locking people up under miserable conditions, it is not the best way to transform their behavior when they are released. And if a better way to accomplish that purpose can be found, as the practitioners of behavior modification claim, then there is no point in not making that option available for those who want to exercise it.

(2) As for the complaint that behavior control "used with the intention or purpose of altering the subject's behavior [directly]," without "altering the subject's conscious cognitive states" is not true rehabilitation, it can be refuted by the same line of reasoning as the one already set forth in Chapter 4. What a person *does* is an inseparable part of who she *is*, and if her behavior is improved she is in some very important sense re-formed as a person. If her *agency*—that is, what she causes as an agent—is changed for the better, she is a better person; she is to some extent rehabilitated. If she is so perverse as to

regret the improvement in her behavior, then it has to be admitted that her will (and, if you insist, her nature as a moral being) remains unrehabilitated. But so long as her antisocial behavior is not repeated and so long as she was in fact willing to undergo the behavior modification process she had to undergo in order to escape incarceration (and is willing, further, to undergo a "refresher" process, if necessary, to stay out of prison), then both the social protection and the rehabilitation functions of the criminal correction system have been well served by EBC.

## FAIR AND OPEN ACCESS

It is ironic that attention gravitates so quickly to fears of oppression when the question of the political ramifications of EBC is raised. Oppressive abuses must be avoided, of course—but the sum total of evil that is likely to occur because of them may be very small in comparison with the amount of good that could result from the adoption of political measures to insure fair and open access to the benefits of EBC. The structure of the analysis of this side of the coin in the second half of the chapter will be similar to that in the first half: Just as our analysis of the problem of oppression took the form of an argument to the effect that although externally imposed control by EBC would be bad in principle and must be prevented, certain kinds of control in particular circumstances (e.g., crime control) would be good, even so our analysis of access must take the form of endorsing *these* restrictions but not *those*. The argument will be, in fact, that although society (acting primarily through government) should offer certain protections against the marketing of demonstrably *unsafe* EBC agents and procedures, it should nevertheless refrain from enforcing paternalistic judgments about *efficacy* by establishing unwarranted sanctions on consumer freedom. The danger is that society may not offer *enough* control over hazardous substances and techniques and that it may interfere *too much* in areas where danger is not the issue, and where—therefore—individual desires should be allowed free play. I shall also argue that society, through government, should not only *offer protection* against certain perils, but should also *promote* certain things that are in the public interest (e.g., consumer education, human benefit-oriented research, and distributive justice).

## Protection Against Health and Safety Hazards

The enactment of the Pure Food and Drug Act of 1906 represented our nation's acknowledgment of the fact that access to chemical substances should not be unrestricted. The establishment of premarket clearance requirements in 1938 and of the Federal Drug Administration (FDA) in 1940, acknowledged the need for a testing and certification process by means of which to ensure that unsafe drug products were not marketed in the U.S. Like all of the other regulatory agencies of the federal government, the FDA has from time to time been a political football, and it has had to face recurrent charges from both ends of the political spectrum that it is either too soft or too tough in its handling of applications for the approval of new drugs. In the past two decades, the agency seems to have leaned in the direction of dominant trends in American politics: In the 1960s (partly as a result of publicity arising from the thalidomide scare), it veered in the direction of greater caution; in the 1980s (under an administration that prides itself on eliminating "governmental interference in the economy"), it has been accused of entering into "a cynical 'partnership in crime'" with the pharmaceutical industry—that is, of perpetrating a "major scandal of failed law enforcement which threatens the lives and health of all of us."[25]

A great deal seems to hinge on the enactment, in 1962, of the Kefauver-Harris amendments:

> These amendments repealed the automatic approval clause of the 1938 statute, broadened the definition of new drugs, required the submission of the investigational new drug application before testing on humans, and required proof of *efficacy*, in addition to the proof of safety called for by the 1938 act [italics added].[26]

Opponents of the efficacy provision contend that it contributes decisively to an excessive bureaucratic bias that forces Americans to wait too long for access to many beneficial products and discourages innovation by pharmaceutical houses. Application of this standard calls for

> comparison of the efficacy and risks of a new drug with the efficacy and risks of other drugs as well as with procedures including surgery, evaluation of suspected or potential adverse effects, and evaluation of the risk from intentional abuse and use for purposes other than those listed

on the label. [All these requirements] could greatly increase the cost of research and clinical testing and prolong the approval process.[27]

As a result, say the critics, people in this country are "denied the benefits of significant new therapeutic agents for substantial periods of time," and drug companies must spend *forty* times as much money to develop a new drug as they had to spend in 1960![28] The effects of the 1962 amendments may be summarized as follows:

> The 1962 amendments required documented scientific evidence of the efficacy of new drugs, and as a result, the FDA has frequently required additional clinical testing. The FDA was given discretionary authority over the investigational new drug process for the first time, and manufacturers were required to furnish the results of prior animal tests and to obtain FDA approval of protocols for testing in human subjects. The FDA may prohibit or delay testing to obtain different testing procedures or out of concern for risk to volunteers. The FDA set fairly specific and increasingly difficult standards for animal toxicology control over the preclinical state of drug testing. Only about one in ten to fifteen drugs can be expected to complete clinical testing....
>
> The span of time from discovery of a drug through its approval by the FDA has increased from two or two and a half years prior to 1962 to about ten years at the present time. Similarly, the cost of developing a new chemical entity has increased from approximately $1.3 million in 1960 to about $50 million now according to various estimates.... Additional regulation has increased the burden of supporting the new drug application, and one recent application is said to have required 124 volumes, running to 40,242 pages. The annual rate of approval for new chemical entities in the thirteen years ending in 1962 averaged forty-two, but for the thirteen years beginning in 1963 the average rate of approvals per year was fourteen.[29]

Supporters of the 1962 amendments maintain that the "drug lag" caused by close scrutiny of applications for approval of new drugs is simply a part of the not exorbitant price we must pay to create a "death lag"—that is, to prevent the deaths, deformities, and other kinds of damages that would result from lax standards. They cite the too hasty and ill-advised approval of Oraflex—an antiarthritis "miracle drug" that had to be withdrawn from the market by the manufacturer (who feared a barrage of lawsuits) less than four months after its approval by the FDA—as an example of the folly of the two-thirds drop in enforcement actions undertaken by the FDA since President Reagan took office. According to Dr. Sidney Wolfe, Director of the Nader Health Research Group, there exists within the FDA a hands-off attitude similar to that which prevailed in the Department of the Interior under James Watt and in the Environmental Protection Agency under Ann Gorsuch:

> It is an attitude in which there is this emphasis in doing things on a "voluntary" basis. The signal this sends out to the drug industry is that "We're not really serious about enforcing the laws—you [drug companies] take it from there."[30]

It may well be that both sides are right. Perhaps *safety* is a matter in which the level of acceptable risk is very low and in which enforcement standards should be stringent. When safety is concerned, no short cuts in the approval process should be countenanced, and firms that submit false research data in order to secure approval—as Eli Lilly was accused of doing in the Oraflex case—should be penalized severely.

But *efficacy* may be a different matter. The FDA could prevent unwarranted claims in the advertising of a new drug—indeed, it could insist on appropriate disclaimers in package inserts—without withholding a *safe* new drug from the market. Thus, consumers could enjoy the healing effects (even the placebo effects) of new drugs without lengthy delays while efficacy tests were still being carried out, and the benefits of quicker release might far outweigh the bad effects of disappointment caused by the marketing of new drugs that are no more—*but also no less*—beneficial than other available substances or therapies.

## Abuses by Individuals

From the standpoint of political philosophy, the issue here seems to be that of *legal paternalism*. The right and duty of the state to limit freedom in cases in which it is being used in such a way as to harm *others* is well established. That's why it is appropriate for a government agency such as the FDA to safeguard the public against products that constitute a threat to health and safety. But does the state have a right to limit the freedom of citizens who are doing something that somebody *else*—scientists, priests, or even a majority of other citizens—has labelled injurious to *themselves*? The main body of opinion in Anglo-American political philosophy says no. The government may seek to *persuade* citizens not to do certain things through consumer education campaigns (e.g., the warning on cigarette packages and the antismoking messages on TV), but it must stop short of *prohibition*.

There are two reasons for stopping short of paternalistic prohibitions. One is based on the argument that society has no right to dictate to an individual what he or she does if it affects only himself or herself; the other is that it is too much trouble to seek to penalize those involved in "crimes without victims." Thus, some political leaders who are devoutly opposed to pornography admit that the administrative and economic costs of "protecting people against their own base instincts" in regard to sexual titillation is not worth the trouble it would take to make such an attempt.

In any case, the issues raised in connection with paternalism bring us to a second broad area of concern about the political ramifications of EBC; namely, protecting society against the alleged evils caused by widespread use (and abuse) of drugs on the part of individuals. In the first part of the chapter, our attention was focused on making individual citizens safe from misuse of EBC by the state or other large social institutions; now the focus shifts to the presumed threat to society posed by a high level of voluntary individual use.

The following analysis of drug abuse by individuals will be divided into two principal parts: protection of society and redemption of the addict. Included in the former category are an analysis of the rationale for criminalization of illicit drug use, and examination of the indirect harms to third parties caused by the impaired health and irresponsibility of drug abusers and an assessment of the indirect wounds suffered by society as a whole because of the presumed self-degradation drug abuse entails. Consideration of the latter category takes the form of a last look at the case for legal paternalism (i.e., the argument that society has both a right and a duty to protect citizens against themselves by using legal sanctions to prohibit self-degradation).

In the discussion that follows, I am relying heavily on David Richards's splendid new book, *Sex, Drugs, Death and the Law*. Richards's rejection of legal paternalism is based upon what he calls the "autonomy-based interpretation of treating persons as equals"; that is, he grounds his argument on a viewpoint in political philosohy that

accords supreme importance to the principle of individual self-determination and then insists that the rights implied in this principle must
be extended on an equal basis to all citizens. Autonomy-based
equality rules out legal paternalism except in the sense of very specific and precisely limited regulatory laws and policies. Richards puts
his appeal for decriminalization in perspective by concluding it with
this statement:

> Finally, it is important to remind ourselves ... that there are limits to an
> argument grounded in human rights of the kind here presented. To say
> that a person has a human right to do an act is to make a political legal
> claim that certain conduct must be protected by the state from forms of
> coercive prohibition. To assert the existence of such a right is not to
> assert that it should be exercised. The latter is an issue of personal
> morality....
>
> To say, therefore, that people have a human right to use drugs is not to
> conclude that everyone should exercise this right.[31]

## Protecting Society Against
## the Evils of Drug Abuse

The most vehement argument in support of criminalization is the
one that views illicit drugs as the number one cause of street crime in
the nation. It is doubtless true that "to pay the crime tariff on drugs,
users may engage in burglary, theft or robbery, or in services with
their own tariffs, such as prostitution, gambling or drug trafficking."
But the "enlarged scope of organized crime operations" associated
with drug use is not a function of use per se; it is, rather, "a result of
criminalization itself." Furthermore, "there is simply no factual support for the argument that drug use itself releases inhibitions or
criminal tendencies. In short, "arguments of criminogenesis are gen-
erally circular and question-begging; they argue for criminalization of
drug use on the basis of the evils that criminalization, not drug use,
fosters."[32]

A second oft-cited reason for the legitimacy of criminalization is a
response to the unfortunate consequence of the lowered performance and the unreliability of drug abusers. In addition to the sins of
commission charged against criminals, it is argued, there is an equal
or greater amount of harm that must be charged to their sins of omis-

sion: families left without support, employers whose employees either do not show up for work or cannot be counted on to carry out their duties in a competent manner, contracts not honored, and so on. Add to that the personal injury and destruction deliberately wrought in the home or the workplace but never reported or punished as crime and you have a fearful toll to reckon with.

There is doubtless some merit to this argument, and its implied justification of partial regulation (rather than wholesale criminalization) of certain kinds of drug use under certain conditions surely deserves to be honored. As Richards observes,

> Although absolute prohibitions of drug use cannot be sustained on appropriate moral grounds, more limited and circumscribed moral arguments might justify forestalling drug use in specific circumstances.... Consider, for example, moral obligations to third parties (such as those entailed in parental relationships). Parenthood is a role embedded in social institutions of family and education and regulated by principles of justice that assess rights and duties, benefits and burdens, in terms of fairness and equity to parents, children and society in general. Voluntarily undertaking parenthood gives rise to ... a social obligation to perform one's just parental role.... It is a prima facie violation of such moral obligations to take drugs that impair the well-being of the unborn child. To the extent that grave effects of such kinds may occur, drug taking by parents during the relevant period of risk may be appropriately regulated.[33]

But regulation-legitimating circumstances of this kind are a special case. The general rule is that society does not have "property rights" in individual citizens that would allow it to proscribe putatively self-destructive or self-limiting behavior. To describe drug use as a form of suicide (as Benjamin Rush does), and to infer from that debatable assumption that such behavior "violates the citizen's duty of service to the state, which has an interest akin to a property right in the lives and services of its citizens," is untenable. For

> if the autonomy-based interpretation of treating persons as equals means anything, it means that the idea that other persons or institutions may have property rights in our lives is radically misplaced.... There are means by which society may encourage performance for the public good. Money and status may be used as incentives. But as a free and rational being, a person has a right to choose a way of life in which such

performance plays no central role, assuming minimal obligations of citi-
zenship are met.[34]

Certainly, criminalization of such conduct is profoundly unjust, tantamount to a violation of human rights. Criminalization on the basis of
the property rights principle would constitute, in fact, a negative form
of technological Calvinism: It would imply that any and all forms of
pleasure that detract from maximum mobilization of energy for full
production are morally illicit and may be forbidden by the state.

A particularly egregious form of this line of thought declares that
criminalization is necessary as a function of "the right of existing institutions to protect themselves from subversion." It was this kind of
thinking that identified the use of liquor with Catholic immigrants and
their subversive (i.e., non-Protestant) values, or heroin (when it first
came under attack in this country) with Chinese influences, marijuana with Hispanics, and cocaine with blacks. But these assumptions are patently absurd: "From the perspective of fundamental
moral theory, [these claims] assume what should be in dispute, the
moral legitimacy of existing institutions," and they "can be fairly
credited only after we have evaluated the legitimacy of existing institutions and their policies regarding drug use." Richards concludes,

> These claims are transparently baseless. Some forms of currently
> criminal drug use would, if decriminalized, probably have little effect
> on current American aims and aspirations; if anything, there might be
> benign shifts to these drugs from currently legal drugs such as alcohol.
> In addition, the values invoked against certain forms of drug use are
> themselves subject to criticism. For example, the current division in
> American law between legal and illegal drugs distinguishes between
> drugs that influence levels of arousal (the stimulants and depressants)
> and those that affect the information processing systems (the
> hallucinogens) ... : the former tend to be legal, the latter illegal.... This
> distinction reflects an underlying value of facilitating work at particular
> tasks.[35]

To make the same point in the language of Theodore Roszak's critique of the "objective consciousness" of the scientific-industrial
mind-set, our culture is one that encourages the use of drugs that
make us better able to focus our minds and energies on the
mechanical and bureaucratic tasks it wants us to perform, whereas it

condemns and punishes those drugs (and attitudes) that interfere with this sort of resource mobilization.

The third important argument favoring criminalization as a necessary protection for society is the rather neo-Platonic argument that the self-degradation of drug abusers somehow endangers society by impugning its ideals, especially its ideals of individual productivity and social responsibility. Whenever an addict shows his scorn for conventional notions of respectability (says this argument), he jeopardizes the devotion of others to this ideal and thereby harms society because he is "scandalizing the faithful."

It cannot be denied, of course, that there is an element of truth here: All cultural ideals and culturally institutionalized behavior patterns are precarious in the sense that they become problematic when they are not supported by the "probability structures" of everyday life. But one of the cardinal tenets of political philosophy in a pluralistic society is that no one should be required to do certain things, or to refrain from doing things, simply because somebody else may feel uncomfortable as a result. That is why the entire history of religious freedom in Western civilization is the history of a movement away from requiring every member of society to believe approved doctrine and conform his or her behavior to this doctrine, lest the gods be offended and send a plague upon the city and all its inhabitants.

## Legal Paternalism

The final argument concerning society's need to protect itself against illicit drug use is already a form of the argument for legal paternalism. The theory of legal paternalism asserts that protecting people against themselves (philosophical paternalism) is a principle that ought to be expressed in legal sanctions: You not only *tell* people that they ought not to do certain things (for their own good); you go a step further and make it *against the law* for them to do these things. You try, in other words, to make every sin into a crime.

According to Richards, legal paternalism appears in two forms. "Interference on the basis of facts unknown to the agent, in order to save the agent from harms he would wish to avoid," is the first form, and it is valid. It leads logically to the establishment of agencies such as the FDA that are responsible for guarding citizens against and advising them about health hazards of which they might otherwise be ignorant. But the second kind of legal paternalism—"interference on the basis of values that the agent himself does not share"—constitutes "a violation of human rights." It cannot legitimately be used to "justify the kind of interference in choices to use drugs that is involved in the current criminalization of many forms of drug use." In sum,

> At most, paternalistic concern for forms of irreparable harm might dictate appropriate forms of regulation to insure that drugs are available only to mature persons who understand, critically evaluate and voluntarily accept such risks. To minimize pointless risks, such regulations might insure that certain drugs, LSD, for example, are taken only under appropriate supervision. In general, however, there is no ground of just paternalism for an absolute prohibition of such drugs.[36]

But the passion of those who believe in paternalism is not easily quenched. Despite familiarity with rational expositions of political philosophy such as Richards's, their gut feelings continue to force them to demand that self-degradation be prohibited. They genuinely believe that an addict ought to be saved from depravity by a society that "knows better"—that is, a society that knows better than he does what is good for him and what he really ought to want, if he were in his right mind. Robert Neville articulates his convictions on this point in the following words:

> Among the things highly valued in our society ... is a habit of taking care of people so that they live within a range of locally accepted human amenities. Harmful drugs might be justified in being controlled, therefore, because their uncontrolled availability would allow users to sink to socially shameful depths of abject filth, mindlessness and disorder.... If we could eliminate the criminal costs to society [by legalizing addiction, and thus making crime unnecessary as a means to "feed one's habit"], would we allow the abject victims of drug use to rot in their autonomy? I suspect not.... The reasons we cite for these attempts are that they are humanitarian, that it is inhumane for society to let people victimize themselves to the extent common in the drug scene. This reflects not so much a principle of paternalism as a principle of social responsibility, of identification with the plight of the abject.[37]

One of the particulars cited here is the contention that drug abuse causes dreadful physical harm. The scenario usually invoked is that of the big-city heroin user; it features hepatitis, tetanus abcesses at the place where needles are inserted, and the spread of communicable diseases (such as malaria) that sometimes result from addicts sharing tainted paraphernalia. Yet, the horrors of this scenario do not amount to a convincing case for criminalization, but rather for the intelligent regulation and explanation of proper use that is a feature of the legal traffic in drugs:

> Many of the harms cited as the basis for criminalization could be avoided by the same forms of regulation that are applied to presently legal drugs. For example, because the FDA does not regulate the sale of heroin, the buyer is never sure of what he is getting.... The lack of appropriate medical supervision over the sterilization of hypodermic needles ... accounts for the disease found at the site of the injection. In addition, the illegality of drug use discourages the addict from seeing a physician, [although] a physician, if consulted, might detect symptoms of illness (such as malnutrition) that are masked by the addiction. In short, the evils of heroin use that are alleged as a ground for criminalization are produced or fostered by such criminalization; all these dangers could be reduced appreciably if heroin use were made legal and regulated.[38]

But the heart of the paternalistic view is not its concern for the physical self-destruction of the addict. It is, rather, spiritual self-destruction, an effacing of the image of God in the self. How can anyone be so lacking in compassion, asks the advocate of paternalism, as to ignore this ultimate tragedy? How can mere theory in political philosophy—even one as ostensibly noble as that of "autonomy-based equality," justify failure to redeem the addict from this abyss?

The most important answer to these questions has already been given in Chapter 3. Just as the absolutely fundamental importance of the right of free speech may persuade persons of elevated mind and goodwill to support the right of Nazis to march in Skokie, the even more fundamental right to self-determination justifies decriminalization as the ruling guideline in public policy regarding EBC. There are two reasons for this. The first has to do with the nature of addiction; the second, with the positive values of EBC and with the ways in which these positive values may be taken into account in calculating the trade-offs between using and not using certain specific forms of EBC.

## Addiction

As the history of the concept reveals, addiction does not "turn on physiological factors like tolerance and dependence, but on a certain kind of psychological centrality." Addiction is a word that was originally used to describe the passionate devotion of lovers, and this kind of "addiction"—like addiction to wealth—is viewed critically only when the psychological centrality of the attachment is blind or disproportionate. Thus (as the analysis of addiction in Chapter 3 implies), "liking something a lot" is morally problematic only when it diminishes one's "capacity for appreciation of and ability to deal with other things in [one's] environment, or in oneself, so that [one becomes] increasingly dependent on that experience as his only source of gratification."[39]

Moreover, "careful empirical studies of the causes of drug devotion . . . demonstrate the importance, not of physiological dependence, but of social and psychological factors." The excessive psychological centrality of drug use is often aggravated (or even engendered) by the sociological aspects of addiction, notably by stigmatization. So if the stigma of heavy use were to be lifted through decriminalization, the pressures reinforcing addiction would relax substantially. Once again, then, the facts often pointed to as a reason for making drug use illegal may actually be better interpreted as support for the opposite policy apropos the legal status of drug use. The irony of criminalization is compounded by the fact that it has "decisively shaped . . . the composition of the drug-using population" in this country, creating a greater disproportion of addiction in the least privileged classes. There is something astonishingly counterproductive about the argument that decriminalization would increase the misery of the poor by encouraging increased use of the most powerful and destructive euphorics (by letting them, in other words, have easy access to a real "opiate of the people"), which worsens "the passive vulnerability of the poor to exploitation."[40]

### The Positive Value of
### Nontherapeutic Drug Use

Another crucial reason for endorsing decriminalization is suggested by James Bakalar and Lester Grinspoon in their thought-provoking article, "Why Drug Policy Is So Harsh." Bakalar and Grinspoon aver that policy on such matters as antipollution laws and safety regulations (e.g., on protective guards for chain saws) are usually based on an assessment of acceptable risk that considers the trade-offs between the valuable uses of a product or a process and requirements of reasonable public health and safety. Our society's conclusion in these matters is usually based on a commonsense balancing of costs and benefits. Even the repeal of Prohibition fits this model, for repeal was based on the conclusion that the *benefits* derived from use of alcohol by millions of people were so great that some abuse could be tolerated (and specific abuses, such as drunk driving or public disorderliness, could be deterred by legal penalties). This mix of benefits and abuses was considered preferable to the corruption and chaos occasioned by vain efforts to enforce total prohibition. But curiously enough, say Bakalar and Grinspoon, public thinking is on the whole unwilling to grant that the taking of mood- or sensation-enhancing drugs yields a significant benefit that deserves to be taken into account and balanced with risks of abuse:

> There is probably more confusion than hypocrisy here. In modern society experiences and behavior that are hard to classify make us anxious. Drug use for work or pleasure is both a cement for the social order and a threat to it; the drug user is free and yet often, somehow, compelled; the drugs are medicine, but also vice or even a kind of infectious disease. The existing system of drug control is entirely a product of our century, both institutionally and conceptually. Facing a problem of technology and social change, we have allayed our anxiety by fixing certain legal and social categories, different for different drugs. If they seem hard to justify in the abstract, perhaps they represent some collective historical wisdom. Only marginal changes are likely. But we may at least be able to use these categories more wisely, flexibly, and humanely if we remember what was left out in formulating them.

> We should recognize our own confusion in the judgment of the average person and the recuperative powers of the community; if any drug could destroy the fabric of society, alcohol would have done it by now. Historians have been quick to see the elements of a "symbolic crusade" and "moral entrepreneurship" in the campaign for prohibition of alcohol, but not where other drugs are concerned. We have to restrain the imagery of epidemics and legal moralism and concentrate on health and safety hazards that can be clearly shown to be a product of drug abuse. As we become more conscious of our implicit models and analogies, we can acknowledge that it is not as simple as it seems to

justify subjecting drug use to harsher legal restraints than other forms of risk taking.[41]

For those who feel the need of a stronger argument on philosophical principle, the analysis adumbrated by Thomas Szasz is instructive. Szasz bases his thesis concerning "The Ethics of Addiction" on the assumption that social policy is usually legitimated on the basis of tradition or (especially in our day and time) science. "Whatever a social practice might be," he observes, "if people engage in it, generation after generation, then the practice becomes accepted not only as necessary but also as good. Slavery is an example." He continues,

> Many opponents of illegal drugs admit that tobacco may be more harmful to health than marijuana; nevertheless, they urge that smoking tobacco should be legal but that smoking marijuana should not be, because the former habit is socially accepted while the latter is not. This is a perfectly reasonable argument. But let us understand it for what it is: a plea for legitimizing old and accepted practices, and for illegitimizing novel and unaccepted ones. It is a justification that rests on precedence, not on evidence.

> The other basis for legitimizing policy, increasingly more important in the modern world, is science. In matters of health—a vast and increasingly elastic category—physicians thus play important roles not only as healers, but also as legitimizers, and as illegitimizers. One result is that, regardless of the pharmacological effects of a drug on the person who takes it, if he obtains it through a physician and uses it under medical supervision, that use is ipso facto legitimate and proper, but if he obtains it through nonmedical channels and uses it without medical supervision (and especially if the drug is illegal and the individual uses it solely for the purpose of altering his mental state), then that use is ipso facto illegitimate and improper. In short, being medicated by a doctor is drug use, while self-medication (especially with certain classes of drugs) is drug abuse.

> Again, it is perfectly reasonable to insist on such an arrangement. But let us understand it for what it is: a plea for legitimizing what doctors do, because they do it with "good therapeutic" intent, and for illegitimizing what laymen do, because they do it with bad self-abusive (masturbatory) intent. This justification rests on the principle of professionalism, not of pharmacology. Hence it is that we applaud the systematic medical use of methadone and call it "treatment for heroin addiction,"

but decry the occasional nonmedical use of marijuana and call it "dangerous drug abuse."

Our present concept of drug abuse thus articulates and symbolizes a fundamental policy of Scientific Medicine: namely, that a layman should not medicate his own body but should place its medical care under the supervision of a duly accredited physician. Before the Reformation, the practice of True Christianity rested on a similar policy: namely, that a layman should not himself commune with God but should place his spiritual care under the supervision of a duly accredited priest.[42]

In short, Szasz proclaims that self-medication is a right as fundamental as freedom of speech or religion, although he stipulates that it "should apply only to adults, and it should not be an unqualified right." He ends by asserting the conventional view that one must accept "unqualified responsibility for the effects of one's drug-intoxicated behavior on others," and he registers his approval of laws designed to enforce this limitation on "the right of self-medication."

Szasz's comments on the role played by the medical profession in supporting the philosophy of strict controls are echoed by Bakalar and Grinspoon, who point out that medical professionals are (intentionally or unintentionally) protecting their own power and prestige by insisting that "the rule for taking risks in medicine is different from the rule for taking risks in the pursuit of pleasure or ambition,"[43] and by seeking to proclaim their right to be arbiters of what is permissible in this area. Reflection on this fact should remind us that both regulation and paternalism are matters that must be discussed in connection with clinical practice as conducted by physicians and other therapists, as well as in connection with the government.

## DECRIMINALIZATION AND SOCIAL REFORM

The liberal argument for decriminalization must be complemented by an exhortation to work for the kind of social reform that will mitigate the *causes* (not just the symptoms) of the social and psychological malaise that sometimes drive people to drug abuse. This point is made with admirable clarity by the author of The Biocrats at the conclusion of his explanation of why prohibition of sophisticated forms of EBC will not work and should not be attempted.

Lastly, the key question, will we really be worse off with a cornucopia of drugs that we can dip into easily? Will we be trapped into relying heavily on chemical help to get us through life—as we already have been trapped by cars, cities, houses, television ... ? I do not see why, or rather why it should necessarily be so much more devastating to human dignity ... than those other props of civilization. As long as these props are not actually addictive, do not truly run our lives, we still retain the freedom to rule them and to discard them if we wish—while as long as we do not discard them but do use them we must gain an advantage. Once we get over the emotional reaction that taking little soulless pink pills to manipulate our moods is unnatural—and therefore somehow discreditable—the idea that we might gain becomes easier to accept.

If we are still appalled at the prospect of a vast spread in drug-taking, then of course the challenge is not so much to prevent that spread but to change the social conditions that underpin it.[44]

That's it, of course. If you are unimpressed by the claim that decriminalization will actually lessen the amount of physical and psychological harm suffered by drug addicts and if you are emotionally and morally undone by the prospect of leaving the dispossessed in the pit of self-degradation, then it's up to you to create a political, economic, and cultural environment in which people who flee to the solace of excessive drug use can really improve their lives. Create equality of outcomes in education and employment; overcome the pernicious heritage of status differentials; make everyone in the world happy and secure.

Yes, that's the *best* answer. That's what should be done, and affirming it as an ideal is fine and dandy. More power to all who invest large portions of time, money, and energy into efforts intended to achieve these goals. But when one considers the odds of success in such an enterprise, one can hardly ask the downtrodden to believe in its imminent realization or blame them for choosing the tangible (although ambiguous) rewards of mood-control drugs instead of waiting, hoping, or even working toward systemic social reform. As the author of the above-cited passage from *The Biocrats* goes on to say,

Until we can change all this [i.e., the injustice and inhumanity of societal conditions], perhaps we should bless the fact that the civilizations that are advanced enough to push people into such conditions are also advanced enough to invent the modern range of mind-affecting drugs.[45]

## Practical Safeguards

In the end, though, advocates of decriminalization must do more than simply refute the claims of their opponents. They must give a constructive answer to the question, "How can the health care system operate in such a way as to forestall the dangers associated with drug abuse and promote the solid benefits of proper use of EBC?" On this point, proponents of EBC and health care system reformers can find significant common ground and should join hands in working for many of the same goals.

Among the practical safeguards against abuse that may be instituted in a health care system that respects the autonomy-based equality of all citizens are (1) continued efforts to ameliorate professional paternalism by cultivating better physician-patient relationships, (2) careful screening of the safety of new types of CSB in the light of the medical history and individual makeup of would-be users, and (3) a comprehensive consumer education program.

Critics of "pill pushing" often complain that prescriptions are used as a substitute for vital contact and genuine communication between physician and patient. A similar argument is frequently used against behavior therapy: The quest for treatment is suspected of being an attempt on the part of the family, coworkers, or friends to avoid dealing with the difficulties of complex personalities and relationships, and even successful treatment is regarded as superficial symptom-relief that leaves root causes untouched.

The critics may be wrong (or, at the very least, guilty of exaggeration) in their complaints, but they are probably right in what they recommend: sustained, probing communication between patient and physician/therapist. And this is certainly a recommendation that EBC enthusiasts can join in supporting.

In the poignant words of Arthur Miller's *Death of a Salesman*, "attention must be paid" to the loneliness, bewilderment, and low-key desperation of many ordinary people. And when these people consult doctors or therapists, the feeling that they are getting the genuinely concerned full attention of a healer—the feeling that their miseries are being attended to sympathetically by someone who not only cares about them but will care for them—can in itself have a healing effect.

But what I am calling attention to here is not simply a psychological placebo effect. As a leading figure in medical education recently urged, physicians need to become more adept in "reading" other people and in genuinely "being present" to them. This does not mean a return to the folksy self-presentation (and especially not to the image) of the much-venerated "country doctor." It means, on the contrary, development of at least a rudimentary knowledge of body language, nonverbal communication, and the ability to figure out what patients are trying to say between the lines. It means, furthermore, trying to get them to say what they really want to say more directly and informatively. The kind of rapport the physician establishes if she cultivates these skills is not just "good PR" (that will lessen the likelihood of a malpractice suit later on, should something go wrong); it is a source of oftentimes decisively important information, the kind that can lead to substantially improved treatment.[46]

Although some safeguards against harmful side effects are *general* —for example, package inserts explaining counterindications such as high blood pressure, old age, or pregnancy—optimal protection requires individually tailored analysis and advice provided by a physician who knows the medical history of the person concerned. The risks involved in experimenting with EBC could be reduced to very acceptable limits by getting physicians to screen new drugs for use by particular clients. Screening would be made all the more feasible by the use of the computerized information networks that are making it easier and easier for physicians and pharmacists to monitor the results of nationwide use of a new drug, or the overall use pattern of a single individual.[47] (Incidentally, being intelligently wary about new EBC products by asking one's physician to carry out a screening process is not the sort of ignominious capitulation to the godlike authority of a physician-priest that Szasz rightly fears. It's just good sense.)

Some observers are worried about what might be called "the ethics of clinical intervention," particularly in regard to behavior therapy.[48] In addition to more or less routine (but by no means trivial) matters such as well-defined criteria for commencing treatment, limiting treatment, keeping records (so as to maintain confidentiality, e.g.), and ensuring informed consent, there is the question of the applicability of what Edward Erwin calls "the basic model" of therapeutic intervention. This model of treatment asserts that "the practice of behavior therapy needs no moral foundation except for the following: It is right (permissible or obligatory) to help people who request help."[49] Erwin rightly argues that this model is unsatisfactory unless its meaning is clarified by a stipulation that whatever is done (or not done) must aim at making the client better-off *in terms of his or her own values.* (This stipulation is derived from the work of Carl Rogers, who comes very close to defining enhanced well-being in terms of greater personal autonomy and strength. Erwin agrees that any therapy that increases the freedom of the client is probably beneficial, but he emphasizes that freedom is certainly not the only personal goal worth attaining.)

It is clearly wrong for the therapist to decieve the client about what a particular process involves (especially if it's aversive) and is intended to achieve. It is obviously wrong for a therapist to use aversive procedures gratuitously in order to gratify sadistic proclivities of his or her own. It is certainly wrong to use patients as guinea pigs without their knowledge or consent, particularly if vital therapy is neglected in order to further research goals. What is less clear, some would say, is the exact status of the client's "right to be treated." The therapist cannot be asked to carry out a procedure he does not believe in or to devise a procedure to produce results she does not endorse. Does she have a *right* to try to dissuade the client from undertaking a desired treatment or from pursuing a desired goal? an *obligation* to do so?

In a healthy therapist-client relationship, she does have a right to endeavor to dissuade and even a right to seek legislation or a court ruling to prohibit some form of treatment she considers illegitimate. What she does *not* have a right to do is to trick the client by pretending to be in agreement and promising to do X but doing Y instead. Harmon L. Smith, the highly regarded medical ethicist from Duke University, is correct in insisting that the principle that must always be a part of the picture is *accountability*: The modifier must always accept a large measure of responsibility for the outcomes that emerge from treatment and must maintain a faithful and morally accountable relationship with the modifiee until treatment has run its course and both parties are released from the contract into which they entered when treatment was begun.[50]

If paternalism is a danger, one of the best defenses against it is a well-informed and confident public whose members may be counted upon to assert their wishes and rights to the management of their own health, experience, and behavior. It should be clear that consumer self-assertion is a third major source of countervailing power against possible misuse of EBC: some protections and stimuli are best provided by government; some, by self-regulation on the part of health care professionals; some, by people in general, who are, after all, finally more able to influence their own destinies than any other single force acting upon them.

But ordinary persons are not in a very good position to make decisions, set goals or choose means (particularly in scientific matters) unless they have adequate knowledge. Thus, consumer education in regard to the opportunities and risks of EBC is of the utmost importance and ought to be a matter of interest and program effort on the part of many institutions in our society, ranging from governments to corporations and labor unions to professional associations to schools and colleges to voluntary associations of all kinds. Only if ordinary citizen-clients know how to discount advertisements, read drug package inserts, and understand FDA ratings of efficacy or limitations on safe use will the work of that agency be optimally effective. Only if average people know what to ask for and about will physicians and pharmacists be fully responsive to client needs and fully responsible in defining their own performance. Only if people know "how bad things are" or how much better they might be, will they be able to influence social policy instead of merely making the best of it.[51]

A final note on this point. As any student of the pharmaceutical industry knows, health care professionals themselves are consumers, and it is said that most of what the average physician knows about drugs comes from what he or she has been told by the "detail men" (salespersons) from the pharmaceutical houses who visit regularly to bring free samples and up-to-date information on the latest miracles produced by their companies.[52] When speaking of consumer education in the field of health care, then, we should not forget Robert Neville's reminder that one of our society's most imperative needs is to "educate physicians not to be bamboozled by greedy advertisements or pathetic pleas from patients wanting attention."[53]

## Promotion of Desirable Products, Processes, and Outcomes

The philosophical principle of distributive justice requires that all economic resources and all technological benefits should be equitably disseminated to all who are entitled to share in these goods. Because this is a topic unto itself, a topic on which innumerable learned tomes have already been written (with but sadly partial and inconclusive results in the "real" world), it cannot be developed here. But it is applicable to EBC and nothing is more important in the ethics of experience and behavior control than a fair distribution of its benefits.

There are two principal ways in which this policy goal can be sought. On the one hand, the legal and administrative mechanisms by means of which most modern industrial societies seek to mitigate extremes of wealth and poverty (such as a progressive tax structure, full employment guidelines, transfer payments to the unemployed and the disadvantaged, etc.) must be strengthened. Ours is not a commonwealth that has ever been attempted to establish thorough-going across-the-board numerical equality of income, and there are some tenable pragmatic reasons for this. But we must do a better job than we have in the past of promoting "fairness of outcomes" instead of an unavailing (and fundamentally hypocritical) "equality of opportunity." And unless we do a better job than we ever have done in satisfying John Rawls's "difference principle" (which declares that inequality in a given society can only be justified if the least advantaged citizens are better off in this society than they would otherwise be), we can hardly claim to be a country that provides meaningful liberty and justice for all.[54]

It may well be that our best hope for distributive justice lies in the quest for "productive justice"—that is, it may well be that the best way to ensure that human need is met on a global scale is by producing a bigger pie, not simply by seeking to slice up the pie we have more equally.[55] This is to say that the best means of promoting full access to the benefits of EBC lies in the area of research. A truly sensible and humane technology assessment process would allocate research funds and brain power to projects designed to yield the most important payoff for the citizenry as a whole, not those that promise maximum profits to the stockholders of particular companies. Thus, one specific tactic worth pursuing is to invest a significant portion of the government's research and development capital in projects of this kind. As for the private sector, its research funds will be more likely to flow in the right directions if the mechanisms described in the previous paragraph have given adequate buying power to even the most disadvantaged members of our society.

## NOTES

1. George Orwell, *1984*, pp. 13-16.
2. Vance Packard, *The People Shapers*, p. 164.

3. Jose Delgado, *Physical Control of the Mind,* p. 193.

4. Frank Ervin, "Biological Intervention Technologies and Social Control," *American Behavioral Scientist,* Vol. 18, No. 5 (May/June 1975), p. 627.

5. *Ibid.*

6. *Ibid.*, p. 634.

7. Nicholas Kittrie, *The Right to be Different,* pp. 3, 41.

8. H. Morris, "Persons and Punishment," *The Monist,* Vol. 52 (October 1968), p. 500. Cited in Alan R. Mabe, "Coerced Therapy, Social Protection and Moral Autonomy," *American Behavioral Scientist,* Vol. 18, No. 5 (May/June 1975), p. 612.

9. Kittrie, *Right,* pp. 43-44.

10. *Ibid.*, p. 44.

11. Elizabeth Dalton and Kim Hopper, "Ethical Issues in Behavior Control," *Man and Medicine,* Vol. II, No. 1 (1976), p. 25.

12. Mabe, "Coerced Therapy," p. 612, quoting H. Morris, "Persons and Punishment," *The Monist,* Vol. 52 (October 1968), p. 500.

13. Ludmilla Thorne, "Inside Russia's Psychiatric Jails," *New York Times Magazine* (June 12, 1977), p. 27.

14. Stanley Milgram, "Behavioral Study of Obedience," *Journal of Abnormal and Social Psychology,* Vol. 67 (1963), pp. 371-378.

15. James Jones, *Bad Blood, passim.* See especially pp. 124-131.

16. Kittrie, *Right,* pp. 386ff., 391.

17. *Ibid.*, p. 393.

18. Langdon Winner, "Autonomous Technology in Humanistic Perspective," an address delivered at the University of Southern California, October 9, 1978. Cf. Winner, *Autonomous Technology,* Chapter 7.

19. Michael Shapiro, "Legislating the Control of Behavior Control," *Southern California Law Review* (February 1974), p. 86.

20. David B. Wexler (1973) "Token and Taboo: Behavior Modification, Token Economies and the Law." *California Law Review,* Vol. 61, No. 1 (January 1973), p. 91.

21. Conversation with Dr. Kenneth Clark, Durham, NC, October 1971. Dr. Clark said that the two largest groups of persons who responded to his appeal for a chemical solution to violence were clergymen (who denounced him) and prisoners, many of whom said they would be grateful for the opportunity to take "antiviolence pills" and equally willing to volunteer for the research necessary to develop such pharmaceutical products.

22. Adam Bedau, "Physiological Interventions to Alter Behavior in a Punitive Environment," *American Behavioral Scientist,* Vol. 18, No. 5, pp. 674, 677.

23. Joseph Neyer, "Individualism and Socialism in Durkheim," in Kurt Wolff [ed.], Emile Durkheim et al: *Essays on Sociology and Philosophy,* p. 34.

24. Shapiro, "Legislating," p. 86.

25. Allan Parachini, "FDA Hit on Arthritis Drug," *Los Angeles Times,* August 31, 1982, Part V, p. 8.

26. American Enterprise Institute, Proposals to Reform Drug Regulation Laws, p. 2.

27. *Ibid.*, p. 39.

28. *Ibid.*, p. 34.

29. *Ibid.*, pp. 34-35.

30. Parachini, "FDA Hit," p. 8.

31. David Richards, *Sex, Drugs, Death, and the Law,* p. 188.

32. *Ibid.*, pp. 166-167.

33. *Ibid.*, p. 178.

34. *Ibid.*, p. 179.

35. *Ibid.*, pp. 179-180.

36. *Ibid.*, p. 184.

37. Robert Neville, "The State's Intervention in Individuals' Drug Use: A Normative Account," p. 9.

38. Richards, *Sex, Drugs,* pp. 167, 168.

39. *Ibid.*, p. 175.

40. *Ibid.*, p. 181.

41. James Bakalar and Lester Grinspoon, "Drug Abuse Policy and Social Attitudes to Risk-Taking," *Hastings Report 13,* 4: 21-22.

42. Thomas Szasz, "The Ethics of Addiction," *American Journal of Psychiatry,* Vol. 128 (1971), pp. 542-543.

43. Bakalar and Grinspoon, "Risk-Taking," p. 18.

44. Gerald Leach, *The Biocrats,* pp. 57, 59.

45. *Ibid.*, p. 59.

46. Comments made at a conference on "The Medical Malpractice Insurance Crisis," University of California at Los Angeles, March 1976.

47. T. Donald Rucker, "Public Policy Considerations in the Use of Psychotherapeutic Drugs," pp. 9-11.

48. Dalton and Hopper, "Ethical Issues," pp. 18ff.

49. Erwin, *Therapy,* p. 173.

50. Harmon L. Smith, "Ethics and Behavior Modification," *Social Responsibility,* Vol. II (1976), pp. 102f.

51. Janice Mall, "About Women: Center Focuses on Prescription Drugs," *Los Angeles Times* (November 22, 1981), Part VI, p. 21.

52. Silverman, Milton and Philip R. Lee, *Pills, Profits and Politics,* pp. 48-80.

53. Neville, "Intervention," pp. 17-18.

54. John Rawls, *A Theory of Justice,* pp. 60-83.

55. Howard Richards, "Productive Justice," in William Aiken and Hugh LaFollette [eds.], *World Hunger and Moral Obligation.* Reprinted in Tom Beauchamp and Norman Bowie [eds.], *Ethical Theory and Business,* pp. 112-119.

# Chapter 7

# A NORMATIVE VIEW OF HUMAN NATURE AND DESTINY

Readers who have followed the argument of the preceding chapters will understand that its fundamental thrust may be summarized as follows:

*(1) All three components of the good life can be increased through EBC.* A great variety of pleasurable sensations and delightful moods can be created artificially, and both physical and emotional pain can be greatly reduced or in some sense alleviated. Our happiness in interpersonal relationships can be augmented by techniques of behavior therapy that iron out many routine difficulties in human interaction and that clear up many of the internal states of mind that cause a given individual to have difficulty in relating smoothly to others. Even fulfillment can be increased by EBC-generated peak experiences, including memorable experiences of transcendence or long-lasting transformation of self-awareness. All of this can occur, furthermore, as one *supplementary* aspect of *balanced* lives that in no sense degenerate into "besotted hedonism."

*(2) Extraordinary goodness is obtainable in two forms:* the extinction of specific behaviors deemed undesirable (i.e., morally un-

worthy) by the person concerned and the inculcation of general behavior patterns and points of view considered morally worthy by the person concerned. The choice to generate these behavioral and attitudinal manifestations of goodness through EBC does not represent a dehumanizing forfeiture of human conscience or consciousness; on the contrary, the need to exercise ethical reflection regarding what behavioral goals to seek is as necessary and as important as ever, and awareness of the need for moral choice and one's accountability in regard to such choice is keener than ever.

(3) *Human capacities can be upgraded in many ways.* This technological capability raises once again the perennial moral question of *ethical rigorism* (or, as it is referred to in Chapter 5, "technological Calvinism"): If productivity for good purposes *can* be substantially increased through EBC, to what extent must one feel *obligated* to use experience and behavior control techniques for this purpose?

Even the reader who *wants* to believe in the benevolence of EBC and who wants to be convinced that its benefits can enrich human life enormously may be aware of lingering doubts. Anything that sounds this good must have a catch to it, right?

Our nagging fear that something must be wrong is in part a healthy sense of caution that we ought to cherish. It will motivate us to be appropriately tough-minded about demanding rigorous tests of safety, strong legal and political safeguards against political abuses, and a staunch unwillingness ever to allow our *use* of EBC to become wholesale *dependence* on it. On the other hand, I believe that our hesitancy is in part unnecessary and woefully misguided—and I believe that this aspect of our hesitancy is rooted in misplaced allegiance to a traditional image of human nature and destiny that we would be wise to reexamine and renounce. Enthralled by an exaggerated reverence for the conventional wisdom concerning the American Dream and character formation, we remain blind to the ambiguities inherent in these cultural ideals and we lack the moral imagination to reshape them in accordance with the new realities of our era.

## THE SIGNIFICANCE
## OF VALUE REFINEMENT

Thus, the final chapter of this book is devoted to a critique of the mistaken value assumptions that might prevent us from taking optimal advantage of the opportunities for a better life afforded by EBC. It is an exercise in *value refinement* that is undertaken in response to a particular set of new technological possibilities, but as such it is an example of the more general cultural evolution that needs to occur in order for us to move smoothly into what might be called the technological humanism of the future.

The task of refining our notions of humanness to make the most of new technological developments is formidable, but it is by no means overwhelming. We are from time to time momentarily disoriented by future shock and we make many mistakes—but we also manage to make many necessary or desirable adjustments rather successfully. Consider, for example, the revisions in our attitudes toward sexual morality and family life and the revisions in our attitudes toward economic activity that have been taking place during the past two or three decades.

To enjoy fully the beneficial possibilities for the liberation of women provided by an improved technology of contraception, we had to revise a number of traditional patriarchal assumptions; that is, we had to get a new vision of the full-fledged humanity of women. Effective contraception made it *possible* for women to transcend "biology as fate," but few women were actually *able* to do so until significant changes in cultural attitudes about "a woman's place" and in the legal status of women transpired.

Something similar is also true in the economic sphere. The environmental damage wrought by heedless technological and economic expansion was caused in part by the Western glorification of productive labor ("the exploitation of the world to the glory of God" in Calvinist thought),[1] and until new cultural attitudes favoring "appropriate technology" in production processes and "voluntary simplicity" in life-styles become more widespread our society will be in serious danger of exceeding the limits to growth.

Similar adjustments in cultural attitudes and expectations regarding artificially increased happiness, goodness, and human capacity ought to be readily attainable. What our culture needs is a revised view of the human potential that neither demands too much nor tolerates too little. We need a cultural ego-ideal that does not pointlessly deprive us of pleasure by demanding impossible standards of achievement or of passive heroism. We need an understanding of ethics that refuses to tolerate unjust or inhumane behavior in the name of counterproductive notions of moral goodness and character development. We need a view of technology that allows us to make optimal use of the blessings it has to offer as well as a view of human nature and destiny that enables us to protect ourselves against its dangers. In ordinary parlance, we need more "looseness" on the part of those who are unnecessarily "uptight" regarding the legitimacy of pleasure as an intrinsically valid element in human experience, and more "solidity"—that is, disciplined goal orientation and moral stamina—on the part of those who are lax in the fulfillment of civic duties and the many other tasks social responsibility imposes on ethically sensitive persons. We can allow a somewhat greater portion of our energies to be absorbed in the direct enjoyment of pleasure (whether naturally or artificially achieved) and in so doing, our work-oriented energies will be recreated for the new productive efforts when we return from the "vacations in Eden" provided by pleasurable experiences. At the same time, we must focus a considerably larger portion of our vitalities on effective attainment of a just and humane society. In all of this, increased capacities of intellect, intuition, and physical well-being will be helpful—and all three of the applications of EBC technology highlighted in this book will be usable and useful.

What we need, above all, is to stop wasting our resources in battles that cannot be won and need not be fought. There is no point in struggling heroically against our elemental desire for pleasure, as if the enjoyment of the flesh and the world were a trick of the devil designed to ensnare our souls. Nor is there any point in being perfectionistic about socially constructive behavior, insisting that it should be the expression of a pure heart and an unambiguous will, not the product of the manipulations of laws, economic incentives, or EBC.

## New Rules

Readers who are skeptical of the likelihood of cultural value change should also be instructed by the findings reported in Daniel Yankelovich's recent book, *New Rules*. Long regarded as one of America's foremost public opinion pollsters, Yankelovich summarizes the results of a decade of research by asserting that people in the United States are moving toward an "ethic of commitment" that is a synthesis of the "ethic of self-denial" characteristic of nineteenth-and early twentieth-century America and of the "ethic of duty to self" characteristic of the 1960s and 1970s.[2]

The data reported by Yankelovich and the interpretation put upon these data are consistent with the thesis advanced in this book pertaining to the changes in cultural values that are likely to occur *and are needed* if we are to take full advantage of the technologies of EBC. *New Rules* demonstrates that value change in America for the past thirty years has followed this path:

(1) Most people continue to cling tenaciously to many traditional values, yet those who do so simultaneously affirm certain new values. People are selective about both retention of the old and adoption of the new; not very many people make a wholesale shift from the old rules to the new.

(2) Those who are initially bewildered or upset by value change typically move from generalized resistance to threatening change to pragmatic experimentation with and appropriation of new values and patterns of conduct that they see working in the lives of children, friends, and people they know (or various segments of the population whom they know about through the mass media).

(3) There is, then, a "both/and" principle operative in the revised equilibrium toward which a majority of citizens move. And that is why Yankelovich predicts the emergence in the 1980s and 1990s of a new ethic of commitment that contains some of the best features of the two preceding ethics.

(4) Yankelovich stresses, finally, the importance of "picking up societal signals" in a population's value shifts. Imagining that one could have *more* made sense in the period of relative affluence we enjoyed in the 1950s and 1960s and the oppressiveness of what Marcuse calls "surplus repressions" (see later in this chapter) was bound to seem both intolerable and unnecessary to many Americans who enjoyed affluence during these years. Thus, the emergence of an aggressively assertive duty-to-self ethic was in part a response to socioeconomic factors that were genuinely new and powerfully felt. Similarly, the retreat from the duty-to-self ethic in the 1970s—the attack upon narcissism and the rise of neoconservatism—constitutes in part an adjustment to new economic and political realities that transmit rather different signals, *as well as* an adjustment to the chastening disappointments and disillusionments of those who went too far in following the duty-to-self ethic as a moral guideline.

I believe that a sensible response to the situation created by the availability of EBC will follow a similar pattern (and, indeed, that it *should* follow such a pattern). People will cautiously, gradually, and selectively use EBC as a means to achieve the goals dictated by their values. Use will gradually become more widespread as the qualms and misgivings of the cautious are dissolved by their observation of the ways in which others successfully generate experience and shape behavior in accordance with their own desires *and* as slightly different values come to be accepted. People will very quickly perceive that it is possible both to enjoy the direct access to pleasure offered by experience control and to live up to the ethical values they affirm through behavior control. In all this, people will be responding to both supply and demand cues: The availability of refined EBC technologies makes a new level of achieved values possible, and the imperatives of an increasingly interdependent world in which crime and injustice are more dangerous than ever before in history make wise use of EBC increasingly necessary.

## The Conventional Wisdom

Many of the ideas about happiness and goodness that arouse anxiety and resistance in the opponents of EBC are actually counterproductive—and this leads to an ironic situation in which the critics are actually defeating their own purposes by clinging to dubious concepts of moral excellence. The irony of the critics' position is all the more poignant because their fears of dehumanization are rooted in a philosophically and morally commendable desire to preserve an element of *nobility* in human existence. I am in full agreement with this desire, but I disagree with their assumption that conventional notions of achievement, success, and honor are valid ingredients in grandeur. These notions are, on the contrary, a part of an erroneous concept of heroism and an exaggerated version of the Challenge/Response motif that hold us back instead of leading us forward to the best kind of human fulfillment. Clutching at these familiar notions of *virtù*, the critics cry, "But how can we indulge ourselves in artificial happiness or lower ourselves to artificial goodness without losing our humanity?" When I look at the prevailing models of fulfillment—and especially when I look at the empirical life patterns resulting from subservience to this model—I ask, "But how human are we now?"

Analysis of the conventional wisdom begins with an exposition of the so-called official model of the attainment of happiness and goodness on which contemporary American culture is based. It continues with an analysis of the "debased" and "pathetic" versions of the official model actually lived out by most people in our country today. Then we take a closer look at the dark side of the prevailing ideal of character development, and at the preoccupation with death, will-to-meaning, and credit/blame that feeds the hubris of Western man. Finally, we offer an alternative perspective on human nature and destiny.

## The Official Model

The official model of the path to fulfillment recommended in the American Dream is depicted in Figure 4. "Happiness" is supposed to be the by-product of a well-ordered pattern of sequential states of being that begins with hard work and proceeds from competence to achievement, which leads in turn to a good reputation. One is expected to have high standards of competence that blossom, with achievement, into a sense of honor that includes a measure of justifiable pride—and if one's abilities and energies are sufficiently great and one's standards sufficiently demanding, one may even aspire (one *ought* to aspire) to a measure of fame. This usually translates into hope for one of the three kinds of immortality traditionally viewed as legitimate objects of hope: the immortality of a heavenly reward, of fame, or of progeny. A rational life plan constructed along these lines is capable of stirring many a youthful heart and the dream that breathes inspiration into the early seasons of a person's life, when he is the eager protégé of some influential Mentor, is often shaped according to this model.[3]

Happiness (especially the felicity of hoped-for immortality) is also viewed to some extent as a reward for goodness, which even before the Reformation but especially since the Renaissance, is dependent in no small measure on hard work, competence, and achievement in one's vocation. Often, however, goodness in a moral or theological sense has been understood to be the outcome of good character and conscience infused by grace that is bestowed upon pious persons of faith whose lives are ordered in obedience to God's revelation in Scripture and Church. The philosophical variant of the official model of goodness emphasizes reason or intuition that yield the knowledge that is tantamount to virtue in creatures who may be born ignorant but are not caught in the web of sin. Goodness, as we have seen in Chapter 4, is the happy fruit of good character formed through the cultivation of virtue in accordance with grace and/or knowledge of the Good.

However, as suggested in Figure 5 and explained in the discussion of "the dark side of character development" that follows, even when

## I   The Official Model

| Hard Work | Competence (based on high standards of excellence) | Achievement (generating a sense of pride and honor) | Good Repute (extending even to immortality through fame, pro- geny, or a life beyond) |
|---|---|---|---|

Payoff: Happiness as a by-product of virtue (exemplified in faithful performance of duty and capable exercise of vocation)

## II   The Pathetic Model

| Exploitation | Subsistence | Respectability (based on—futile—heroic perseverance) |
|---|---|---|

Result: "The hidden injuries of class"

## III   The Debased Model

| Cultivation of Image (based on "figuring the angles" and "knowing the score") | Enjoyment of Status (based on the secondary pleasures of conscpicuous consumption and faddish life-style imitation) |
|---|---|

Result: Malaise of identity diffusion compounded by anxieties resulting from the uncertainties of competition and the limitations of external satisfactions

Figure 4   The American Dream of Social Mobility

the official model works to the genuine satisfaction of the individuals concerned, a number of ethical objections can be posed. Social analysts contend that it robs people of the warmth of community by making them too individualistic and too competitive.[4] Psychologists worry about the one-sidedness of the "objective consciousness" encouraged (even demanded) by bureaucratic industrial life, arguing that it alienates us from the nonrational side of our own being.[5] Historians and ecologists declare that it alienates us from other forms of life and Nature in general by telling us that we can exploit natural resources recklessly for the sake of our own convenience.[6] And social philosophers condemn the inequalities that result from the economic systems of all parts of the urban industrial world.

## The Pathetic Model

The heartrending deficiencies of what I have called the pathetic model are a reflection of the inequalities that coexist along with the burgeoning Gross National Product of the technologically advanced world. The word "exploitation" is appropriate in describing the psychological situation (and in many cases the economic plight) of white and blue collar workers who are led to believe that everyone in our society has a chance to achieve upward mobility to a point of stable security and comfort, but who are in fact doomed by market realities to spend their lives on a treadmill of unremitting toil that has many opportunities for a slip downward but precious few opportunities for a decisive leap upward. Cobb and Sennett's book, *The Hidden Injuries of Class,* is a portrait of working-class people in the Boston area who fit this description. The sample was composed of bright, industrious persons who followed the advice of their admiring teachers and worked hard to obtain the education that would supposedly open the doors of middle-class affluence and status to them. Their adoption of mainstream American values alienated them from their families and neighborhood friends, but did not quite give them the kind of success they had hoped for: Even though they had more education and better jobs than their parents, they found that making payments on their modest suburban house always made it necessary for the principal breadwinner to moonlight or for both partners to be gainfully employed outside the home. Instead of enjoying a feeling of secure satisfaction, they lived in perpetual terror of the next (unpredictable) round of layoffs and the next increase in taxes, inflation, or both. Yet they could not admit that the American Dream that they had bought into was at best misleading for people like themselves. They blamed only *themselves* for the failure of the dream, flagellating themselves with the thought that if they had been a little more diligent, a little more thrifty, or a little bit smarter, they would have made it. The injuries they suffer are self-inflicted; they remain hidden because "seeing the light" would be too painful. (It would force them to admit they had been suckered into buying a badly flawed bill of goods by the disingenuous purveyors of the myth of easy upward mobility.) Most pathetic of all, perhaps, is their wistful envy of those who are slightly above them in education and what we call "cultural privileges": They tend to imagine that those who went to Harvard instead of Worcester Poly have a serene comprehension of economics, politics, art, and life that yields immunity from the bewilderment, rage, and despair in which they are mired.[7]

Theirs is the static heroism of simply holding on, of gritting your teeth and refusing to drop out of a game whose rules you can now see were stacked against you from the beginning. Their fate is similar to that of the pitiful marathon dancers in *They Shoot Horses, Don't They?* who have to keep dragging their exhausted bodies back onto the floor for one more round of aimless movement under the lash of the master of ceremonies' reminder that "you mustn't finish last," and (above all) "you mustn't be a quitter."

In so far as those whose lives fit the pathetic model still have hope, it is likely to be the kind of hope that springs eternal in the heart of a gambler. According to a brilliant article entitled "Status Orientation Among Shipyard Workers," written during World War II, the average blue-collar worker in this country has a "gambler's view of life." Because he has practically no sense of class consciousness, his hope lies not in collective action on the part of all similarly situated workers to develop the countervailing power necessary to improve their lot as a group; instead, he dreams of a fabulous stroke of good fortune that will lift him as an individual out of his dull existence and place him high above his former peers:

> The shipyard worker had no faith in his ability to plod to wealth and idleness. Wealth, he believed, was neither to be earned nor patiently entreated, and it had little to do with talent. Wealth was either ... a product of cunning to which the worker denied his readiness to stoop, or, like a royal flush in poker, it merely came by chance to a few—a few no more deserving then himself....
>
> The triumph which the shipyard worker pictured ... was the triumph of an individual chosen by chance from all the world. Since it implied and accepted the disappointment of the mass of men as a concomitant of the happiness of one, it was, in truth, the triumph of the gambler, whose winnings are inevitably a compound of the losses of many others. [The workers with whom I talked] blandly viewed the phenomena of competition between individuals for social place and the balancing of the success of a few against the failure of the many as the natural elements of a cruel and bloody universe.[8]

## The Debased Model

Life in accordance with the pathetic model is anything but an inspiring portrait of human fulfillment. Unfortunately, the same has to be said of life in accordance with the debased model—although the people who fall into this category may have more money, their involvement in what French sociologist Alain Touraine calls "dependent participation" is almost as inhumane.[9] Many of those who would tell an opinion pollster that they were very satisfied with the level of happiness and goodness they have reached are conning themselves. (After all, how many of us would in fact admit to a stranger with a clipboard that we are unhappy and wicked?)

The analysis of the debased model suggested some thirty years ago in David Riesman's The Lonely Crowd is still sadly accurate. The other-directed character type is apt to be an inside dopester instead of a person of clear moral insight, and he all too often substitutes "figuring the angles" or "knowing the score"—in short, "playing ball"—for hard work and competence.[10] In Erik Erikson's terms, he loses vital identity (and the satisfaction of a clear inner sense of identity) in a succession of role-performances from which there is no "psychosocial moratorium" to allow soul-searching questions to be raised about who he really is and what he really wants to be.[11] So instead of genuine achievement or a solid reputation based thereon, he acquires nothing more than the appearance of success, which leaves him grasping at the straws of image and status instead of having a secure hold on standards and a sense of honor he can stand by proudly. Because image and status are frequently fragile in the extreme, they can sometimes be grasped only through conspicuous consumption or the kinds of "secondary pleasures" that are pursued only because you think other people will think you are happy, not because you derive authentic personal satisfaction from obtaining them. And because the triumphs attained through competition offer satisfactions less stable than achievements based on honorable competence, the creature of the debased model is far less secure than he was led to expect he would be and his anxieties may be compounded by angry disillusionment when he meditates on his fate.

The pejorative adjectives usually employed to criticize successful followers of the debased model are "materialistic" or "hedonistic." But these words fail to acknowledge that the gratifications procured by people of this kind are all too often derivative from the endorsement of others who are supposed to want such gratifications for themselves and who, therefore, will be envious of those who have acquired them. One of the penalties of other-direction, then, is what psychologist Ernest Schachtel calls "the Midas syndrome." Increasingly, says Schachtel, affluent people in high consumption societies tend to experience everything in terms of cliches, cliches implanted in their minds by pictures they have seen in advertisements or stories they have become acquainted with through popular culture:

> There are people who experience a party, a visit to the movies, a play, a concert, a trip in the very words in which they are going to tell their friends about it; in fact, quite often, they anticipate such an experience in these words. The experience is predigested, as it were, even before they have tasted it. Like the unfortunate Midas, whose touch turned everything into gold so that he could not eat or drink, these people turn the potential nourishment of the anticipated experience into the sterile currency of the conventional phrase with which later they will report to their friends the "exciting time" they have had.... But while Midas suffered tortures of starvation, the people under whose eyes every experience turns into a barren cliche do not know that they starve. Their starvation manifests itself merely in boredom or in restless activity and incapacity for any real enjoyment.[12]

No wonder W. H. Auden satirized "our bland picnic on the heath/ Of the agreeable, where we bask,/Agreed on what we will not ask," and that his eloquent commentary on "September 1, 1939" describes the heirs of European civilization as:

> Children afraid of the night
> Who have never been happy or good.

No wonder, too, that the same poem links the blight of totalitarianism and the tragedy of war to unhappiness and moral incompetence—for it is no accident that attempting to follow the official model in our culture so often results in the injustices of the pathetic model or the futility of the debased model. We are less happy than we might be and less good than we ought to be, and can be, because the official model is gravely flawed.

The fundamental flaw is Western man's passion for grandeur; more precisely, it is a pretentious definition of grandeur that misguides our quest for happiness and corrupts our efforts to be good. A false understanding of happiness makes us pursue it by attempting to dominate our fellow human beings and glory over them. That's why we tend to scorn the elemental pleasures of sensory experience and of common amiability and to scorn ourselves if we enjoy these simple

goods very much. That's why we demand an ever larger accumulation of the secondary satisfactions of material possessions and status
symbols. As Veblen saw, the point of conspicuous consumption and
conspicuous leisure is to demonstrate one's *power* and thus to
display a grandeur that seems to lift one above the common herd and
its less exalted lot in life.[13]

Needless to say, defenders of the conventional wisdom are not
oblivious to the shortcomings of our society, and they would concede that the official model often deteriorates into a pathetic or a debased caricature of itself. They are not unaware of the deplorable
consequences for millions of their fellow citizens; indeed, some of
the staunchest advocates of the conventions are those who suffer
most because of them. But they are afraid to surrender their faith in
the official model because they are terrified at the thought of ques-
tioning the established verities regarding character formation. If it
could be shown convincingly that their ideal of character and the
process by means of which it is cultivated are mistaken, their resistance might lessen decisively. If they could be persuaded that the
ironically sado-masochistic elements of the official doctrine of moral
education typically produce consequences that are the exact opposite of what is intended, they might be more willing to accept the
alternative perspective advocated in this book and the judicious use
of EBC called for in that perspective.

## THE DARK SIDE
## OF CHARACTER DEVELOPMENT

The case for the claim that traditional notions about moral education are counterproductive (even sadomasochistic) is founded on
three main lines of argument: Berger and Luckmann's concept of
alienation, the Freudian view of the conflict between id and superego, and the notion of the authoritarian personality elaborated by a
number of philosophers and social scientists during the past half-
century. Each of these arguments is highly debatable, of course, but
insofar as each contains a significant measure of truth, the implications are sobering (see Figure 5).

What actually happens when moral ideals are internalized? What
actually happens when, in the words of moralists from Aristotle to
Kant and Durkheim, a person tried to define true freedom as
acknowledgment of his or her duties and faithful performance of

HUMAN NATURE

|   | I   The Official Model | |
|---|---|---|
| A. Religious version:<br>Revelation | Faith, piety | Grace |
| B. Philosophical version:<br>Reason<br>(or "Moral Sentiment") | Knowledge of the Good,<br>dialectic | Conscience,<br>character,<br>virtue |

II   The Dark Side

| Conformity-oriented<br>socialization process<br>(in which "socially<br>constructed reality"<br>is legitimated and<br>internalized) | Alienation (from one's<br>emotional/feeling side<br>and one's true self) | Antagonistic cooperation,<br>repressed hostility,<br>social inequality |
|---|---|---|

Result: An ironic failure to promote either internal well-being or consistently benevolent external behavior (as the frustrations and sense of self-betrayal of the
alienated person often manifest themselves in covert sabotage—for example,
bureaucratic legalism or "lip service" morality, harassment of underlings,
*Schadenfreude,* scapegoating, etc.)

Figure 5   The Traditional Concept of Character Formation

them? Granted that internalization of this concept of virtue can be viewed as the crowning humanization of an individual, the process through which she develops that noble understanding of the good and a steady disposition to do the good, does it not also have a darker side?

The fact is, the process can be viewed as crippling instead of humanizing. Moreover (following Berger and Luckmann), as the cosmized objectivations—that is, the cardinal beliefs—of traditional theology and philosophy have increasingly lost their authority in recent decades, the traditional model of character development has become more and more problematic. One might even go so far as to contend that continuing reliance on a theory of moral education that has become increasingly unrealistic, inapplicable, and in these ways *phony* is a perfect illustration of what sociologists call "patterned evasion." Why? Because everyone continues to pay lip service to a norm (in this case, a socialization process that is supposed to be viewed as "normal" and proper) that is consistently evaded and/or contradicted in actual experience and practice. Even those who are (in secret, behind the scenes) most contemptuous of the norm often pay tribute to it by continuing to offer symbolic recognition of its validity.[14]

(1) According to Berger and Luckmann's thesis concerning the social construction of reality, the traditional approach to character formation leads inevitably to alienation.[15] Unfortunately, there is a curious irony surrounding use of this term—for in common parlance, to be "alienated" is to be "out of tune" with society and its conventional wisdom, its customary requirements and its prevailing assumptions. The alienated person, in this view, is the one who raises impudent questions about why things are the way they are, the one who refuses to "fit in," the angry rebel, the defiant nonconformist, the sulking deviant. Accordingly, the perfect example of alienation in contemporary American society is the inquisitive college student who is smart enough to perceive the problematic character of the legitimations advanced to justify existing institutions, roles, and rules and who is also free enough to challenge all this. "Growing up" is supposed to override his alienation as he becomes wise enough to understand the rightness (or least the benevolent authority) of the established way of doing things, and to accept a recognized place in society.

But Berger and Luckmann use the word "alienation" in a different (and directly contrary) sense. They apply it to any individual who accepts socially constructed reality as the way things *really* are and *have* (or *ought*) to be and who therefore fits in all too smoothly and unquestioningly. Such a person is alienated from his or her own true being—for to be human, in their book, is to be aware of the radical freedom of the self to define and shape reality according to one's own unique perceptions and value-commitments. The dependence of the self on society is acknowledged and indeed society's "mothering" of the individual is interpreted as in part an absolutely necessary and in many ways benign reality of life. However, like the relationship with one's actual mother, it is also seen as partly a bondage that must be understood, challenged, and outgrown if one is to attain maturity as an independent self.

(2) The Freudian theory of id-superego conflict parallels this concept of alienation and carries it a step further by observing that the tension between Nature and Civilization is irremediably painful.[16] Whatever the defects of Freud's treatment of the Oedipal situation, it has the merit of dramatizing the cruel conflict within every social unit and within every individual between "father" and "son"—that is, the

conflict between a growing individual self and the enforcers of social reality. Every maturing person has to learn that his desires for pleasure and power must be curbed internally because they will certainly be curbed by those who control access to these goods; every young person has to learn to give some kind of concession to the demand of the elders of the tribe for delay, deference, and submission to their will as a precondition for access. The concept of the superego is an accurate reminder that the ultimate form of "parental" authority (whether the "parent" in question is one's father, mother, boss, priest, or God) is internalized authority, the little policeman within who forbids and punishes even more relentlessly and, sometimes, more ferociously and destructively than any external authority would dare to do.

The more subtle the pressures to conform in attitude as well as in behavior, the more tyrannical the reign of the inner cop. A study of contrasting styles of child rearing in different socioeconomic classes makes this point by highlighting "threatened withdrawal of love" as the key weapon in middle-class parenting:

> Middle-class parents have made "love" of supreme importance in their relation to the child, theirs for him and his for them, partly because of the love-complex of our time, ... and partly as a compensation for the many sacrifices they have made.... Now, the more ambivalent the parents are toward the child, the more seriously is the "trouble" he causes them interpreted. He should not act [badly] because of the sacrifices they have made in his behalf, and the least he can do is show his gratitude by "loving" them in turn, i.e., keeping out of trouble. When the trouble inevitably occurs, *the most effective punishment imaginable is the threat to withdraw their love from him....* To the extent that a child's personality has been absorbed, he will be thrown into a panic by this sort of treatment, and develop guilt-feelings to help prevent himself from getting into further trouble.[17]

As a child who has been handled in this manner grows into adolescence, even subtle expressions of parental disapproval operate directly on his emerging sense of self to threaten his sense of self-respect. The "personality absorption" that takes place as a result of the threatened withdrawal of love tends to make the young person "feel small, insignificant, and unworthy." The destructiveness of this kind of manipulation of the emotions is appalling, and its effects are carried into adult life in the terrible conflict between guilt and rage, between submission and assertiveness, that many people never cease to experience.

As Barrington Moore observed many years ago in an essay entitled "Reflections on the Future of the Family" (long before the ambiguities of the nuclear family were as fully acknowledged as they are today), nothing is more infuriating than a social system that requires its victims to appear to be (and, yes, genuinely to *feel themselves to be*) grateful to parents or other authority figures for the oppression visited upon them.[18]

(3) One of the sadistic aspects of the socialization process is already evident in the description of middle-class child rearing just cited. But the best analysis of the sadistic results of the inculcation of an "authoritarian conscience" is provided by Erich Fromm in his highly regarded *Man for Himself*. Fromm maintains that moral education based on the internalization of authority that is experienced as alien and punitive cannot be very effective in producing consistently good behavior. If the moral requirements of one's conscience are experienced as commands made by an unduly restrictive outside authority and if these commands derive their force from the explicit or implicit threat of punishment, they will be powerfully resented even when they are obeyed. Over a period of time, this "antagonistic cooperation" with the resented authority will result in a large accumulation of frustration and repressed hostility that must find outlets, sooner or later, in one way or another, consciously or subconsciously. Thus, Fromm offers the concept of the authoritarian conscience as an explanation for the high-strung nervousness, the pent-up anxiety and fury, and the sometimes overt, sometimes subtle, cruelty of legalistically "good" persons.[19]

The thesis is obviously complex and the inferences drawn from it by Fromm are not self-evident. One's position in regard to these matters will depend in large measure on one's opinion concerning the rules enforced by an authoritarian conscience and on the degree to which one accepts Fromm's belief in the ability of the presumably nonrepressive "humanistic conscience" he favors to guide people to attitudes and behavior that are more ethically satisfactory than legalistic prescriptions and proscriptions. If one believes, for example, that humans are creatures whose id and ego normally erupt in such a disorderly will-to-pleasure and will-to-power that only a harsh internal policeman can prevent moral chaos, then the discomfiture of individuals with an authoritarian conscience will seem a regrettable, but necessary, price to pay. If, on the other hand, one is convinced that a nonrepressive conscience can inspire its possessor to behave ethically because doing so is "really what she wants to do" in light of a freely affirmed moral vision of the kind of human being she really wants to be, then one will probably believe also that people will be *better* as well as happier (and better in part *because* they are happier) with a humanistic conscience. In this case, the conventional approach to moral education will be seen as being in need of drastic alterations, and the unintended sadism of this approach may be counted as a decisive reason for rejection of it.

So the question must be asked, "How human are we now?" Persons of sound mind and goodwill may disagree in the verdict they render on this point, but unless one totally discounts the line of reasoning advanced here, enough has been said to call into serious question the simplistic point of view that puts the *entire* burden of proof on advocates of "artificial" happiness and goodness through EBC, as if the "naturalness" of present methods of socializing the membership of the tribe were a guarantee of its perpetual all-sufficiency.

The irony of single-minded faith in the traditional approach is striking. Apologists for this way of producing goodness are often very much aware that it comes at a high price. But instead of seeing this fact as a drawback—and this is the masochistic element in the conventional model, they *glory* in it. For they believe that the nobility of moral goodness shines all the brighter if it requires heroic self-extension (that is, if it puts the doer of good *on the rack*). But if the quantity and the quality of the "goodness" generated by all that painful self-denial and superhuman endeavor is not beyond dispute, then what's it all for? and who needs it? Doubts of this kind are the seeds of further rage, but also of renewed self-discipline, more self-righteous indignation, and/or subtle mistreatment of others ... and ever deeper involvement in the maelstrom of the authoritarian conscience.

To recapitulate, I contend that the traditional process of character development is too counterproductive to be praised as crucial to the enoblement of humankind. On the contrary, I submit that it is in practice a sadomasochistic menace to individual and societal well-being. To accept society's definition of the world and of life is to incur alienation; to subject oneself to all of the restraints imposed in the

name of civilization is to be oppressed—and the all too common outcome of the usual socialization process is aggression against others as
a fruit of alienation and repression.[20]

Fortunately, the dark side of character formation is not something
we have to learn to live with indefinitely. Just as Yankelovich's research encourages us to believe that value refinement on a large
scale is always possible in contemporary society, even so it is possible
to identify the flaws in the socialization process and correct some of
them. An optimistic assessment of this dimension of the problem
rests mainly on Herbert Marcuse's concept of surplus-repression and
Peter Berger's view of dealienation.

Freud's gloomy conclusions about the inevitability of the conflict
between Civilization and Nature have been substantially qualified in
revisionist Freudian thought, notably in Marcuse's doctrine of
surplus-repression. In *Civilization and its Discontents,* Freud argued
that the conflict between our instinctual drives toward self-gratifica-
tion and society's need for self-restraint and order was a fact of life (a
manifestation of the "reality principle") that simply could not be
avoided or resolved. The human animal was doomed to ineluctable
frustration: Civilization *has* to oppress and repress the limitless will-
to-power and will-to-pleasure of individual citizens.

Marcuse denies this assumption. He maintains that many of the repressions that made life unpalatable in the past are no longer necessary. The taboos on sexual activity that were thought to be essential
in order to insure that conception would only occur within patriarchal marriages are now superfluous; men and women alike can
enjoy the pleasures of the flesh without regard to procreation. If
repression of sexual self-expression endures, it is because certain
individuals or groups *want* to enforce this repression, not because it
is essential for the health of society. By the same token, it is no longer
necessary for every member of the tribe to contribute his or her labor
to the production of the wherewithal for survival—and if the rule that
"those who do not work shall not eat" continues to be enforced, that
is because somebody *wants* it to be this way (and in some sense
*profits* from keeping it this way), not because it has to be thus.[21]

Peter Berger offers the antidote to his own bleak picture of socially
constructed reality in his concept of dealienation. The alienated self
achieves health and maturity by adopting a personal identity from the
perspective of which the internalized objectivations furnished by
society are screened and evaluated. This entails a self-conscious pro-

cess of enlightenment that enables one to develop, assert, and give expression to a self that is aware both of the blessings bestowed by society and of the limits beyond which its claims cannot legitimately be pressed. Berger describes the import of dealienation in a lovely simile that likens each human being to a puppet whose limbs are moved by strings that are attached to levers operating in the semi-darkness above its head. Homo sapiens, he declares, is a being who can look up and see where the strings are coming from and what kind of lever is causing various movements—and when we do this, we are capable of either accepting and cooperating with the motions initiated by the strings or, on the other hand, cutting the strings and initiating other movements of our own choosing.[22]

The implications of this analysis of the human situation are simple in principle, yet complex and far-reaching in detail. The basic thrust of the concept is simply an assertion of a core of human independence, freedom, and responsibility underneath all the layers of sociological and psychological conditioning piled on by the socialization process. In regard to moral education, it suggests that there will inevitably be—and *ought* to be—a tension between the moral demands of a society and the self-definition of an awake, aware, alive individual. She understands why the strings have been attached and the purpose of their attempt to move her limbs (or prevent their moving) in certain ways at various times; moreover, she may decide to leave most of the strings intact (or even to retie some of them after having cut them). But it will be *her* decision whether to leave intact, cut, or retie: She claims this as a basic right (an inalienable right that she cannot give away and no society can justly deprive her of) and she accepts full responsibility for the tensions and difficulties her decisions may cause.

In sum, my argument about the traditional character development process is this. There is a great deal of evidence to suggest that society's attempt to produce civilized behavior by means of an internalized policeman have proved to be woefully unreliable and counterproductive. This process creates inner conflict and self-estrangement, a form of unhappiness that is all the more onerous because it cannot be openly acknowledged: One must pretend to be devoted to moral guidelines one is inwardly resentful of and in rebellion against. Furthermore, it doesn't often guarantee the kind of benevolence or beneficence toward others it is supposed to; indeed, it leads to antagonistic cooperation, displaced hostility, and aggression.

Thus, the same question posed at the beginning of this chapter must be asked again in a slightly different form. Given the unsatisfactoriness of conventional modes of attaining happiness and goodness—and given the fact that alternatives are available (both in the form of value-refinement concepts such as dealienation and surplus-repression and in the form of EBC)—why is resistance to these alternatives so adamant in some circles? Exactly what form or depth of "dehumanization" is feared?

The answer to that question must be sought in a careful investigation of the proposition that human beings are destined for heroic *grandeur*. Exponents of the traditional humanistic view of man cannot abide the prospect of giving up certain illusions about human nature and destiny: They would rather pay the price of continuing to live with these illusions than accept what they see as an ignoble conception of human being. They would rather continue to suffer the disadvantages of these illusions than accept a more modest conception of humanity and the benefits that can be obtained through EBC. So it is the notion of grandeur that we must now examine, giving particular attention to the emphasis on immortality and moral credit that are a function of its preoccupation with humankind's allegedly universal fear of death and meaninglessness.

## PREOCCUPATION WITH DEATH AND MEANINGLESSNESS

The most troublesome tenet of Western thought concerning human nature and destiny is one the modern secular mind might well imagine it has no more use for; namely, a yearning for immortality (or, in a broader sense, preoccupation with death and will-to-meaning). For the absolutely fundamental desire of many people in our culture is the desire for meaning in terms of human significance. According to anthropologist Clifford Geertz, the will-to-meaning is biologically rooted: The larger brain of the human animal requires satisfaction of certain higher order needs for psychological order that arise from the brain's capacity for symbolizing activity. Thus, philosophy, religion, and art are not *optional* enterprises; they are as necessary for the mental health of the species as agriculture is for physical health.

In harmony with this assumption, Peter Berger defines religion as "man's audacious attempt to make the whole universe humanly significant."[23] Despite an element of hyperbole, that is a statement that illuminates a great deal of the pretentious imagery of both religious and philosophical thought on the nature and destiny of humankind. The paired concepts of sin/virtue are designed to make human beings feel that their moral failings are a matter of cosmic importance: *God Himself* pays attention and metes out weighty rewards or punishments befitting the excellence or depravity revealed in moral action. Attitudes and rituals surrounding death reflect a desire to believe that its implacable victory over life cannot make a mockery of all our efforts, sufferings, and dreams: Our frailty and grief are pitied and will be compensated for somewhere, sometime, in some sense, by the power of Something or Somebody in whose eyes we may be judged worthy. Even if this compensation is nothing more than the pale comfort to be found in fame, progeny, or the elemental fact that human beings are aware that they are going to die, a consolation of sorts is provided. In these ways, and in so many others, people seem to prefer the pain of guilt and the risk of unending torment to the abyss of meaninglessness. In this sense it may be true that our most formidable terror is fear of chaos and that the primordial task of religion, art, and philosophy is to create ordered perceptions, interpretations, and symbolic experiences that deliver us from it.

A fascinating debate between two anthropologists is very instructive on this point—namely, the debate between Malinowski and Radcliffe-Brown concerning the relation between certain magical or religious ceremonies and the metaphysical beliefs associated with them. The former held (along with most functional analysts of religion) that the belief system of a religion expresses the psychological and social needs of a collectivity and that the rituals of religion are designed to give reassurance in response to the anxiety aroused by uncertainty regarding the satisfaction of these needs.[24] The latter contended that

> for certain rites it would be easy to maintain with equal plausibility an exactly contrary theory, namely, that if it were not for the existence of the rite and the beliefs associated with it the individual would feel no anxiety, and that the psychological effect of the rite is to create in him a sense of insecurity or danger....

Thus, while one anthropological theory is that magic and religion give men confidence, comfort and a sense of security, it could equally well be argued that they give men fears and anxieties from which they would otherwise be free.[25]

The issue at stake here pertains to the "naturalness" of religion and the presumed cosmic bewilderment and loneliness that religion claims to heal. If Radcliffe-Brown is right, religion is "necessary" only in the sense that its potential ability to heal certain wounds, comfort certain sorrows, and meet certain needs may come in handy after religion itself has already generated or intensified (and, in many cases, raised to the status of a psycho-cultural problem) these same wounds, sorrows, and needs. From this point of view, the Challenge/ Response motif exudes a marvelous aroma of nobility—but its claim to reverence is somewhat dubious, for it may also cause a waste of energy that might have been used directly to solve avoidable prob- lems in ordinary life (or at least to cope with them more efficaciously).

From this point of view, what appears to be masochism may be a not entirely pointless choice. The choice in favor of cosmic dignity may be worth its utilitarian price, for it yields a gratifying answer to the thousand natural shocks that flesh is heir to. To be noticed, and indeed to see oneself as worthy of notice, is a psychic good that may justify any price it exacts in emotional and spiritual anguish. The autobiographical hero of Arthur Miller's *After the Fall* doubtless speaks for many members of the species when he declares that the most intolerable thought of all is the suspicion that there is no Final Judgment at the end of life, or any final judge to tally up the balance sheet of all our strivings and all our sorrows. The unspoken fear may be that there is no chance, after all, to win approval for all the pains we bear and all the pains we take, no mama to take us to her bosom and tell us we ran a good race and she's proud of us, and no papa to put his hand on our shoulder and say, "Well done, thou good and faithful servant."

## AN ALTERNATIVE VIEW

The analysis of Western man's dread of insignificance in Chapter 5 is pertinent in this connection. To the extent that one gives assent to Ernest Becker's thesis concerning the perils of hubris, preoccupation with the will-to-meaning and its insistence on credit and blame is a lamentable excess—a *dangerous* excess that we would be smart to avoid. Yet, Becker's thesis is itself extreme and (as argued in Chapter 5) it is certainly possible to avoid cosmic pretentiousness without abandoning the dream of progress in human affairs and diligent exertions to promote it.

Following this line of argument, we can certainly put to rest the fears of those for whom the most offensive aspect of EBC is its shift of the focus of moral analysis from character to consequences and, therefore, its tendency to undermine the emphasis on credit and blame that has always pervaded our culture's approach to morality. If what counts most is what happens rather than how or what makes it happen, then character formation through instilling reverence for the Challenge/Response motif is not necessarily the crux of ethical behavior and the credit or blame associated with right action, conscience and virtue become less important than the calculation of the means that will produce the desired consequences most effectively. Thus, rationality appears to replace morality, and the heroic struggles for growth that have heretofore been seen as evidence of praiseworthy spiritual stature may now be viewed as unnecessary, ineffective, and undeserving of praise. The misery of man may be diminished—but what will become of the possibilities for grandeur?

Fear not. There is still plenty of opportunity for grandeur, for one can reject the excesses of the prevailing model of character development without casting aside altogether a refined ideal of heroic virtue. One can avoid the silly posturing of "dreaming the impossible dream" without forfeiting one's chances to play the part of Prometheus or Sisyphus.

A good point of entry in elaborating this argument may be found in the world of sports. There is certainly nothing inherently evil in competitive sports, even contact sports (provided the spirit of the rules is enforced by coaches as well as the letter of the rules by referees). George Sauer, explaining his decision to retire from professional football at the height of his career as star flanker on a team that had just won the Super Bowl, summarizes his thinking on this matter in the following interview with Jake Scott:

> SCOTT: Looking back on your years in sport, can you think of a particular occasion where sport existed as you believe it ought to exist, even if just for a fleeting moment?

SAUER: I probably could think of more, but one of the outstanding ones in my mind is an incident that happened between Butch Byrd of Buffalo and myself in a game we played in Shea Stadium in 1969. The previous years, 1966, 1967 and 1968, I had pretty much what we call "owned" Butch. Even though he was always known as a hard-nosed player, I think he had a lot of respect for me. He was the kind of guy who wouldn't mind trying to intimidate you by occasionally giving you a cheap shot. Still, from mutual respect, we had built rapport, even an affection for each other that carried off the field as well as on. In 1969 he changed his style of playing me and he shut me out for the first game of the 1969 season. In the second game he shut me out for the first half, but in the third quarter I caught a long pass over his head and he tackled me from behind. Given my speed, anybody could have. We rolled over, and as we started to get up, he looked at me and stuck out his hand. There is no way really to explain it. We just shook hands right there in the middle of the field. It was a very warm, human moment, and I think the story bears witness to the fact that opponents can get along as human beings, because once Butch got over the stage of trying to intimidate me and really concentrated on working on me, he was able to cover me more effectively. His excellence grew with respect for my humanity. That one moment, which no one else probably understood, to me that was one of my most fulfilling experiences in football.[26]

The salient points in Sauer's testimony are these: First, fierce competition is not incompatible with the best kind of comradeship between competitors. If you really understand that the point of competitive sports is to help each participant learn how to "drag the best out of him/herself," then you will respect your opponent's determination to beat you and you will admire the strength and ingenuity displayed in trying to do so. Thus, you will forge with him a bond of mutual appreciation—and, with a larger group of competitors and teammates, a *community* of respect for one another's *virtù*—that is surely one of the most rewarding experiences anyone can have in life. Second, all of this can be corrupted by emphasis on *winning* or by putting a premium on entertainment that compromises true excellence in performance by subordinating it to the demands of "show biz."

One can see an analogy, I believe, between this commentary on the potential value of sports and the enduring worth of the Western view of human nature and destiny when the corrupting aspects of that view have been stripped away. The remainder of this chapter is devoted to an exposition of a "purified" version of our culture's conception of essential humanity and to some final comments on the relation between EBC and this normative view of human nature and destiny.

## Cosmic Heroism and Technological Humanism

The psychological and social pressures that are an inevitable part of civilized existence cannot be expected to disappear. But certain kinds of EBC are capable of easing the burden significantly by providing a way to elicit good behaviors from ourselves without the loss of psychic energy entailed in struggle with an inner policeman whom we resent and want to elude. In those areas of behavior where one decides that he genuinely affirms what the superego decrees (in order to be the kind of person he wants to be), he can *do* it instead of undergoing the demoralization of continually saying he wants to but never doing so. And those who follow this path can enjoy an abundance of pleasure, happiness, and fulfillment that will be more satisfying than the fruits afforded by the prevailing model of human striving.

What we need in addition to the technologies of EBC is a rather different concept of human nature and destiny. It is a concept that might well be elaborated along the lines indicated in Figure 6. It contrasts the troublesome elements of the traditional view of the good life with a slightly different view that could serve as a basis for the technological humanism of the twenty-first century.

## The Old View

The picture given so far of the traditional view may be summed up under three main categories: the rational life-plan, "immortality" and the will-to-meaning. Included in the rational life plan are competence, achievement, success, honor, and (however modestly conceived, on the neighborhood level, or the professional reference group level, or the institutional level) a measure of fame. Fame, of course, is a life goal that could be considered as an aspect of immortality—but whether it is or not, the crucial point at stake is that of *wanting to be remembered* and remembered because of what one has *done* to reflect *credit* upon oneself.

Being famous, or just being remembered (long enough, by the right people), is a kind of immortality and many outstanding people have wanted this type of historical flattery very much indeed. Others —notably Kant—have insisted that virtue requires being remembered and rewarded by God with transhistorical immortality and this wish is a part of the popular mentality. Common folk have often been satisfied with the kind of immortality afforded by progeny or by the continued flourishing of the tribe or the nation. Whatever form it takes, one of the deepest longings of the human animal seems to be a longing for some degree of *permanence* and some kind of *reward*, which can be construed as triumph over death and sin.

Permanence, reward, and triumph—these are the concerns of a mentality characterized by a strong will-to-meaning. And of the three great anxieties postulated by Tillich in his widely acclaimed *The Courage to Be*, it is probably the anxiety of meaninglessness that bothers most people even more than the anxieties occasioned by guilt and death. A desire for meaning, a sense of pattern and coherence that can make even the heaviest burden or the deepest sorrows bearable—that may be, after all, the ultimate *human* characteristic ... or the ultimate idolatry.

In any case, let me now oppose to these attributes of the traditional Western view of man (on the left side of the diagram in Figure 6) a different set of attributes for a new and refined view of human nature and destiny.

## A New Vision

There is nothing wrong with thinking about the developing course of one's life and having a sense of direction about it. But the concept of the "rational life plan" connotes a high degree of rigidity. It might be better to speak of a reflective orientation with certain differences in its particulars, one of which is that it is more flexible and more whole than a *rational* life plan. Pursuing this direction calls for the development of competence and productivity. But the concern for competence and productivity is not focused, in this case, on achievement for the sake of pride or honor and it certainly isn't focused on "success" according to the usual sense of that word in contemporary America. It is focused instead on a concern to make a *contribution* to the ongoing experience of the human family over the generations. *Integrity* in using one's competence to contribute is what matters, not

| The Old View | A New Vision |
|---|---|
| 1. Rational life plan<br>—competence<br>—achievement<br>—"success"<br>—honor<br>—fame | 1'. A direction (a steady, yet somewhat flexible, orientation to life)<br>—competence<br>—productivity<br>—contribution to life<br>—integrity |
| 2. Immortality<br>—progeny<br>—heavenly reward | 2'. Solidarity with the human family and Nature<br>—"enlightened self-interest" (in the sense of "integrity as its own reward") |
| 3. Will-to-meaning<br>—certainty<br>—vindication | 3'. Playful self-consciousness<br>—life view, not worldview (much less a *Totalweltanschauung)*<br>—self-certifying value-commitment |

Figure 6   A Normative View of Cosmic Heroism for the Age of Technological Humanism

external recognition, much less fame. If there is such a thing as the soul of the individual, a *daimon*, a unique genius, an inbuilt *entelechy* that is somehow given in one's unique being and meant to be cherished, cultivated, and brought to flower, thinking of it in terms of integrity is much better than thinking of it in terms of success, pride, and honor that all too readily come to be translated into selfish, self-indulgent, and even callous or cruel behavior.[27]

Inner awareness of having made a contribution, or of having endeavored to do so with integrity, is more desirable as an ideal than preoccupation with immortality. If it means anything at all valid to say that virtue is its own reward, this is what it ought to mean: Integrity is intrinsically rewarding, and without it no amount of external rewards (including fame) can bring real satisfaction.[28] Moreover, there are two very important corollaries of this point:

(1) Goods do not have to be eternal in order to be good. The demand for perpetuity is an expression of the excessive atomistic individuality characteristic of Western thought since Locke, Adam Smith, and Rousseau. A richer sense of human solidarity over time and of the fact that one is never really an autonomous self, but always a self-in-society, would ease the anxiety of death and expose the irrelevance of personal immortality, whether in an afterlife, through fame, or through children. In doing so, it might deliver us from some of the horrors wrought by those who seek extension of their lives through

the adulation of the crowd or through emulation by a son or a daughter.

(2) Thinking of one's contribution and integrity as a matter of enlightened self-interest is both more dignified and less dangerous than thinking of these life goals as moral duties performed in the hope of reward. Focusing attention on the hoped-for reward is apt to lead to self-righteousness or self-pity (or both)—and these traits are apt to be counter-productive.

Perhaps the best way to summarize this brief on behalf of integrity as its own reward is likewise the best way to suggest the sort of flexibility needed in our understanding of the will-to-meaning. Self-consciousness about the unique worth of one's own being is wholesome if it manifests itself as a sense of being a part of Nature rather than as an obsessively individualistic ego-awareness, and the interpretation of life experience as a sense of the whole (the wholeness of one's life, over the whole of its course) is one of the richest experiences life can give us. But this is very different from an insistence that everything (absolutely everything) must fit into place, without error or mystery. Everyone needs a life view, but this is much more modest and more realistic than a worldview, especially a *Totalweltanschauung*, which demands immortality or certainty as a guarantee of the payoff of virtue or as a solace for failure, defeat, deprivation, or misunderstanding.[29] We can empathize with those who feel that the lack of a final Judge or a Final Judgment is a final cosmic insult, but we can also smile at such self-preoccupation and recognize its folly. We can be joyously playful without being frivolous, and it is possible to be seriously committed to significant projects of benefit to humankind without being deadly serious about their success or the credit one is entitled to receive because of one's efforts. Value commitment may be all we know for sure in this life—but maybe that's all anyone really needs if he or she has a clear sense of identity and integrity. It's enough for any person who has been liberated from the hubris of wanting to be a god instead of a human being.

The changes that are needed in our normative view of fulfillment and the benefits of these changes, may be summarized as follows:

—We need the good sense to use limited and precise technologies of EBC in humane ways to achieve optimal productivity without turning ourselves into machines obsessed with maximum productivity.

—We must retain a vigorous sense of ethical responsibility without the guilt and anxiety that have so often been its unwelcome companions (that is, we need the ability to work hard for good purposes without being afraid of play and playfulness and without being suspicious of a lusty appetite for pleasure—knowing that pleasure can and should and must be viewed, not as the enemy of goodness, but rather as an ally that is an essential component of balanced human fulfillment).

—We must preserve our zeal for accomplishing something excellent and for making a decent contribution to the world without being hung up on success or fame. We need heroic devotion to noble causes without preoccupation with our own noble stature as heroes or heroines.

—If we find ourselves exhilarated by the notion of God, we need to be able to have a lively sense of His or Her lovingkindness without yearning for cosmic rewards or fearing cosmic punishments, and to revere Him or Her in the context of the doctrine of cocreatorship. According to this theological notion, God deliberately left the world incomplete and imperfect so that human beings could rise to the heights intended for them by having a part in the finishing of the work of creation. Thus, our status as beings formed in the image of God finds its most profound expression in our opportunity to contribute to the final fashioning of the world and it is our duty to do so. And the doctrine of cocreatorship, paradoxically enough, delivers us from the seductions of hubris by focusing attention upon the advancement of the Creation and its creatures, not upon ourselves as heroic agents of this creative activity.

## A FINAL WORD

Because I am an ethicist, it is only fitting that the last chapter of this book on the ethics of experience and behavior control should focus on a new understanding of human fulfillment and that it should sketch a new model of human excellence. All that remains to be done is to reiterate the link between these normative reflections on essential humanity and EBC.

Of the three applications of EBC that are highlighted here, one is clearly more important than the other two. I have tried to make a case for the moral *legitimacy* of artificial happiness because I think that enjoyment of the pleasures available through EBC is much healthier than the pursuit of happiness in accordance with the debased and pathetic models. And I have tried to show the *promise* of increased capacity because I believe that if one's abilities and energies are directed toward worthy ends, then there's a lot to be said for extending and expanding them. But it must be evident that in my mind the most significant use of EBC is for the purpose of enhancing goodness, and my attack upon the self-defeating pretentiousness of traditional notions about moral heroism is mainly intended to refine and promote a superior ideal of goodness.

*Pace* Skinner, the concepts of human freedom and dignity do not have to be banished along with the excessive hubris of the conventional wisdom. There is ample substance left in a chastened view of heroism after all pseudoheroic nonsense has been purged. Nothing in the above attack upon spurious conceptions of honor makes the experience of energetic striving problematic (including the rich experience of attempting to formulate a meaningful life view). Nothing in the attack belies the reality of human choice: It merely recommends choosing *not* to maintain a destructive self-image, or to compete in futile games, or to engage in counterproductive energy investments. Nothing in the above denies the validity of certain kinds of commitment and action: It simply advises that the focus of attention needs to be kept on the cause being served, not on one's own admirable poses, gestures, and inspiring countenance as Glorious Hero.

We come, at last, to a final word about goodness. How can it be understood in such a way as to escape the spurious "goods" formerly associated with the concept, without losing what is rightly essential to it?

The perceptive reader will have noticed, of course, that many of the concerns normally categorized as moral concerns have already been analyzed. In subsuming "honor" under "happiness" and in viewing the right kind of integrity and cocreatorship as ingredients of enlightened self-interest, we have already dealt with certain elements of the soul that are often viewed as all-important in ethics. The internal dimensions of goodness have been explored; what remains are the external dimensions (that traditional moralists might regard as being of only secondary importance, but that are regarded here as being of primary significance).

Precisely. For one of the convictions operating in the mind of the author of this book throughout is that goodness ought properly to be understood as mainly a matter of *actions taken* to enhance the well-being of other human beings. Morality is horizontal, not vertical; it has to do with how people treat each other on this earth during this lifetime, not with conjectures regarding the soul in its presumed relationship with a presumed Deity, or its probable fate in an existance yet to come. Ethics is external, not internal: It pertains more to behavior than to internal feeling states, attitudes, or dispositions, and the measure of goodness is consequences rather than purity of motivation or means.

The most impressive single fact about goodness in the second half of the twentieth century is the fact that we cannot do without it. To quote once again from Auden's reflections on "the low, dishonest decade" that reached its unholy climax in the war that began on September 1, 1939:

> There is no such thing as the State
> And no one exists alone;
> Hunger allows no choice
> To the citizen or the police;
> We must love one another or die.

This does not mean that we must have jolly sentiments about each other, although international understanding and appreciation are certainly worthy goals to seek. It means that survival of the human race requires mutual restraint, respect for orderly processes, and cooperation among individuals, groups, and nations. If freedom is defined as rampant individualism devoid of a reasoned sense of social solidarity and responsibility, the social contract dissolves (and becomes nothing more than the barbaric atavism proposed by Konrad Lorenz and by the Social Darwinists before him).[30] Certainly some individualistically conceived freedoms must be given up by all members of society so that the most important goods may be preserved, cultivated, developed, and furnished to all. Humankind is a global village that must promote justice or it will not even be able to enjoy order. It must establish reliable mechanisms for creating ecosanity and planning cooperatively the best use of resources as well as acceptable limits to industrial growth and population increases. Otherwise, civilization will either explode with the bang of nuclear holocaust or else it will die with a whimper of totalitarian oppression.

Thankfully, there is no compelling evidence that the crises that surround us cannot be solved. Despair is not the only logical stance a thoughtful person can take—and there's a lot more the passengers can do than simply "stay on the bus until the last stop." It is one thing to acknowledge that "in the long run we are all dead," or that (human finitude and orneriness being what they are) each three steps toward a more tolerably just and humane world are usually followed by two (or more) steps backward. It is quite another thing—and a terribly mistaken, ignominious thing it is—to dismiss the significance of modest improvements in specific life situations. Such modest gains may be insufficient and they are always subject to reversal. But they are not without meaning, for unless we conclude that the alleviation of human suffering, the mitigation of injustice, and the significantly increased well-being of even a small number of persons are totally *worthless*, why, then, incremental betterments are not to be scorned. To say that all effort is futile is the ultimate betrayal of the human family and the ultimate disgrace.

If we allow this interesting cosmic experiment (the evolution of Homo sapiens) to fail because we turn out to be incapable of developing into full humanity, it will be a shame, and the shame of failure will rest on our heads. The least we can do is give it our best shot—and our *best* shot will require the wise use of EBC. The humanism of the future must be a technological humanism.

## NOTES

1. Lynn White, Jr., "The Historical Roots of Our Ecological Crisis," in Garrett DeBell [ed.], *The Environmental Handbook*, pp. 12-16.

2. Daniel Yankelovich, *New Rules*, pp. 250-263.

3. Daniel Levinson, *The Seasons of a Man's Life*.

4. This charge has been made by innumerable critics of "mass society," an analytical concept that Daniel Bell calls "a romantic protest against modernity." A high water mark in this literature was reached in Charles Reich's *The Greening of America* in 1970. See Daniel Bell, *The End of Ideology*, pp. 21-36; cf. Maurice Stein, *The Eclipse of Community*.

5. Theodore Roszak, *Where the Wasteland Ends*, especially pp. 68-241.

6. White, Jr., "Historical Roots," pp. 15-26.

7. Richard Sennett and Jonathan Cobb, *The Hidden Injuries of Class*, pp. 160-183.

8. Katherine Archibald, "Status Orientations Among Shipyard Workers," in Reinhard Bendix and Seymour Martin Lipset [eds.], *Class, Status, Power*, pp. 395-403.

9. Alain Touraine, *The Post-Industrial Society*, pp. 9-13.

10. David Riesman, *The Lonely Crowd*; cf. Louis Kronenberger, *Company Manners*.

11. Erik Erikson, "The Problem of Ego-Identity," in Maurice Stein and Arthur Vidich [eds.], *Identity and Anxiety*, pp. 37-87.

12. Stein, *Eclipse*, p. 259.

13. Thorstein Veblen, *The Theory of the Leisure Class.*

14. Edwin M. Schur, *Crimes Without Victims*, pp. 176-179.

15. Peter Berger and Thomas Luckmann, *The Social Construction of Reality*, pp. 85ff.

16. Sigmund Freud, *Civilization and its Discontents.*

17. Arnold W. Green, "The Middle-Class Male Child and Neurosis," in Reinhard Bendix and S. M. Lipset [eds.], *Class, Status and Power*, p. 297.

18. Barrington Moore, "Reflections on the Future of the Family," in Stein and Vidich, *Identity*, pp. 391-401.

19. Erich Fromm, *Man for Himself.*

20. It is in this connection, of course, that the ordinary socialization processes of middle-class society are most strikingly akin to thought reform in China. See Chapter 4.

21. Herbert Marcuse, *Eros and Civilization*, pp. 32ff.

22. Peter Berger, *Invitation to Sociology*, p. 176.

23. Peter Berger, *The Sacred Canopy*, p. 28.

24. Bronislaw Malinowski, *Magic, Science and Religion*, pp. 96-111.

25. Alfred R. Radcliffe-Brown, *Structure and Function in Primitive Society*, pp. 136-152.

26. Jake Scott, "The Souring of George Sauer," *Intellectual Digest* (December 1971), p. 55.

27. Paul Tillich, *The Courage to Be*, pp. 40-57.

28. Rollo May, *Love and Will*, pp. 123-129.

29. For a fuller account of this idea, see Henry Clark, *The Ethical Mysticism of Albert Schweitzer*, pp. 28f.

30. For a helpful summary of the view of human nature espoused by Lorenz and his school, see Anthony Storr, *Human Aggression.*

# BIBLIOGRAPHY

Adler, Nathan (1972) The Underground Stream. New York: Harper & Row.

Aiken, William and Hugh LaFollette [eds.] (1977) World Hunger and Moral Obligation. Englewood Cliffs, NJ: Prentice-Hall.

American Enterprise Institute (1979) Proposals to Reform Drug Regulation Laws. Washington, DC: Author.

Archibald, Katherine (1953) "Status Orientations Among Shipyard Workers," in Reinhard Bendix and Seymour Martin Lipset [eds.] Class, Status, Power. New York: Free Press.

Baier, Kurt and Nicholas Rescher [eds.] (1969) Values and the Future. New York: Free Press.

Bakalar, James and Lester Grinspoon (1983) "Drug Abuse Policy and Social Attitudes to Risk-Taking." Hastings Report 13, 4: 35-39.

Balter, Michael B. et al. (1974) "Cross-National Study of the Extent of Anti-Anxiety Sedative Drug Use." New England Journal of Medicine 290, 14: 769-774.

Beauchamp, Tom and Norman Bowie [eds.] (1979) Ethical Theory and Business. Englewood Cliffs, NJ: Prentice-Hall.

Becker, Ernest (1973) The Denial of Death. New York: Free Press.

——— (1976) Escape From Evil. New York: Free Press.

Bedau, Adam (1975) "Physiological Interventions to Alter Behavior in a Punitive Environment." American Behavioral Scientist 18, 5: 657-678.

Bell, Daniel (1962) The End of Ideology. New York: Free Press.

Bellah, Robert N. et al. (1985) Habits of the Heart. Berkeley: University of California Press.

Bendix, Reinhard and Seymour Martin Lipset [eds.] (1953) Class, Status and Power. New York: Free Press.

Bennett, Edward L. et al. (1964) "Chemical and Anatomical Plasticity of the Brain." Science, pp. 610-619.

Berger, Peter L. (1967) The Sacred Canopy. Garden City, NY: Doubleday.

——— (1963) Invitation to Sociology. Garden City, NY: Doubleday.

——— and Thomas Luckmann (1966) The Social Construction of Reality. Garden City, NY: Doubleday.

Berlyne, D. E. and K. B. Madsen [eds.] (1963) Pleasure, Reward and Preference. New York: Academic Press.

Bernstein, Arnold and Henry L. Lennard (1973) "The American Way of Drugging." Society 10, 4: 14-25.

Betz, Barbara J. (1979) "Some Neurophysiologic Aspects of Individual Behavior." American Journal of Psychiatry 136, 10: 1251-1255.

224

Blackwell, Barry (1973) "Psychotropic Drugs in Use Today." Journal of the American Medical Association 225, 13: 1637-1641.

Block, Alex Ben (1977) "The Sputnik of the Classrooms." New West, pp. 36-43.

Block, Sidney and Paul Chodoff [eds.] (1981) Psychiatric Ethics. New York: Oxford University Press.

Blum, Richard H. [ed.] (1974) Society and Drugs. San Francisco: Jossey-Bass.

Bresler, David (1980) "The Treatment of Pain." Los Angeles Times Book Review Section, July 8, p. 4.

——— and Richard Trubo (1980) Free Yourself From Pain. New York: Simon & Schuster.

Brock, Dan W. (1983) "Can Pleasure Be Bad For You?" Hastings Report 18, 4: 30-34. (Based on an earlier unpublished position paper entitled "The Use of Drugs for Pleasure.")

Brown, Barbara (1974) New Mind, New Body. New York: Harper & Row.

Brown, Norman O. (1959) Life Against Death: The Psychoanalytical Meaning of History. Middletown, CT: Wesleyan University Press.

Buytendijk, F. J. J. (1961) Pain. London: Hutchinson & Co.

Campbell, H. J. (1973) The Pleasure Areas. London: Eyre Methuen.

Canetti, Elia (1962) Crowds and Power. New York: Viking Press.

Cassirer, Ernest (1972) The Individual and the Cosmos in Renaissance Philosophy. Philadelphia: University of Pennsylvania Press.

Chorover, Stephan L. (1979) From Genesis to Genocide. Cambridge: MIT Press.

Clark, Henry (1962) The Ethical Mysticism of Albert Schweitzer. Boston: Beacon.

Clark, Kenneth (1971) "The Pathos of Power." American Psychologist 26, 12: 1047-1057.

——— (1971) Personal communication (October).

Cochrane, Charles (1957) Christianity and Classical Culture. New York: Oxford University Press.

Collier, Bernard Law (1971) "Brain Power: The Case for Bio-Feedback Training." Saturday Review 54, 14: 10-13, 58.

Dalton, Elizabeth and Kim Hopper (1976) "Ethical Issues in Behavior Control." Man and Medicine 2, 1: 13.

Davison, Gerald and G. T. Wilson (1975) "A Road to Self-Control." Psychology Today 9, 5: 60.

DeBell, Garrett [ed.] (1970) The Environmental Handbook. New York: Ballantine.

Delgado, Jose (1969) Physical Control of the Mind. New York: Harper & Row.

——— (1979) "Triunism: A Transmaterial Brain-Mind Theory," p. 392 in Brain and Mind. Ciba Foundation, Series 69. New York: Elsevier, North Holland/Excerpta Medica.

——— (1982) Personal communication (June).

Deutsch, J. Anthony (1972) "Brain Reward: ESB and Ecstasy." Psychology Today 6, 2: 45-48.

Durkheim, Emile (1961) Moral Education. New York: Free Press.

Dyer, Alan (1975) Personal communication (June).

Eiduson, Samuel (1967) "The Biochemistry of Behavior." Science Journal 3, 5: 113-117.

Einstein, Stanley and Gerald DeAngelis (1972) The Non-Medical Use of Drugs. Farmingdale, NY: Baywood.

Ellul, Jacques (1964) The Technological Society. New York: Knopf.

Englehardt, H. Tristram, Jr. and Daniel Callahan (1977) Knowledge, Value and Belief. Hastings-on-Hudson, NY: Institute of Society, Ethics and the Life Sciences.

Erikson, Erik (1958) "The Problem of Ego-Identity," pp. 37-87 in Maurice Stein and Arthur Vidich [eds.] Identity and Anxiety. New York: Free Press.

Ervin, Frank (1975) "Biological Intervention Technologies and Social Control." American Behavioral Scientist 18, 5: 617-636.

Erwin, Edward (1978) Behavior Therapy: Scientific, Philosophical and Moral Foundations. London: Cambridge University Press.

Evans, Wayne O. (1975) "The Psychopharmacology of the Normal Human," in D. Efron [ed.] A Review of Progress. Washington, DC: Government Printing Office.

Feallock, Richard and L. Keith Miller (1976) "Design and Evaluation of a Worksharing System for Experimental Group Living." Journal of Applied Behavior Analysis 9: 277-288.

Fenichel, Otto (1941) "The Ego and Its Affects." Psychoanalytical Review 28: 47.

——— (1945) The Psychoanalytic Theory of Neurosis. New York: Norton.

Ferguson, Marilyn (1980) The Aquarian Conspiracy. New York: St. Martin's Press.

Fieve, Roland (1977) "Medicine for Melancholy," in Albert Rosenfeld [ed.], p. 229 in Mind and Supermind. New York: Holt, Rinehart & Winston.

Fletcher, Joseph (1974) The Ethics of Genetic Control. Garden City, NY: Doubleday.

Fordyce, W. et al. (1973) "Operant Conditioning in the Treatment of Chronic Pain." Archives of Physical Medicine and Rehabilitation 54: 399-408.

Foreman, Judy (1981) "Mind-Body Separation Has Become Obsolete." Los Angeles Times, December 27, Part VII, 24-25.

Forrell, George (1954) Faith Active in Love. Minneapolis: Augsburg.

Frankl, Viktor (1955) The Doctor and the Soul. New York: Knopf.

Freud, Sigmund (1957) Civilization and Its Discontents. London: Hogarth Press.

Friedberg, John (1975) "Let's Stop Blasting the Brain." Psychology Today 9, 10: 18-23, 98-100.

Fromm, Erich (1947) Man for Himself. New York: Rinehart.

——— (1973) The Anatomy of Human Destructiveness. Greenwich, CT: Fawcett.

Gaylin, Willard M. et al. (1975) Operating on the Mind. New York: Basic Books.

Glover, Jonathan (1984) What Sort of People Should There Be? Middlesex, England: Penguin.

Green, Arnold W. (1946) "The Middle-Class Male Child and Neurosis," pp. 292-300 in Reinhard Bendix and S. M. Lipset [eds.] (1953) Class, Status and Power. New York: Free Press.

Greenspan, P. S. (1978) "Behavior Control and Freedom of Action." The Philosophical Review 87, 2: 225-240.

Grinspoon, Lester and James Bakalar (1979) Psychedelic Drugs Reconsidered. New York: Basic Books.

Gross, Bertram (1980) Friendly Fascism. New York: M. Evans.

Halleck, Seymour (1973) The Politics of Therapy. New York: New American Library.

Haring, Bernard (1975) The Ethics of Manipulation. New York: Seabury.

Heath, Robert [ed.] (1964) The Role of Pleasure in the Brain. New York: Harper & Row.

Hirsch, Madelyn and Richard Wurtman (1978) "Lecithin Consumption Increases Acetylcholine Concentrations in Rat Brain and Adrenal Gland." Science 202, 13: 223-225.

Holland, James (1976) "Ethical Considerations in Behavior Modification." Journal of Humanistic Psychology 16, 3: 71-78.

Horrobin, Daniel (1977) Medical Hubris. Toronto: Eden Press.

Houston, Jean (1975) "Putting the First Man on Earth." Saturday Review 2, 11: 28-32, 53.

Hughes, Richard and Robert Brewin (1979) The Tranquilizing of America. New York: Harcourt Brace Jovanovich.

Hunt, Morton M. (1967) "A Neurosis Is 'Just' a Bad Habit." New York Times Magazine, June 4, pp. 38-48.

Huxley, Aldous (1962) Island. New York: Harper & Row.

Hyde, Margaret O. [ed.] (1981) Mind Drugs. New York: McGraw-Hill.

Illich, Ivan (1976) Medical Nemesis. New York: Pantheon.

James, William (1956) "The Will to Believe." The Will To Believe. New York: Dover.

Jeffrey, C. R. and Ina A. Jeffrey (1975) "Psychosurgery and Behavior Modification." American Behavioral Scientist 18, 5: 685-722.

Jonas, Gerald (1974) "The Human Brain." The New Yorker 50, 19: 52-69.

——— (1981) Visceral Learning. New York: Free Press.

Jones, James (1981) Bad Blood. New York: Free Press.

Kant, Immanuel (1959) Foundations of the Metaphysic of Morals. New York: Liberal Arts Press.

Kierkegaard, Soeren (1954) Fear and Trembling. Garden City, NY: Doubleday.

Kinkade, Kathleen (1973) Twin Oaks: A Walden II Experiment. New York: Morrow.

Kittrie, Nicholas (1971) The Right To Be Different. Baltimore: Johns Hopkins University Press.

Klerman, Gerald (1974) "Psychotropic Drugs as Therapeutic Agents." Hastings Center Studies 2, 1: 81-93.

Kline, Nathan S. (1971) "The Future of Drugs and Drugs of the Future." Journal of Social Issues 27, 3: 73-87.

——— (1974) From Sad to Glad. New York: Putnam.

Koestler, Arthur (1968) The Ghost in the Machine. New York: Macmillan.

Krech, David (1968) Testimony given before the Congress of the United States (April 2) p. 7.

Krieger, Dorothy T. and Joseph B. Martin (1981) "Peptides." New England Journal of Medicine 304, 15: 944-951.

Kronenberger, Louis (1951) Company Manners. New York: Bobbs-Merrill.

Leach, Gerald (1972) The Biocrats. Baltimore: Penguin.

Lennard, Henry L. et al. (1971) Mystification and Drug Misuse. San Francisco: Jossey-Bass.

Leonard, George (1975) "In God's Image." Saturday Review 2, 11: 12-14.

Levinson, Daniel (1978) The Seasons of a Man's Life. New York: Alfred Knopf.

London, Perry (1969) Behavior Control. New York: Harper & Row.

——— (1976) Observations made at a conference on "The Ethics of Experience and Behavior Control" at the University of Southern California (February 12).

——— and Gerald Klerman (1976) "Mental Health and Behavior Control." Institute for Society, Ethics and the Life Sciences, pp. 142-143. (unpublished)

Louria, Donald B. (1968) The Drug Scene. New York: McGraw-Hill.

——— (1978) "The Future of the Drug Scene." The Futurist, June, p. 151.

Lowrance, William W. (1976) Of Acceptable Risk. Los Altos, CA: William Kaufmann.

Mabe, Alan R. (1975) "Coerced Therapy, Social Protection and Moral Autonomy." American Behavioral Scientist 18, 5: 519-616.

MacIntyre, Alasdair (1981) After Virtue. Notre Dame, IN: University of Notre Dame Press.

Mackay, Donald (1973) "Brain Surgery to Control Behavior." Ebony 28, 4: 24-27.

Macklin, Ruth (1973) "Values in Psychoanalysis and Psychotherapy. American Journal of Psychoanalysis 33: 133-150.

——— (1982) Man, Mind and Morality. Englewood Cliffs, NJ: Prentice-Hall.

Malinowski, Bonislaw (1948) Magic, Science and Religion. Boston: Beacon.

Mall, Janice (1981) "About Women: Center Focuses on Prescription Drugs." Los Angeles Times, November 22, Part VI, p. 21.

Manheimer, Dean I. et al. (1974) "Popular Attitudes and Beliefs About Tranquilizers." American Journal of Psychiatry 130, 11: 1246-1254.

Marcuse, Herbert (1955) Eros and Civilization. Boston: Beacon.

May, Rollo (1969) Love and Will. New York: Norton.

Melzack, Ronald (1968) The Puzzle of Pain. New York: Viking.

——— (1975) "The Promise of Biofeedback: Don't Hold the Party Yet." Psychology Today 9, 2: 18-22, 80-81.

Mendelsohn, Everett et al. [eds.] (1971) Human Aspects of Biomedical Innovation. Cambridge: Harvard University Press.

Menninger, Karl (1968) The Crime of Punishment. New York: Viking.

Meyer, Victor (1982) Personal communication (March).

Miles, John et al. (1974) "Pain Relief by Implanted Electrical Stimulators." The Lancet I (April 27): 777-779.

Milgrim, Stanley (1963) "Behavioral Study of Obedience." Journal of Abnormal and Social Psychology 67: 371-378.

Mill, John Stuart (1971) Utilitarianism. Indianapolis: Bobbs-Merrill.

Miller, Russell R. (1973) "Prescribing Habits of Physicians." Drug Intelligence and Clinical Pharmacy 7: 492-500.

Mitford, Jessica (1974) Kind and Usual Punishment. New York: Vintage.

Moore, Barrington (1958) "Reflections on the Future of the Family," pp. 391-401 in Maurice Stein and Arthur Vidich [eds.] Identity and Anxiety. New York: Free Press.

Morris, H. (1968) "Persons and Punishment," The Monist, October, p. 500.

Moskin, J. Robert (1970) "Drugs: We Are Just Plain Ignorant." LOOK, October, pp. 108-112.

Murray, Thomas H. (1983) "The Coercive Power of Drugs in Sports." Hastings Center Report 18, 4: 24-30.

Neville, Robert (1976) "The State's Intervention in Individuals' Drug Use: A Normative Account." Paper prepared for The Hastings Institute, Hastings-on-Hudson, New York. (unpublished)

——— and Sidney Cohen (1978) "Drug Use," pp. 326-338 in Encyclopedia of Bioethics. New York: Free Press.

Niebuhr, Reinhold (1943) The Nature and Destiny of Man. New York: Scribner.

Nozick, Robert (1974) Anarchy, State and Utopia. New York: Basic Books.

Nuttin, J. R. (1963) "Pleasure and Reward in Human Motivation and Learning," in D. E. Berlyne and K. B. Madsen [eds.] Pleasure, Reward and Preference. New York: Academic Press.

Olds, James (1967) "Emotional Centres in the Brain," Science Journal 3, 5: 87-92.

——— (1975) "Ten Milliseconds into the Brain." Psychology Today 8, 12: 45-48.

Orwell, George (1950) 1984. New York: New American Library.

Packard, Vance (1977) The People Shapers. Boston: Little, Brown.

Panati, Charles (1980) The Book of Breakthroughs. Boston: Houghton Mifflin.

Parachini, Allan (1982) "FDA Hit on Arthritis Drug." Los Angeles Times, August 31, Part V: 1, 8.

Parry, Hugh et al. (1973) "National Patterns of Psychotherapeutic Drug Use." Archives of General Psychiatry 28: 769-784.

Peele, Stanton (1975) Love and Addiction. New York: New American Library.

Pfeiffer, Carl C. (1975) Mental and Elemental Nutrients. New Canaan, CT. Keats.

Pines, Maya (1973) The Brain Changers. New York: Harcourt Brace Jovanovich.

Presthus, Richard (1962) The Organizational Society, New York: Knopf.

Pritchard, E. R. [ed.] (1977) The Family and Death. New York: Columbia University Press.

Rachman, Stanley and G. T. Wilson (1980) The Effects of Psychological Therapy. New York: Pergamon.

Radcliffe-Brown, Alfred (1980) Structure and Function in Primitive Society. New York: Pergamon.

Rawls, John (1971) A Theory of Justice. Cambridge: Harvard University Press.

Restak, Richard (1977) "The Brain Makes Its Own Narcotics." Saturday Review 4, 9: 7-11.

Richards, David (1982) Sex, Drugs, Death and the Law. Totowa, NJ: Rowman & Littlefield.

Richards, Howard (1977) "Productive Justice," in William Aiken and Hugh LaFollette [eds.] in World Hunger and Moral Obligation. Englewood Cliffs, NJ: Prentice-Hall.

Riesman, David (1950) The Lonely Crowd. New Haven, CT: Yale.

Robb, J. Wesley (1981) "The Christian and the New Biology." Encounter 42, 3: 197-205.

Rodgers, Joann (1976) "The Great Megavitamin Flap." Saturday Review, February 21, 3, 10: 33-36.

Rorvik, David M. (1970) "Brain Waves: The Wave of the Future." LOOK, October 6, pp. 88-98.

Rosenfeld, Albert (1969) The Second Genesis. Englewood Cliffs, NJ: Prentice-Hall.

——— (1977) Mind and Supermind. New York: Holt, Rinehart & Winston.

Roszak, Theodore (1972) Where the Wasteland Ends. Garden City, NY: Doubleday.

Routtenberg, Aryeh (1979) "The Reward System of the Brain." Scientific American 239, 5: 154-165.

Royal Commission into the Non-Medical Use of Drugs of South Australia (1976) The Social Control of Drug Use.

Rucker, T. Donald et al. (1974) "Public Policy Considerations in the Use of Psycho-
    therapeutic Drugs." College Park: Department of Psychiatry, University of Mary-
    land School of Medicine.
Scarf, Maggie (1970) "Brain Researcher Jose Delgado Asks, 'What Kind of Humans
    Would We Like To Construct?'" New York Times Magazine, November 15, pp.
    46-47, 154-172.
Scheflin, Alan W. and Edward M. Opton, Jr. (1978) The Mind Manipulators. London.
    Paddington.
Schrag, Peter and Diane Dworkin (1975) The Myth of the Hyperactive Child. New
    York: Pantheon.
Schur, Edwin M. (1965) Crimes Without Victims. Englewood Cliffs, NJ: Prentice-Hall.
Scott, Jake (1971) "The Souring of George Sauer." Intellectual Digest, December,
    p. 55.
Sennett, Richard and Jonathan Cobb (1972) The Hidden Injuries of Class. New York:
    Knopf.
Shaffer, Richard A. (1977) "Mastering the Mind." The Wall Street Journal 97, 30: 1, 18.
Shapiro, Michael (1974) "Legislating the Control of Behavior." Southern California
    Law Review 47, 2: 72-95.
Shearman, John (1973) Mannerism. London: Penguin Books.
Sherlock, Richard K. et al. (1982) "Saying 'No' to Electroshock." Hastings Center Re-
    port 12, 6: 18-20.
Silberman, Charles (1978) Criminal Violence, Criminal Justice. New York: Random
    House.
Silverman, Milton and Philip R. Lee (1974) Pills, Profits and Politics. Berkeley: Uni-
    versity of California Press.
Smith, Harmon L. (1976) "Ethics and Behavior Modification." Social Responsibility 2:
    88-104.
Spengler, Oswald (1928) The Decline of the West. London: Allen & Unwin.
Stein, Maurice (1960) The Eclipse of Community. Princeton, NJ: Princeton University
    Press.
Stevens, John (1973) Medieval Romance. New York: Norton.
Storr, Anthony (1968) Human Aggression. New York: Atheneum.
Sullivan, William M. (1982) Reconstructing Public Philosophy. Berkeley: University of
    California Press.
Szasz, Thomas (1971) "The Ethics of Addiction." American Journal of Psychiatry 128:
    541-546.
——— (1975) Pain and Pleasure. New York: Basic Books.
Taylor, John G. (1971) The Shape of Minds to Come. Baltimore: Penguin.
Thorne, Ludmilla (1977) "Inside Russia's Psychiatric Jails." New York Times Magazine,
    June 12, pp. 24-27.
Tillich, Paul (1952) The Courage To Be. New Haven, CT: Yale University Press.
Timnick, Lois (1977) "Brain Pacemaker Success Reported." Los Angeles Times, June 3,
    Part I: 1, 31.
Touraine, Alain (1971) The Post-Industrial Society. New York: Random House.
Trinkhaus, Charles (1940) Adversity's Noblemen. New York: Columbia University
    Press.

Twycross, Robert G. et al. (1978) "Pain and Analgesics." Current Medical Research and Opinion 5, 7: 497-505.

——— (n.d.) "Principles and Practice of Pain Relief in Terminal Cancer." Available from St. Christopher's Hospice, London.

Valenstein, Eliot (1973) Brain Control. New York: John Wiley.

Veatch, Robert (1974) "Competing Drug Ethics." Hastings Center Studies 2, 1: 68-80.

Veblen, Thorstein (1973) The Theory of the Leisure Class. Boston: Houghton Mifflin.

Weber, Max (1958) The Protestant Ethic and the Spirit of Capitalism. New York: Scribner.

Wender, Paul H. and Donald F. Klein (1981) Mind, Mood and Medicine: A Guide to the New Biopsychiatry. New York: Farrar, Straus & Giroux.

Wexler, David B. (1973) "Token and Taboo: Behavior Modification, Token Economies and the Law." California Law Review 61, 1: 81-109.

Wheeler, Harvey (1973) Beyond the Punitive Society. San Francisco: Freeman.

White, J. C. and W. H. Sweet (1977) Pain: Its Mechanisms and Neurological Control. Cambridge: MIT Press.

White, Lynn, Jr. (1970) "The Historical Roots of Our Ecological Crisis," in Garrett De-Bell [ed.] pp. 12-26 in The Environmental Handbook. New York: Ballantine.

Wilson, G. Terence and Gerald C. Davison (1975) "Behavior Therapy: A Road to Self-Control." Psychology Today 9, 5: 54-60.

Winner, Langdon (1977) Autonomous Technology. Cambridge: MIT Press.

Wise, Roy A. (1983) "Pleasure and the Brain." Queen's Quarterly 90, 1: 74-87.

Wolff, Kurt H. [ed.] (1960) Emile Durkheim et al.: Essays on Sociology and Philosophy. New York: Harper & Row.

Yankelovich, Daniel (1981) New Rules. New York: Random House.

Young, Jack (1971) The Drugtakers: The Social Meaning of Drug Use. London: Granada.

# Index

# ABOUT THE AUTHOR

Henry Clark received his education at Duke University (B.A.), Universitat Bern (Switzerland), Union Theological Seminary in New York (M. Div.), and Yale University (Ph.D.). He has taught at Howard University, Union Theological Seminary, Duke University, and the University of Southern California, where he has been Professor of Social Ethics since 1975. During that period he also served as Coordinator of Urban Affairs at the National Council of Churches (1966-1967). On sabbatical leaves he studied Renaissance art and philosophy at I Tatti in Florence (1973-1974) and did research for this book at the University of London (1982).

Clark has published sixteen books and numerous essays and scholarly articles. His book, *The Ethical Mysticism of Albert Schweitzer,* has been called "the finest book in the English language on the thought of Schweitzer," and *Ministries of Dialogue* won a Christopher Award as one of the best nonfiction books of the year in 1972. His writing addresses issues of racial and economic justice, ethics and technology, and the relationship between the humanities and public policy. From 1975 to 1983 Clark served as Coordinator for Humanities and the Professions at the USC Center for the Humanities, and in 1979 he was named Distinguished Humanist of the Year by the California Council for the Humanities.

# NOTES

# NOTES

# NOTES

# NOTES